T0294967

# The Republic of Football

# THE REPUBLIC OF FOOTBALL

## *Legends of the Texas High School Game*

### CHAD S. CONINE

University of Texas Press ◆ Austin

Requests for permission to reproduce material
from this work should be sent to:
Permissions
University of Texas Press
P.O. Box 7819
Austin, TX 78713-7819
http://utpress.utexas.edu/index.php/rp-form

The paper used in this book meets the minimum requirements
of ANSI/NISO Z39.48-1992 (R1997) (Permanence of Paper). ∞


Library of Congress Cataloging-in-Publication Data

Names: Conine, Chad S. (Samuel), 1977–, author.
Title: The republic of football : legends of the Texas high school game / Chad S. Conine.
Description: First edition. Austin : University of Texas Press, 2016.
Includes bibliographical references and index.
Identifiers: LCCN 2016000147
ISBN 9781477303719 (cloth : alk. paper)
ISBN 9781477310489 (library e-book)
ISBN 9781477310472 (nonlibrary e-book)
Subjects: LCSH: Football—Texas—History. School sports—Texas—History.
Football players—Texas—Biography.
Classification: LCC GV959.52.T4 C66 2016
DDC 796.3309764—dc23
LC record available at http://lccn.loc.gov/2016000147.


doi:10.7560/303719

*In memory of Odell Lowe and Milton Conine*

# Contents

# Introduction

I remember being nervous as hell as I walked through my high school's wide main corridor on an August morning in 1993.

As a sixteen-year-old sophomore, I already knew I wanted to be a sportswriter. I was pumped to have been named the sports editor of the *Midway Panther Post*. I was excited because the beginning of football season loomed, only days away. But mostly I was trying to suppress that anxious feeling in my gut as I walked down the main hall, through the cafeteria, and into the gym. I had my first assignment: introduce myself to the head football coach, Kent Bachtel, and tell him I would be covering the football team that fall.

It turned out I had nothing to worry about.

Bachtel couldn't have been better suited or more willing to help me along my chosen career path. I know of a couple of coaches who would've nodded politely and told me they could try to help, but they were actually very busy. Not Coach Bachtel. He enthusiastically shook my hand and we figured out a game plan. I would come to his office on Saturday mornings after the team had met to watch film and I would interview the coach about the previous night's game.

I would write down a few questions, but mostly we would have an open-ended conversation about football. More than two decades later, when I began working on this book, I used pretty much the same formula.

When I went to college, I talked the *Lubbock Avalanche-Journal*'s sports editor, Doug Hensley, into sending me out to high school football games on Friday nights. I had a bulky Toshiba laptop that would connect to the Internet by using a dial-up service called Juno, which was just e-mail. That was about a million communication revolutions ago. Of course, my older sportswriter friends would say I had it easy, since I never had to lug around a "Trash-80" (the TRS-80 was an early personal computer made by Tandy–Radio Shack). Anyway, when the football game ended, there would be a mad dash to write a game story and find a phone line to connect to and send the story via e-mail. I would find myself at the Springlake-Earth coach's house or behind the counter of a Blockbuster Video after begging the clerk to let me use the analog fax line. Desperate times called for desperate measures, but it was a thrill to be learning to be a sportswriter through the trials of covering high school football in West Texas.

Since that time, I've spent every Friday night during football season at football stadiums from the Panhandle and South Plains to Dallas–Fort Worth to Central Texas and wherever the playoff wind blows. Plenty of Saturday afternoons and nights, too. I've seen a few thrillers, one of which is included in these pages. I've also seen lots of duds. The duds aren't so bad, really. When it's 42–0 at halftime, I bang out the requisite number of paragraphs while the two marching bands fill up the twenty-eight minutes between the second and third quarters. Many times, I'm happy to file my game story and then meet up with friends for a beer. An ordinary ending to an ordinary night.

I'll admit, there are even times when spending Friday night at a high school football field is a tiny bit of drudgery. Just like everything else in life, it's not always magical. High school football can be the very definition of ordinary American life.

When it's special, it's electric. And that's the theme throughout these forty-one chapters.

I attempted to capture as many angles as possible from as many points of the high school football experience as I could. LaDainian Tomlinson's breakthrough game, the first nondistrict game of his senior season, came on a sweltering Thursday night when the Waco University Trojans kicked off the season against Austin LBJ. Colt McCoy showed his first flash of brilliance in his first seventh-grade game. Robert Griffin woke up one Saturday morning, the playoffs looming a week away, and found himself struggling to walk. There are stories of dynasties that won multiple state titles, and there are stories of teams whose dreams died hard early in the playoffs.

Collectively, the stories give proof to a couple of bold statements. Anywhere football is played, Texas has influence. It leads the nation in producing college and NFL stars, and has for decades. Its powerhouse programs, which combine progressive ideas with traditional fundamentals, set the tone for how to build a winner. The evidence couldn't be contained in a dozen volumes, and I certainly didn't set out to write a comprehensive account. I was able to talk football and tell some of the stories passed along to me by Hayden Fry, Spike Dykes, Bob McQueen, Lovie Smith, Art Briles, Lawrence Elkins, Warren McVea, Ray Rhodes, Dat Nguyen, Zach Thomas, Drew Brees, Johnathan Gray, and many others.

While interviewing, researching, and writing, I camped out in the moments that we crave as fans. The phrase "Friday night lights" has become ubiquitous in relation to Texas high school football. But I'm here to tell you that the game is at its absolute best on sunny, crisp Saturday afternoons in December: that time of year when the teams on both sidelines believe it's their destiny and birthright to move on to the next round. The fans in the stands cheer their heads off, partly to stay warm but mostly because they want the ride to continue forever, or at least right up until Christmas.

While traveling to NFL training camps for this project, I found myself in a hotel room in Chicago in late July. While preparing to drive to Detroit to interview Lions quarterback Matthew Stafford, I discovered a YouTube video with thirteen minutes of highlights of a Highland Park versus Stephenville game from the mid-2000s. The sound track was simply the crowd at the game. Listening to those fans scream and those Stephenville fans shake their propane-tank-filled-with-ball-bearings noise contraptions for dear life, I was transported from that hotel room back to Texas in December, where football is as rich and electric as it ever gets.

I knew right then that that was the game Stafford and I would talk about the next day. That game and so many others like it are the reason I'll never stop covering high school football.

Those are the moments featured in this book.

# The Republic of Football

# HAMLIN

## 1984

### *The Tie That Doomed the Pied Pipers*

It's so easy to connect the dots from a Class 2A football game in 1984 to Baylor's rise to relevance in the Big 12 that it seems like a massive oversimplification.

As I sat in Baylor coach Art Briles's state-of-the-art, modern-deco office, the connection was as clear and straightforward as the man himself. Briles looked out the window at Baylor's nearly finished $250 million McLane Stadium while describing the Works Progress Administration–era rock stadium in Childress, Texas, and a picture developed that encompassed everything that's happened between then and now. Briles's philosophy, his plan for how his football players were going to beat your football players, was born in the wake of a 7–7 tie versus the Panhandle Panthers on December 7, 1984.

"It was a real cold, kinda windy night in Childress, Texas, in December," Briles said. "Cool stadium. Rock stadium kind of like Cleburne and a few of the others."

Briles remembers details like that from this particular playoff game. He was in his first season as head coach of the Hamlin Pied Pipers, who were 13–0 as they faced off against Panhandle, which also came in 13–0.

When I spoke to Briles in the spring of 2014, the story of the Hamlin versus Panhandle game was familiar to me. Several sources, including a sportswriter from Amarillo named Lance Lahnert, who covered the game, described it for me. For three quarters, Hamlin traded punches with the Panthers. The Pied Pipers piled up 158 yards and gained seven first downs in three quarters of knock-'em-down-drag-'em-out warfare.

Now Briles was describing it to me in his office. Taking a short break from the whirlwind schedule of an in-demand major college football coach, he told me how he noticed a flaw in the Panhandle defense and how he decided to exploit it.

"It took me a little while to finally see that's what they're doing," Briles said. "They're manning it up instead of playing Cover 3."

Briles brought it back like the play had happened yesterday. He began drawing on an imaginary dry-erase board, once again breaking down the Panhandle defense.

"I finally figured out how to attack the defense," Briles said, and it was as if he were sitting in the field house in Hamlin again. "Because we were going to run what we called 'Loaded 12 Throw Back Fly.' The safety is manned up on the tight end, this corner is manned up on the flanker, this corner is manned up on this receiver. I'm going to take the left halfback and send him right down the center of the field, because the linebacker is manned up on him. We're throwing the ball to him right there, manned up with the backer, and hitting him for a touchdown."

The only problem was that Briles figured it out one play too late. Hamlin faced a fourth-and-long with time running out in the third quarter. So Briles called timeout, enabling punter Mike Howerton to kick with the wind at his back. Howerton boomed a sixty-one-yard kick that put the Panthers' backs against their own goal line as time expired in the third.

"We punt the ball, get it down there, and it rolls dead on their one-yard line," Briles said. "And then they kept it the whole fourth quarter. I knew if we ever got the ball back, we were going to score. But we never got it back."

That's not an exaggeration. Panhandle started the fourth quarter at its one and ended on the Hamlin eleven. By the time the clock struck zeroes, the Panthers had fourteen first downs to Hamlin's seven. Panhandle racked up 205 rushing yards, a huge chunk of them coming in the fourth quarter as it played keep-away from the Pied Pipers. And most importantly, Panhandle crossed Hamlin's twenty-yard line to win the penetrations battle 2–1.

That's how the game was decided. No coin flip. No sudden-death overtime. No lining up on the opponent's twenty-five. In the event of a tie, the game was decided by the number of penetrations of the opponent's twenty-yard line. And that's as far as Panhandle had to go. Game over. More than a decade passed before high schools adopted an overtime system in which the game was settled with extra play.

In the decisive fourth quarter, Panhandle slowly bulldozed ahead behind running back Shane Mecaskey, who ran eighteen times for seventy-six yards on a twenty-three-play drive. The Panthers employed a heavy dose of straight-ahead power football with a sprinkle of big plays when they had to have them.

"We put them in some pretty bad spots," said Brooks Eoff, a junior offensive and defensive lineman for Hamlin. "It would be third and way long, and they'd come up with a miraculous play to make a first down."

Jerry Don Woods, a senior fullback and linebacker, still has the game film and a copy of the *Hamlin Herald*'s special section commemorating the Pied Pipers 1984 football team. He still has a difficult time believing his team's season ended with a 13–0–1 record. "It's just a bittersweet thing," Woods said. "We were the only team that was undefeated through fourteen games, and [we were] going home."

It's the kind of game that no one forgets, even if they only heard about it. To that end, Briles has done his part, telling the story often enough that it's become legendary.

Through Briles's tour around Texas from Hamlin to Georgetown to Stephenville, from Texas Tech to Houston to Baylor, the Hamlin-Panhandle game has taken on a life of its own. Buffalo Bills quarterback Kevin Kolb hails from Stephenville, where Briles's career took flight, and Kolb played for Briles at Houston. When Kolb met Woods, the NFL quarterback had to hear the story again.

"I introduced myself and told him I played for Art Briles in his first season as a head coach," Woods said. "He said 'Did you play in that damn game when they kept the ball the whole fourth quarter?' He sat down and said, 'Tell me about it.'"

Woods and his teammates can tell tall tales about the game. Each of the players I spoke with gushed about Briles and his impact on their lives. The final game of the 1984 season is their moment, and it still resonates in much larger football circles as Briles's career has flourished. The players on the team remember bits of the story like a vivid dream.

Howerton was the last Hamlin player to touch the ball, when he punted on the final play of the third quarter.

"I got a kick away, and it rolled dead on the one-yard line," Howerton said. "I remember the referee saying, 'Nice kick, kid.' And I thought, 'We've got this game won.' If we just got the ball back, I think we had 'em."

But Briles remembers the details because they are bricks in his coaching house. He said he considered every alternative while Panhandle chewed up the clock in the fourth quarter. He even seriously pondered the almost unthinkable possibility of letting the Panthers score.

"I remember looking at Bo Smith, who was my defensive coordinator, and I'm saying, 'We've got to let 'em score,'" Briles said. "Our only chance is to let them score and kick the extra point, and then we go and score and go for two and make it and beat 'em. It's not doing any good to play defense and hold them for the last three plays, because they're ahead on penetrations. And we talked about it, and I can remember saying, 'Ah, we can't do it.' It's our first year there. We weren't that solid in with the people in town. We weren't established. It's my first head-coaching job. You know? 'This guy lets 'em score.' So we decided not to do it."

The players I talked to said they felt the worst for Woods and the other seniors. But at the same time, they knew how good they could be in 1985.

They just didn't know how influential they would be.

In the aftermath of the loss to Panhandle, Briles began to consider a new way of doing things. He had a fast team, but it wasn't a bunch of brutes. Panhandle clearly demonstrated that a team could defeat Briles's squad by bulldozing them and holding on to the ball. So Briles decided to spread things out and tilt the field in his favor.

"I saw that as you go on in the playoffs, you're going to come up against people that are better than you, that have better personnel," Briles said. "So you've got to do something to equalize the unequal field. I thought if we were ever going to win a state championship, then we had to do something different."

The next season, Briles's Pied Pipers threw the ball around the field and threw a baffling combination of formations at their opponents, with amazing success. The Briles biography *Looking Up* notes that Hamlin outscored its opponents 416–26 in the ten-game regular season. Hamlin's regular-season showdown came at home against the Stamford Bulldogs; both teams were state ranked. But it wasn't much of a hurdle for the Pied Pipers, who stomped the Bulldogs 31–6.

That's the way it went almost all season, so much so that Howerton recalls feeling sorry for opposing defenses.

"Even the referees were looking around like, 'What are you guys doing?'" he said.

Mitch Hall, a member of both the 1984 and 1985 Pied Piper teams, told me he can see the footprint of his senior squad anytime he watches Briles's current teams. "It caught some people off guard, and he's still doing it today," Hall said. "He had a way to take what talent he had and improve it. He had you playing like you were seven foot tall."

Hamlin went 14–1 and reached the 2A state semifinals before being defeated by eventual state champion Electra. It was Briles's last season at Hamlin. After he compiled a 27–1–1 record in his first two seasons as a head coach, he went on to Class 4A Georgetown and then to Stephenville in 1988.

In Stephenville, Briles's spread offense took hold and launched the Yellow Jackets to the heights for which Briles had designed his offense. Stephenville won state championships in 1993, 1994, 1998, and 1999.

Mike Leach hired Briles to coach running backs at Texas Tech starting in 2000. Three years later, Houston hired Briles as its head coach, and Baylor stole him away five years after that. Briles's innovative style took Baylor to unthinkable heights as Robert Griffin III won the Heisman in 2011 and the Bears claimed their first Big 12 football championship in 2013.

There's no way Briles could have foreseen early in 1985 that the changes he was making would transform high school and college football in Texas. The one thing he can see in hindsight is that if the Pied Pipers had regained possession of the football in time to defeat Panhandle, it would have altered the future.

I asked him what he thought would have happened if he had noticed the hole in Panhandle's defense earlier in the game or if the Panthers had failed to come up with a first down somewhere along the way in the final quarter. Or if they had fumbled, or any of an endless list of events that could have changed the outcome that night. "If we'd have won that game in '84, it probably would've taken a little while longer," Briles said. "Because the thing you've got to be careful about when you win is that everything's OK."

Stephenville and Baylor fans can thank their lucky stars that the Panhandle Panthers held on so tightly to the ball that night in 1984 in Childress, Texas.

As for the players wearing Hamlin jerseys, they credit Briles with a playbook full of life lessons. But they don't see much of a silver lining in Panhandle's tremendous ball control on that famous night.

"I never want to see it again unless it's the team I'm rooting for," Hall said.

# 2

# ODESSA

## 1946

### *Hayden Fry Leads the Bronchos*

While walking the two miles from wherever the bus dropped him off to his family's house, a teenage kid had time to do some pondering.

As the kid walked along the flat, dusty terrain, surrounded by mesquite bushes outside Odessa, his mind was on football. He thought about the kids he played with and how they played and where that could take them. He and the Odessa High Bronchos had finished 11–1 in 1945, losing their only game of the season against Wichita Falls in the state quarterfinals. There was one state champion for all of Texas at that time, and Odessa and Wichita Falls and Sweetwater and the like were lumped in with city schools from Dallas and Houston and elsewhere. So the kid schemed about how he and his boys could compete. He also thought about the black kids he played with in the town's sandlots. The kid considered how unfair it was that the best players in town couldn't dream of going on to play at Baylor or Texas or, well, anywhere white kids played. They couldn't even play for Odessa High. On those long walks to his family's house, he had plenty of time to think through all these things and to make some decisions. Of course, he had no idea where the sport of football and his thoughts about it might take him. How could he? It was 1946, and the game as it existed bore little resemblance to the phenomenon he would help create.

Still, Hayden Fry had a plan up his sleeve.

This was before Fry became synonymous with Iowa football.

This was before he was the inspiration for the character Hayden Fox on the popular ABC television show *Coach*.

This was before he mentored coaches such as Bill Snyder, Bob Stoops, Barry Alvarez, and Bret Bielema.

And this was even a couple of decades before, as a first-time head coach at SMU, he recruited and signed the first African American player to a scholarship in the Southwest Conference.

Before any of that, Fry was just a kid walking home to his family's farmhouse and hatching a scheme.

He knew how strongly folks around Odessa felt about football and winning at it. When he and his classmates were on the ninth-grade team, they were undefeated until they lost at Midland. So their coach drove the bus home by himself, leaving the players to hitchhike the twenty miles back to Odessa as punishment.

Be careful what kinds of lessons you teach a visionary, because he just might do something about it. Fry's senior season ended in 1945 with a quarterfinal loss to Wichita Falls. But not yet ready to be done with football, he figured out how to stay with it.

"I was the quarterback and the senior class president," Fry said. "They had a crazy rule back then that if you weren't nineteen before September the first, and you hadn't graduated, you could still have eligibility for football. So ten of the starters on the team [in 1945] were seniors. I talked them all into dropping their English class to keep from graduating."

Fry told me this story the first time I had the honor of speaking with him on the phone. Since I had called just to set up a proper interview, I wondered for a few weeks whether he would go right back to that story. Sure enough, it was etched in his memory as a vital component of his high school days. Later, when I went to the Ector County Library to further research the 1946 Bronchos, all the evidence was right there in the 1946–1947 yearbook.

So I asked Fry how difficult it had been to talk his friends into taking that leap. The answer that followed described high school football in the post World War II era with vivid and poignant succinctness.

"We lived in a little oil field town of Odessa, about 9,000 people, and there was only one division then," Fry said. "The little schools like Odessa, you played the big schools like Dallas and San Antonio, Lubbock and Amarillo, and all of those places. We were like family. We were very close. Black kids couldn't even come to our school. They were the best athletes in our town, probably. They couldn't even come to our school and play. We had a great group of young men. We were like brothers. Since I was the quarterback and president of the class, the other guys, the other nine guys that were seniors . . . It wasn't a difficult thing to do to persuade everybody."

Odessa began the 1946 season with ten fifth-year seniors in the starting lineup on both sides of the ball (everyone started both ways), plus a dynamo junior fullback-linebacker in Byron "Santone" Townsend. "He transferred from San Antonio to Odessa," Fry said. "His daddy worked in the oil field. We nicknamed him 'Santone.'"

Townsend, who went on to earn all–Southwest Conference and all-American honors at Texas, and was inducted into the Texas High School Football Hall of Fame in 1991, fit in perfectly with the talented squad. Fry said four members of the 1946 Bronchos—Townsend, guard-linebacker Herman Foster, tight end Billy Moorman, and himself—earned first-team all-state honors at a time when that team included only eleven spots.

The Odessa team clicked from the beginning of the season, kicking it off with a 13–0 victory over Lubbock High. Next up was a 26–0 thumping of El Paso High, then a 40–7 walloping of Hollis High School in Oklahoma (Darrell Royal's alma mater). The Bronchos pushed through Big Spring 12–0 to get to 4–0, having allowed only one touchdown through four games.

That would become a trend. Through fourteen games, Odessa gave up a total of seventy-two points (that's less than one touchdown a game). When I spoke to him in the fall of 2014, Fry claimed that the Bronchos never lost a turnover. He said they fumbled three times but recovered all of them, clearly a part of the legend that has grown up around that Bronchos team.

There's no doubt, though, that Odessa had an advantage.

"We were a year older and a little more mature than a normal team," Fry said. "We had great teams in junior high and high school through the years."

Odessa ruled the West Texas region in 1946, ripping through the regular season with a 10–0 record. The big district showdown, according to the *Odessa American*, fell on Armistice Day, when the Bronchos hosted the Sweetwater Mustangs in a Monday-afternoon clash.

As a sportswriter, I get an archetypal thrill from reading game stories from decades past. The game story from the Sweetwater contest was uncredited, though it was likely written by sports editor Roy Scudday, who covered the state championship that season. The first sentence goes on and on in splendid detail: "The Odessa Bronchos, using a savage, down-the-middle-attack coupled with some home-run passes, sailed in with a 33 to 13 victory over a big, hard-fighting crew from Sweetwater yesterday afternoon before a jam-packed throng of better than 13,000 at Fly Field, in the feature event of Odessa's huge Armistice Day celebration."

With the key win over Sweetwater in its back pocket, Odessa went on to defeat Lamesa 35–0 and rival Midland 55–0 to finish the regular season. It was Odessa's second straight undefeated regular season.

The Bronchos raced past their nemesis from the previous year, Wichita Falls, 21–0 to get to Highland Park in the state semifinals, then dumped the Scots 31–13. But Fry and the Odessa seniors had come back for one more time around to try to win a state championship. For a school of Odessa's size, the loophole in the rules allowed them to take aim at bigger schools from bigger cities.

That's what the Bronchos drew in the final in San Antonio Thomas Jefferson. More than sixty years after the contest, Fry recalled the principal characters in the championship game. "The toughest game was probably the state final against San Antonio Thomas Jefferson," Fry said. "They had Kyle Rote, who was an all-American at SMU. He was All-Pro with the New York Giants. And they had Sonny Payne and Pat Knight."

Odessa claimed its perfect 14–0 season with a 21–14 win over Thomas Jefferson. Scudday reported that "a screaming throng of 40,000 people" watched the final at Memorial Stadium in Austin. This, mind you, was long before it was renamed Darrell K Royal–Texas Memorial Stadium, since Royal was a quarterback and defensive back for the Oklahoma Sooners at the time.

Townsend made many of the vital plays for the Bronchos in the state final, as described by Scudday in the *Odessa American*:

Led by brilliant Byron Townsend, and the smashing line play of Harvey (Pug) Gabrel, the red-shirted Bronchos scored early in the second quarter following an 84 yard drive, a plunge touchdown by Gabrel.

They added their second score in the third quarter on a pass from Townsend to Sonny Holderman, and scored their final tally on a plunge by Townsend late in the third period.

It was a slam-bang, offensive show from start to finish. Both clubs were a touchdown threat each time they got the ball.

The *Odessa American* ran the screaming headline "Broncs win schoolboy grid crown!" across the top of the front page and ran an additional Associated Press game story on the sports page. Fry and the Bronchos achieved what they had come back for, and the championship took them far beyond the game played on December 28, 1946.

"Every one of us in the starting lineup got four-year scholarships to play college football," Fry said. "Isn't that amazing? It paid off not only with a state championship but with scholarships for all the guys."

Odessa was coached by Joe Coleman, whose name I uncovered while doing research in the *Odessa American* microfilms. The field at Odessa High is named for Coleman, though the Bronchos play their home games at the city's famed Ratliff Stadium. However, it's difficult not to think of Fry as the team's coach. It was his ingenuity and leadership, on the field and off, that made the difference in a team that lost in the state quarterfinals in 1945 and one that claimed the state title in 1946. Retrospectively, it's easy to transpose Fry's ability to lead men on to Odessa's first championship football team (Odessa Permian won its first state championship in 1965).

In his yearbook picture, the young, square-jawed Fry appears ready to bark instructions to the Iowa Hawkeyes in a Big Ten clash. But there were miles, important ones, to be traveled before Fry arrived in the Big Ten.

After high school, Fry went to Baylor to play college football and earned a degree in psychology (he would later paint the visiting locker room pink at Iowa's Kinnick Stadium). His first foray into coaching came as an assistant at Odessa, then as a player-coach for his Marines football teams.

"I was sent to Korea, and they called me back to Japan to coach and play," Fry said. "We won the all-four service championship. We beat all of them. All I did was coach and play football, basically. When I got back to Odessa, they gave me back my backfield job. The very next year, the head coach retired and I became the head coach at Odessa."

College coaches quickly saw Fry's potential, and he was hired by Baylor as an assistant before Arkansas's Frank Broyles snatched him away in 1961. Fry was on a fast track to becoming a head coach in the college ranks. But his days in Odessa, and his thoughtful nature, made him hold to a revolutionary provision.

"I made my mind up in the ninth grade," Fry said. "Some of my best friends were black guys, and they couldn't play football. My closest friends were a lot of the black kids. We played sandlot football and football out in the street, but they couldn't go to our school. So I made up my mind if I ever got into a position that I could help my black buddies, I was going to do it. That's what motivated me to not take a head coaching job in college until I found a school that would let me recruit a black player."

SMU made Fry its head coach in 1962, and he set about following through with the promise he made to himself. Fry signed Jerry LeVias in the spring of 1965, the first time an African American had signed to play for a Southwest Conference football program. Probably not coincidentally, the Mustangs emerged as a force to be reckoned with and won the SWC with a 6–1 conference record in 1966. LeVias led SMU in receptions with 18, receiving yards with 420, and his 7 receiving scores made him the only Mustang with more than 2 touchdown catches.

The struggle and the impact of LeVias's college career can't be fully detailed in this chapter, but Fry told me he carefully picked the Beaumont Hebert student to be a trailblazer. "He had great speed, and when you met him you just fell in love with him," Fry said. "He was just an outstanding young man."

Fry's bringing LeVias to SMU may have settled his inner turmoil about his black friends in Odessa not being able to attend Odessa High, but it also gave his team an edge against its opponents. "We won the Southwest Conference championship and beat a lot of the great teams, Texas and Arkansas, people like that," Fry said. "By then, I had four or maybe five black players on the team. All those coaches who said they would never have a black player on their team, we started paddling their rumps, and they started recruiting black players."

Fry went on to win 232 games as a college head coach. His Iowa teams claimed three Big Ten titles. Fry's picture in the 1946–1947 Odessa High yearbook includes his ambition "to hunt treasures." I have no way of knowing whether the successes he had at SMU and Iowa, with LeVias and countless others, were the kinds of treasures he dreamed of as he walked the two miles from the bus stop to his family's country house.

It's doubtful that Fry could have foreseen all that, but he knew he would head in that direction. "My daddy had taught me that if you do a good job, the people you work for will take care of you," Fry said. "If you do a bad job, they'll fire you. That was my philosophy. I think being raised that way had a lot to do with it."

# 3

## SNYDER

### 1952

### *Grant Teaff's First Lessons*

Some football coaches can trade stories about *Xs* and *Os* all day long and make the listener understand how the *Xs* and *Os* translate to teamwork and sacrifice and how those virtues transcend the football field to equal success in life. Football coaches worth their salt, at least from the sampling I've been privileged to interview, understand football's place in the hierarchy of social needs. They grasp the paradox that football ranks far below things like God, family, and country. Yet they hold to the belief that the ideals learned make football pretty darn essential to the fabric of our society.

Football shouldn't be the center of your life, but you could do worse than building your life on the foundation of football values. Most of the stories in this book make a case for football creating a ripple effect that changes lives for the better.

But Grant Teaff doesn't have that kind of game story to contribute from his time as a Snyder Tiger.

That came as a surprise to me when I met Teaff at his American Football Coaches Association office, where he has served as the organization's executive director for twenty years. Teaff built a reputation as a motivator of the highest order while making the Baylor Bears a perennial contender in the Southwest Conference during his tenure as their head coach (1972–1992). I have to write that the words of wisdom Teaff offered me in our meeting regarding this project made me ready to run through a wall. At eighty, he could still do that, and it seems as if he'll be doing it for a while longer.

But Teaff's Snyder teams never played for a state championship or had any particularly memorable games. He said he might be a dud. I doubted that when he said it, and by the time I left his office, I knew Teaff had given me an irreplaceable piece for the "remember when" picture.

Because Teaff didn't tell me game stories. He told me about two of his high school coaches—James "Speedy" Moffett and J. M. "Mule" Kaiser—who arrived in Snyder in 1948 and shaped Teaff's life and career. He told me about a math class and an old, dingy coach's office in a WPA-era building in Snyder. He told me about the blue-collar grit he learned from the ground up, which served him well, since he had to scratch and claw to reach his goals.

The only football story Teaff offered was the one from the time his father took him to his first game.

"The rivalries in high school towns were something," Teaff said. "This isn't a game that I played in, but it was a game that I saw because my dad took me to the games."

Teaff's memory is clear and vivid. But it's his words and the sound of his voice that will stop a man in his tracks. There's something about a strong West Texas accent that gives words the weight of bullets. Art Briles from Rule has that tone of voice, and Teaff has it in buckets. As he related stories from more than fifty years ago, I paused my journalistic tendency to have the next question ready. I shut up and listened.

"I had to be eight or nine, probably, and Snyder was playing Colorado City," Teaff said. "In those days, the men, the dads would walk the sideline. They would follow the chains. They would just walk up and down the sideline. We were down on the field. I don't remember anything about the game. I just knew the chains would move, and this mass of men would move, and I was kind of in the middle of it. There was a close rivalry between Snyder and Colorado City. They're about twenty-something miles apart. At the end of the game—I don't know what happened in the game that caused it—all of the men on the sideline and all of their men on the sideline who were right there rushed onto the field. The players, I don't know what happened to them and the coaches. But it was a huge gang fight. I'm looking around, and people are hitting and swinging and down on the field wrestling. Finally, it's over, and I have no idea how they got everybody off the field.

"We're going back to Snyder, and this is the first game I've actually seen. I said, 'Daddy, I really like this game.' He said, 'You do?' I said, 'Yes. I think that's great: they play a while and they fight a while.'"

It turned out to be a good thing that fight was instilled in Teaff at an impressionable age. He made up his mind as a sophomore in high school that he wanted to be a head football coach in the Southwest Conference. To do that, he felt he needed to play college football. The only problem was that the clever but undersized offensive lineman–linebacker didn't have the size, speed, or strength to make him a shoo-in for a college scholarship.

"Coach Moffett had talked to Coach [Joe] Baumgardner, the head coach down there [at Angelo State]," Teaff said. "They had three scholarships, and they were going to have fifty guys come down there for a tryout. Did I want to come down? Heck yeah, I wanted to come down. I'm thinking we're going to go suit up, get helmets on, get out there, and we're going to practice. And I'm going to try to earn me a scholarship. They take us in the gymnasium, and they had two big boxes from Goodfellow Air Force Base. They've got a basketball. They had fifty of us, shorts and tennis shoes. Coach Baumgardner came out there and said, 'We're going to play a little game in here. We call it boxetball. There are two boxes up here. Everybody come up here and get you a pair of boxing gloves on.' I'm standing by a guy, and he said, 'You know, I think the last three guys standing are going to get the scholarships.' He threw the ball up in the air, and a melee broke out. It carried me back to that old time in Colorado City when I saw them all out there fighting. Suffice it to say, I got one of the three scholarships."

Teaff said he laughed with Baumgardner years later; such an otherworldly tryout would get a coach immediately thrown in jail these days. But despite the violent nature of the proving ground, Teaff looks back on it as an implementation of the lessons he had learned up to that point.

After closely watching his high school coaches, Teaff saw something worth emulating and set about doing just that. Though his parents taught him the necessity of having a hard-nosed work ethic, young Teaff looked at Moffett and Kaiser—both of whom had played college football at Texas Tech, about eighty miles away—and realized where that work ethic could take him. Whether those two men knew it or not, they were up to the task of preparing Teaff.

That is to say, they forged the will to win with fire and a hammer.

"The first really great lesson I remember learning was from Coach Kaiser," Teaff said. "He was a big-boned guy with a long face. In fact, his nickname was 'Mule.' Trust me, I never called him 'Mule' to his face. He was a Renaissance man. This big, tough offensive and defensive line coach, but he's a math teacher. He wrote poetry. He listened to classical music. He was in essence a true Renaissance man. He fascinated me because of that. I guess I had inklings toward that, but that wasn't where I came from. I came from a real work-ethic-type family. Not into the arts, not into the theatre. Into work, work, work.

"One of the first great lessons that he taught me was the foundation for basically everything I've written, everything that I've done, everything that I teach, and it happened in my sophomore math class. He'd given us ten questions on the test. So I finished nine of them. There were about ten minutes left in the class, and the tenth one, I just couldn't get it. I figured, 'Well, 90 percent.' I walked up, put the paper on his desk, turned around, went back, and sat down.

"He just glared at me the whole time. When the class was over, he gave me that one," Teaff impersonated Kaiser slowly, deliberately beckoning with his index finger. The tenth grader nervously walked to his coach's desk. "He said, 'You didn't finish your test,'" Teaff remembered. "I said, 'Well, no, sir, I just couldn't think of that one.' He said, 'You turned it in with ten minutes to go.' 'Well, no, I just couldn't think of it.' He said, 'You quit. Gave up. You're never going to be successful if you give up. You have to finish the test. You have to finish the game. You have to finish life.'

"That's probably one of the reasons I'm eighty years old and still working full-time about eighty hours a week. You finish. Then he said the key to me before I started to leave. 'Grant, remember this: your greatest asset is not your physical abilities, it is your mind.'"

Teaff took that advice and began planning how he was going to use his mind to take him to the places he wanted to go. Coach Kaiser's words were on Teaff's mind when he arrived home from school and realized that his mother embodied a prime example. "It just reminded me that she's always the same," Teaff said. "Consistent. She was always happy. She was always smiling. She was always positive. I thought, 'Foundational is a positive attitude.'"

Teaff's four foundational pillars began with that concept. He said the precepts—a positive attitude, total effort, self-discipline, and the capacity to really care—have informed every decision he's made and action he's taken during his career.

That type of forward thinking was put in overdrive when Coach Moffett pulled Teaff aside for a one-on-one hard-truth pep talk. "He knew my desire to get an education," Teaff said. "He knew how badly I wanted to become a coach, a successful coach. My classmates, by the time we were seniors, knew clearly what my stated goals were. I was going to be a head football coach, and I was going to be a head football coach in the Southwest Conference. It was the biggest thing around.

"[Coach Moffett] called me over to his office, a WPA-built gymnasium out of local fieldstones. Kind of a dingy old place. He had a little bitty office over there, and it was probably eight-by-eight, and he had a cane-bottom chair. He had a squeaky chair. I remember, when he turned, it squeaked. He said, 'I need to see you.' So I said, 'Yes, sir.' He said, 'I know what your goals are. I know what you want to try to accomplish with your goals, and I want to tell you how you can reach your goals.' My heart started beating fast. Here's somebody I really love and respect, and he's going to teach me how I can achieve the goals that I want to achieve. He stopped and looked at me for a moment and he said, 'Effort.' I said, 'Effort.' 'Effort,' he said. 'Every day, every way on every play. Total effort. You can reach every goal you set if you're willing to give the effort.' I said, 'Wow.' He said, 'Are you willing to give total effort? I said, 'Well, I want to reach my goals. I've been taught work ethic. Yeah, I'll do that. I promise I can do that.' He said, 'You'll be successful.'"

"I walk out the door, and just as I put my hand on the knob, he said, 'Grant, you think I'm just talking about on the football field, don't you?' He said, 'No. In the hallway, in the classroom, in the city streets, at home, when you get married, when you go to college, when you have children. Total effort. Every day. Every way on every play.' I said, 'What a foundation!' And it's been true."

It makes a person see how Teaff could inspire generations of football players. When a man who has made more of his physical abilities than should have been possible tells you he knows how you're going to get there, it tends to sink in.

Obviously, it took some fighting—some honest-to-goodness fending off the competition with boxing gloves in a San Angelo gym—to reach his goals. But that's just the color of Teaff's West Texas grit added to the story.

"It intermingles with everything in life," Teaff said. "If you have an emotional ability to care about something, then it triggers everything else. It triggers your effort, your mentality. I cared about a scholarship. I wanted to get an education. I wanted to be a coach. You think anybody else was going to get one of those scholarships? Not on your life. I knew what I wanted, and they gave me a way to get it."

# 4

# BROWNWOOD

## 1960S

### Gordon Wood's Legacy Begins

Part of the myth of high school football includes diners, old codgers sitting around swapping stories of years gone by and sizing up today's boys against the teams of old while a pleasantly saucy waitress pours round after round of coffee.

To be honest, I've never happened upon such a gathering in real life. I've even been assigned to go find it for the sake of a newspaper feature in some place where the ball team hadn't been to the playoffs in decades. The idea was to capture the essence of the town's hopes for a winning football team by catching up with old men who remembered the glory days. Ideally, it's a rich way to tell a story. In reality, it doesn't exist, or at least it isn't nearly as common as in the movies.

But I got lucky on this one when I went digging for stories about Gordon Wood.

If you picked up this book outside Texas, it's possible you're not familiar with Gordon Wood. Simply put, he's the standard-bearer for high school coaches. He won more games than anyone before him. As he built and maintained programs from his start in Rule in 1940 until his retirement after the 1985 season, Wood's legacy ascended with the popularity of football in Texas and the nation. Wood finished his coaching career having led nine teams to state titles in an era when that was much more difficult to do than in later years, when the number of championship trophies began to multiply like rabbits.

I probably could have written a chapter about Gordon Wood's career in Brownwood based on one good interview and the plain historical record. But one Wood player, Roy Spence of Austin, pointed me in the direction of another, Kirk Wall, in Brownwood. Wall helped gather a collection of men who filled my recorder with stories as we sat in an upstairs room of the Gordon Wood Hall of Champions.

Wall met me outside and gave me a quick tour of the hall. Soon after, Walter Croft arrived, and Lawrence Elkins was right behind him.

My friend John Werner, the *Waco Tribune-Herald*'s Baylor beat writer, told me Elkins was priceless as a storyteller, and ole Larry didn't disappoint. He arrived with a manila envelope under his arm. He opened it to reveal a copy of the *Waco Tribune-Herald*'s special all-time Baylor football team section. Elkins couldn't believe he'd made the team ahead of receivers like Kendall Wright, Terrance Williams, and Antwan Goodley. He crowed like a proud rooster, but his selection was justified. Elkins caught 70 passes for Baylor in 1963, an NCAA record then. From here, 70 catches in 1963 seems like 200 in today's game.

After showing off the special sports page, Elkins started in razzing Croft. Despite being almost half a century past their playing days, the men playfully argued over whose Lions team was better. Both had good arguments.

Wall, Croft, and Elkins were joined before long by Jerry Jones, a member with Croft and Wall of the 1965 state championship team. Finally, longtime Wood assistant Kenneth West filled out the group of storytellers. The men treated West with the reverence of kids in the field house who figured if they acted up, the coach might have them running bleachers before they could say, "AARP."

As Werner told me, you don't have to coax a story out of Elkins. We started on the subject of Coach Wood, and Elkins quickly, beautifully depicted the Wood persona. "If somebody made a mistake or fumbled, we didn't have to tell 'em, because the man on the sideline would be waiting for him," Elkins said. "And you were more scared of him than you were of your opponent who was playing opposite you. He could call you out for one play and dress you down so much psychologically that you just wanted to run into the brick wall on the other side of the stadium. He had that penchant. One thing he had as he developed through the years was a brain trust of coaches that was probably smarter than anybody. One of them is right here [West]. One of them is Coach [Morris] Southall. Coach Southall was a genius. It was a good-cop-bad-cop deal. Ole Gordo would blister you, and here comes Morris behind your back, 'It's all right. He didn't mean it. You just do better next time.'"

Coach Wood and his brain trust won seven state titles at Brownwood, including four in Wood's first decade at the helm of the Lions. After the state championships in 1960 and 1965, which we spoke about at the Gordon Wood Hall of Champions, Brownwood went on to win titles in 1967, 1969, 1970, 1978, and 1981.

To tell all the Coach Wood stories, I would need more pages than are in this book. I know this because his autobiography, *Coach of the Century*, weighs in at 462 pages. Coach Wood finished his career with a record of 395–93–15. G. A. Moore eventually surpassed Wood's win total, but Moore was quick to point out that Wood's record stands alone because of the era when it was established. Wood retired after the 1985 season, just three seasons after the University Inter-scholastic League, the governing body for high school competition in Texas, opened the door for the second-place team in each district to participate in the playoffs. For much of Wood's career, the standard was that to make the play-offs, a team had to win a district championship. If Wood had coached in a time when two, three, or four teams from a district made the playoffs, it's easy to imagine him winning two or three more games a year over his forty-four-year coaching career.

By the time Wood arrived in Brownwood, before the start of the 1960 sea-son, he had won a pair of state titles at Stamford. Between his time at Stamford and finishing his career in Brownwood, Wood spent two seasons in Victoria. Needing to move closer to his family in Abilene, Wood applied to be head foot-ball coach at San Angelo Central. When Emory Bellard outflanked Wood for the Central job, Wood found a home in Brownwood.

As fate dictated, Bellard's Central team faced Wood's Lions in the 1960 sea-son opener. Conventional wisdom at the time suggested Brownwood was in for a thumping. In *Coach of the Century*, Wood conjectured that the Bobcats outweighed his team by twenty pounds per man.

But the Lions flipped the script.

"We just ran all over 'em," Elkins said. "We outran 'em, outtoughed 'em, outtackled 'em, outblocked 'em. I've never seen a Bellard team fold, but they folded that night. They were like that dog on that stump. At halftime, they'd had all of us they could stand. At the end of the first nine minutes, it was 22–0, but it wasn't Angelo with the 22. It was 34–0 right after halftime, and those big boys folded. Bellard talked to me later, and he said, 'Elkins, y'all almost cost me a job, and that was my first game in San Angelo.'"

Brownwood claimed a 34–6 victory over San Angelo Central, and the template was set. Later that season, the Lions defeated Breckenridge 18–14, marking the second time Brownwood had beaten Breckenridge in thirty-four games between the two schools, and the first time in twenty-one years. Elkins remembered that game as a turning point that led to the Lions' state title.

Like UCLA's John Wooden, who famously began each season by instructing his players on the proper way to put on their shoes and socks, Wood built his program on a rock-solid base of fundamentals. But also like the Wizard of Westwood, Wood used sharp ingenuity to give his team an edge.

When Brownwood faced the Jacksonville Indians in the 1960 state semifinals, Wood began to ponder the weather forecast for a Saturday-afternoon game at Baylor Stadium in Waco. Seeking an advantage that might turn the game in the second half, Wood figured out how to use the conditions to benefit the Lions.

"He asked the UIL rules committee, 'Can you change uniforms during the game?'" Elkins said. "As long as it's the same number, same color, they had no rule in the book against that. He brought two sets of game stuff. Of course, the other set was older than the hills and ill fitting. We go in there and put a fresh set of uniforms on at halftime. It gave us a fresh attitude, having clean, dry, warm clothes on. We were chattering at the half in that locker room at old Baylor Stadium, and here comes an old set of uniforms, same number, same color but they were throwbacks, I guess from World War II."

The Lions scratched out a 12–6 win, clearly needing every edge they could get on a cold wet day in Waco. Elkins was lined up against the Indians' Pete Lammons, who went on to win a Super Bowl while playing tight end for the New York Jets.

"I asked Lammons years later, 'Hey, Pete, how much did your uniform weigh in the fourth quarter?'" Elkins remembered. "He said, 'About 270 pounds.' I told him about us. He looked at me and said, 'You cheated!'"

The next Friday night, in another frigid game, Brownwood dominated the second half for a 26–6 victory over Port Lavaca for the Class 3A title.

The 1960 Brownwood team not only claimed a state championship but also allowed the town to reinvent itself. The men gathered at the Gordon Wood Hall of Champions described the pre-1960 Hill Country town as "dying on the vine." But with a state championship came a new attitude.

"I've heard business leaders of that era talk about, and it's true, it's funny how things can be tied to sport in a community," said Wall, who was a seventh grader during the 1960 championship run. "In little America, you've got your school system, and you have your faith community, and that's what everything spins around. Pride. There was none about our school sports program. That ball game finished up with bringing home the state championship and bled over into the business community, and business owners and entrepreneurs began to think, 'I can win at what I'm doing.' It was a cultural change overnight."

Decades after playing for Wood, Wall said he realized he needed to employ the principles the coach used to unite his Lions teams. Wood felt it was essential to have four elements present: coaches believing in players, players believing in players, players believing in coaches, and coaches believing in coaches.

The proof of the system was seen in how Brownwood's team success outpaced individual glory. From the Gordon Wood era, there are currently three players (Elkins, Jimmy Carmichael, and Mike Kinsey) and two coaches (Wood and Southall) in the Texas High School Football Hall of Fame. A few Brownwood alums have made it to the NFL, but Elkins is the closest to a bona fide star above the high school level.

"People would ask me, 'How did y'all produce out of that little ole town the consistency of good athletes?'" Wall said. "Are you kidding me? You think we were winning because we had superior talent? We didn't have superior talent. We had average, and in some cases less than. But the formula was in place."

In 1965, Brownwood was still trying to regain the heights reached by the 1960 squad. To that end, the Lions began the season with a huge wave of momentum, particularly on defense. Brownwood shut out its first five opponents, and then came the annual clash with Breckenridge. The Buckaroos limped into the contest with a 2–4 record, but still grabbed an 18–0 lead at halftime. In the locker room, the Lions braced for a tongue lashing from Wood. But it never came.

"Coach never shows up," Wall said.

Years later, Wall remembered that night and asked Wood what happened outside the room.

"He said he and [assistant coach Pete Murray] and Morris were going in, and he stopped them outside the locker room door," Wall said, recalling the story. "[Wood] said, 'They know what they're doing. They came over here with their heads stuck in the clouds. We don't need to change the game plan, we don't need to do nothing. Let 'em sit in there and figure it out. Let's try it.'"

Wall marveled at the insight and willingness to take the risk. "I said, how many times did you do that in your forty-plus years?" Wall remembered asking Wood. "He said, 'That's the only time.' We came back and won the ball game 39–18. But it was a funny halftime, because we're all sitting on those old wooden benches in the locker room. Ain't nobody saying nothing. Even though we're fifteen-, sixteen-, seventeen-year-old kids, we knew."

Since only the district champion made the playoffs in 1965, and a loss to Breckenridge could have cost the Lions a playoff berth, Wood showed tremendous grit in sticking to the "coaches believing in players" pillar of his formula. The Lions made the choice to stand up, though, and when Brownwood reached the state championship game that season, the coaches gave the players another good reason to believe in the brain trust.

The primitive state of video technology at the time and the cagy level of gamesmanship made it almost impossible for Wood to find game film on state-championship foe Bridge City. According to *Coach of the Century*, the Cardinals' coach implored his friends in the coaching business and the other teams in Bridge City's district not to give up film on his team. Finally, Wood discovered that the Cardinals had played a Galveston school that was closing its doors. After the coach at that school agreed to provide the game film, and after waiting two days for the Galveston coach to carry through, Wood finally went into his own pocket to sweeten the deal. Wood told the Galveston coach, "The minute I receive your film and have it in my hands, I'm gonna mail you a fifty-dollar bill." That did the trick, and the fifty-dollar investment paid huge dividends. The Brownwood coaches discovered that Bridge City running back Steve Worster had a tell.

"We knew where he was going all day long," Wall said. "They picked it up on game film. He was a stand-up back in the Power I. They'd come out of the huddle and get set, and if he was going to the left, he had his left foot in front of his right one just a hair, had his push-off foot behind him. If he was going to the right, it was the other way."

Lion defenders flocked to Worster all day, beginning with the Cardinals' first offensive play. "As Worster turned to cut upfield, cornerback Roy Spence, who didn't weigh more than 155 pounds, came flying in to tackle Worster," Wood described in his autobiography. "Spence delivered a crushing blow right at the knees, and the hard impact echoed all across the playing field."

Brownwood defeated Bridge City 14–0 for another 3A state championship. Worster managed eighty-seven yards, not nearly enough for the Cardinals.

"He played four years of high school, four years of college, and that one game's the only game he didn't make 100 yards," said Croft, the 1965 team's bruising middle linebacker.

Brownwood's defensive effort infuriated the Bridge City coach, who wanted an explanation, which Wood was eager to deliver. "When the game was over, the coaches meet in the middle of the field," Wall said. "[The Bridge City coach] was screaming and cussing at Coach Wood, 'Y'all knew where we were going. You were listening to our headset or something. You cheated us.'

"Gordon didn't like to be called a cheater. He said, 'Yeah we knew where you were going. Do you know what your stud running back does?' And he showed him. And Steve's coach didn't even know what the boy was doing. He said, 'You've coached him four years and you don't know what he's doing. Don't call me a cheater.'"

Wood coached forty-four seasons of high school football, the final twenty-six in Brownwood, where he created a culture that carried on for years after he died in 2003. Thanks to his legacy, I finally sat in on that Texas football tradition of a roundtable of old men talking football.

There wasn't any coffee or a saucy waitress, but the tales were as authentic as they were tall.

# 5

# SAN ANTONIO

## 1963

### *The One They Call "The Game"*

Telling the stories of legendary football games, football teams, and football players in the state of Texas means having choices. We've been crowning state champions in Texas for ninety-five years as of this writing, and during the better part of the last two decades, we've been awarding ten or more state championships a year, just among public schools.

Of course, not every great team makes it to a state title game. My notes for this book are full of teams that played their toughest games of the season sometime before the state championship game, not to mention all the teams that never made it to the final stage. Until 1982, only one team from each district made the playoffs, so Texas football lore is full of great ball clubs that didn't qualify for the postseason.

And players? I wanted to fill this book with the biggest stars ever to come out of Texas. Some of them I was able to include (LaDainian Tomlinson, Drew Brees, Hayden Fry, et al.), and some of them were beyond my reach (Earl Campbell, Eric Dickerson, Willie Nelson, et al.).

As for games, the possibilities could fill up a deep ocean with videotape. Every Friday night in dozens of locations from Dalhart to Brownsville, El Paso to West Orange, people experience football games that they will remember for a lifetime. But even in that overwhelming volume of stories, there are games that stand out.

Early on, when I had just embarked on this project, I was standing alongside a youth-football practice field in the spring when a lifelong friend and elder statesman mentioned a game he thought I should include in these pages. Using his smartphone, he found an article he had seen online by the *San Antonio Express-News* columnist Roy Bragg, with the headline "'Biggest game' Turns 50 Today."

I read the article and immediately put it on my list of stories to include.

On November 29, 1963, San Antonio Brackenridge faced off against San Antonio Robert E. Lee. The nation was still in shocked disbelief over the assassination of John F. Kennedy a week earlier. In Texas, the unthinkable horror knocked us off our feet, since it took place on our watch in Dallas. The high school football playoffs were set to begin, but football coaches, players, and fans wondered whether it was permissible to return to sport.

In San Antonio, the defending state champion Brackenridge Eagles drew the Lee Volunteers in the opening round. It was too good a game for football fans to pass up, and so the people of San Antonio gave themselves permission to care about football, at least for a night.

The game sold twenty-two thousand in-demand tickets as hundreds stood in line in the cold November rain even all night some nights, in the week leading up to the Friday-night contest. Many more who failed to obtain a ticket watched the television broadcast on WOAI. Former players recall it as the first bi-district football game ever televised in the state.

I spoke with Linus Baer, one of the key players in the unfolding drama, in his San Antonio office in early February 2015. Before we met, Baer mailed me a copy of a documentary titled simply *The Game*, produced by Gary DeLaune, a Texas Radio Hall of Fame broadcaster. In it, DeLaune unpacks all the elements that made this game special, using interviews with Baer, Brackenridge's Warren McVea, and other members of both teams.

But I still wanted to know more about the environment in the wake of a national tragedy. Having covered high school sports in the uncertain days following the 9/11 terrorist attacks, I wanted to see whether there were parallels. It seems there was the same sense of not knowing exactly how to move on.

Baer said no one wanted to play football a week earlier, on the day of the JFK assassination. He recalled how the teams walked through a ball game on a surreal evening. But a week later, football was something people needed to hold close.

"The Lee-Brack game served as a release, an outlet for people to go to the game or watch it on TV and enjoy it," Baer said. "Get their mind off the Kennedy assassination, give them something else to think about. I think it did that. I think that's one of the reasons people remember it so well."

The Lee-Brackenridge game still resonates with football fans because of a rich collection of ingredients, both between the lines and outside them.

Brackenridge had won the state championship in the state's largest classification in 1962, defeating Borger 30–26 in the 4A title game. The Eagles entered the postseason in 1963 with an 8–2 record, but with a reputation to match that of any undefeated squad. Lee boasted a 10–0 regular season, but approached the game more like an underdog.

Both teams came in with tricks up their sleeves. Brackenridge shifted star running back McVea to quarterback in order to multiply his number of touches. But Lee's philosophy not to punt and to employ only onside kicks was the slightly more dramatic strategy.

Each of those measures influenced the game from its early stages. As I watched the grainy black-and-white film of the contest, it's easy to see why *The Game* electrifies football fans. Though the documentary includes almost the entire game, it still plays like a highlight reel. Before the dust cleared and a winner was declared, the combatants would be smiling at each other on the field, shaking their heads in disbelief at how much fun they were having. They were playing football, but they were also bringing about cultural change.

In 1963, Brackenridge was made up of mostly African American players and a few Hispanic ones, while Lee was all white. Texas was still years away from full-scale integration, and in researching this book, I heard stories of racial hostility at ball games from much later in the tumultuous 1960s.

The Lee-Brack game had it where it mattered most. The storyline was uplifting when people needed it, but the play between the lines made it legendary, and the jaw-dropping action began with the opening series.

Lee marched for a touchdown on its game-opening possession, then recovered its first onside kick attempt. Baer scored to cap the second drive, giving the Volunteers a 14–0 lead before McVea or any of the Brackenridge offensive players had touched the ball.

But the Eagles were wise to Lee's strategy after that, recovering every onside kick attempt the rest of the way. Down 14–0, the Eagles recovered the second one and went to work digging out of a hole.

McVea's first run of the game at once justified both teams' strategy and showed that the early two-touchdown lead wasn't safe. McVea scrambled around the left side of his offensive line and then darted down the sideline for a fifty-four-yard touchdown.

Lee called timeout the first time the Volunteers saw McVea step in at quarterback, but the powwow didn't do much good. "It was a great call for Coach [Weldon] Forren to do that," Baer said. "To get [McVea's] hands on the ball every play was genius, because he could do things with the football that I'd never seen anybody do before."

McVea's high school career made him a sought-after football recruit who received dozens of college scholarship offers. He went on to the University of Houston, where he was the Cougars' first African American player. The Cincinnati Bengals drafted McVea, but traded him to Kansas City after one season. He earned a Super Bowl ring with the Chiefs when they defeated the Vikings in Super Bowl IV.

Viewed retrospectively, it's no wonder that Forren put the ball in McVea's hands on every offensive play on that cold night at Alamo Stadium. McVea told me that Forren pulled him aside during the week leading up to the game and said the only chance the Eagles had was to move him to quarterback. McVea, of course, was on board. Brackenridge simplified its game plan to accommodate the change in strategy. "I only had about four or five plays," McVea said. "That's all we did. We ran Floyd Boone off tackle, Floyd Boone around the end, Floyd Boone up the middle, and then me around the end. That's all we had."

It looked for a moment in the second half as if that would be all the Eagles needed to advance, despite the fact that Lee had taken a 34–19 lead to intermission.

Brackenridge recovered Lee's onside kick to start the second half and began taking control of the scoreboard. McVea scored two touchdowns in the third quarter, helping the Eagles win the third quarter 14–7, marking the first period of the game in which Brackenridge gained an edge. The Eagles went to the fourth quarter trailing 41–33, but holding the momentum.

With seventy-four points on the board going into the final period, the early 1960s contest became the kind of evenly matched offensive slugfest that delights fans. It not only resonated, but also grew like a big fish story.

"If everybody was at that game that said they were at the game, there was like 100,000 people there," Baer said. "Everybody you talked to was at the game or knew somebody who was at the game and always wanted to talk about it. And it was always called 'The Game.'"

The players were loving it, too.

"After the game got going, what's so amazing about that football game is all the guys on both teams started having fun," McVea said. "While we were out there playing, me and Linus were just laughing and saying this is like a track meet."

The Eagles needed a stop to start the fourth quarter in order to pull even with Lee. But Brackenridge made the most crucial tactical mistake up to that point by putting the ball in Baer's hands in the open field.

Baer rushed for 150 yards in the contest and caught two passes for 95 more yards. He finished with four rushing or receiving touchdowns, but his biggest play came on the rare occasion that either team opted to kick deep. He hauled in the kickoff in the first minute of the fourth quarter and found a seam up the left hash mark. Baer and McVea had formed a relationship during track season, and Baer knew that the one player capable of catching him once he cranked up his engine was McVea.

Only McVea, who kicked the ball deep and served as the last line of defense, was wearing human ankle cuffs.

"[A Lee blocker] fell down and crawled over there so I wouldn't see him," McVea recounted. "He had a leg lock, and I couldn't get him loose. I looked down, and the guy had his legs around me in a leg lock. I was like, 'What is going on here, man?' And Linus ran it back for a touchdown. I had a chance to get him, and the referee let it go."

The black-and-white film from DeLaune's documentary confirms McVea's story, though the film is a little too grainy to identify the Lee player.

Baer's kick-return touchdown boosted Lee's lead to 47–33, with more than eleven minutes remaining. Brackenridge wasn't finished, though. McVea, perhaps still riled up from being held, answered with a forty-six-yard touchdown run. On the point after, he grabbed the ball on a fake kick, scrambled to his left, and threw back across the field to complete the two-point conversion pass, cutting Lee's lead to 47–41.

Then came the Eagles' big break as they turned the tables by recovering an onside kick.

On the ensuing drive, McVea handed to Boone, who gained a pair of key first downs, setting up McVea's five-yard touchdown run, which tied it. McVea kicked the extra point to put Brackenridge ahead, and for the first time it appeared as if the defending state champions might survive the battle.

McVea scored the go-ahead touchdown with more than six minutes left. If the game had been played in the early twenty-first century, with both defenses exhausted and quick-strike offenses sensing blood in the water, six minutes would be a virtual eternity. But this was 1960s football, heavy on the run, so the last half of the fourth quarter represented the final gasp of a fantastic game.

Brackenridge came close to stopping Lee when the Eagles forced the Volunteers into a third-and-seven from the Brackenridge twenty-eight. But Lee quarterback Gary Kemph dropped back, pumped once, and then threaded a pass to Eddie Markette over the middle for a sixteen-yard gain to the Eagles' twelve.

From there, the Volunteers plodded forward until fullback Larry Townsend plunged into the end zone from one yard out. A successful two-point conversion put Lee ahead 55–48, with a little more than thirty seconds left.

Though only a few ticks remained, Lee definitely didn't want McVea touching the ball too many times. "It seemed like a whole quarter was left, to me," Baer said. "I did all the kicking. I lined up, and I was going to kick it opposite where McVea was. He lined up in the middle, so I kind of angled over this way, and he moves over this way. Then I line up over there, and he moves over that way. And I just said, 'Ah hell, I'll just kick it.' I kick to this guy, and he laterals it back, and now I've got to catch [McVea]."

The Eagles did corral McVea on the kickoff. Then on the final play, from his own forty-three, McVea scrambled to his right, looking for the kind of hole that had been there so often that night. McVea finished with 215 rushing yards and six touchdowns, but he couldn't get away on his last carry.

Lee tackled McVea and grasped a 55–48 win.

The Volunteers prevailed from the underdog role, but on this night there was no room for chest pounding. The nation had lost its leader a week earlier, and perhaps more meaningfully in the context of the game, a white school and a predominantly black school from San Antonio had won each other's respect through a thrilling football game.

"I'll never forget the fact that after the game, we all met in the center of the field," Brackenridge defensive tackle George Cook recalled on DeLaune's documentary. "I don't even think anyone came together and said, 'Hey, let's meet.' I think automatically we all came together. . . . We all held hands and said a prayer. I think it taught me a lot of character and respect and competitive spirit, and I think I try to use that now as a coach with my kids."

The two principal players had formed a relationship going into the contest, but it was strengthened after the memorable night. They roomed together the next summer at the Texas High School Coaches Association All-Star Game.

Baer, who went on to play college football at Texas, graduated from high school having formed an unusually tight bond with an athlete from another school. "We played basketball against each other, ran track against each other," Baer said. "He'd call me up and ask me to go to parties. We were good friends and had a lot of respect for each other."

San Antonio has long since had the reputation as a culturally and ethnically diverse city. An attempt to explain the reasons and roots of that distinction would fill up another book. But the players involved in the classic football clash of November 29, 1963, credit that experience with playing a huge role in the city's evolution.

"What really, I think, happened is it drew the communities closer together," McVea said. "Robert E. Lee was kind of like the mother ship in all that stuff. They didn't have any black players. The thing that really stood out is how the guys on the other team, how they treated us. They treated us with a lot of respect."

# 6

# LUBBOCK

## 1968

### *The Estacado Matadors' Phenomenal Debut*

Football coaches, the good ones anyway, search for the angle that's going to put them over the top.

Like a gunfighter who makes certain the sun is at his back at the moment of truth, a seasoned football coach will try to find that one determining factor that will allow his team to survive and advance.

Jimmie Keeling thought he had come up with the angle he needed as he prepared his Lubbock Estacado team to face defending 3A state champion Brownwood in the opening round of the 1968 playoffs. The weather forecast called for snow the next day, when the Lions and Matadors would meet at Shotwell Stadium in Abilene. So Keeling called in a favor from Bill Kelly, his friend who worked at Holt Sporting Goods in Lubbock. No matter that it was the middle of the night. Keeling figured his team needed extra-long mud cleats for the game, and he was going to get them.

So Keeling and his coaches acquired the cleats and spent the wee hours of the morning installing them in the team's game shoes.

Sure enough, when they arrived at Shotwell, the field was being blanketed in white. "Hollis Gainey was one of our coaches and Hollis was out on the field the whole [pregame] raking snow off the field over here at Shotwell Stadium," Keeling said. "It was muddy, and as it warmed up, it was a little bit marshy."

Keeling coached high school football in Texas for twenty-four seasons and then moved to the college ranks, where he was Hardin-Simmons's head coach for another two decades. I spoke with him in the spring of 2015 at his Abilene home, where he provided amazing details of the 1968 season. He used the phrase "over here at Shotwell" because he ended up settling practically in the shadow of the famous Abilene stadium.

A coach like Keeling acquires volumes of football tales. It was a rare treat to sit in his living room and hear some of them. I was there to talk about the 1968 Lubbock Estacado Matadors, and it was clear that they were one of Keeling's favorite subjects.

Every now and then, a person gets a chance to do something special at the right time in the right place. When Keeling became the head coach at a new school in Lubbock, he found himself in such a scenario. Overdue and ploddingly, Texas was integrating. Lubbock's strategy for that process meant opening a new school where white, black, and Hispanic students would attend together. In preparing to open Estacado in the fall of 1967, the school district hired Keeling as its head football coach in January of that year.

Keeling, then thirty-one years old, was a relatively new head coach, his previous stops coming at Tulia and Elgin. Hired as the Matadors' coach before they even had a campus, he began by teaching PE (including a square-dancing class) at Lubbock High and holding Estacado's off-season workouts at Alderson Junior High.

David Moody was one of the ninth graders who worked out at Alderson in preparation for the opening of Estacado High School. Moody went on to coach high school and college football in Texas for more than three decades. He was an assistant on Spike Dykes's Texas Tech staff at the inception of the Big 12 conference in 1996, and he turned down opportunities to coach in the NFL and returned to the high school level after Dykes retired in 1999. Moody said it didn't take long to see that bringing together a diverse group of athletes not only was going to work, but also just might thrive.

"We knew we had something special," Moody said. "When you look back at the movie *Remember the Titans*, this was before them, and it was exactly the same type of atmosphere. [Keeling] took people from all races, all ethnicities, all socioeconomic backgrounds, and he meshed them together."

Moody began playing with guys like Joe Rose, a white kid who came from a rough upbringing as the son of a truck driver in East Lubbock. Rose said his family moved after Estacado's first school year to get away from the jurisdiction of the Lubbock school district. But Rose felt so committed to his teammates after their junior varsity season in 1967 that he worked to earn his $200 tuition and attended Estacado anyway. The Matadors finished 9–1 as a JV squad, but Rose saw that the things happening in the Matadors' locker room were bigger than football.

The school lurched and quaked under the pressure and scrutiny of its place in Lubbock's experiment. Students left, and the demographic makeup of the student body shifted. But the football team's core held together. "We purposely didn't allow very inflammatory things around us," Rose said. "Those things flare up, and the whole school is talking about them. We don't let it interfere with what we have to do. We sort of had a kangaroo court. We had a judge and a jury. Fred White was the judge, and David Moody was the jury, and you didn't want to do something wrong."

The bond formed by Keeling's Estacado team was forged by intense pressure. And the situation on the field played to their advantage.

The Matadors' 1967 team was basically a varsity-type squad, made up of the school's best players. But circumstances dictated that the Matadors had to wait until 1968 to play a full-fledged varsity schedule with a chance to advance to the postseason. So for that purpose, Estacado was placed in the largest school classification and took on JV teams from Lubbock High, Monterey, Coronado, and other 4A schools. Except for the anomaly of a hiccup against Amarillo Caprock, the Matadors blazed through that first season, learning to win.

Then, when the UIL slotted Estacado by size into a district for the 1968–1969 school year, the Matadors were put in 3A. From this vantage point, it's obvious Estacado had been primed for its first varsity season as well as it could be. But it was difficult for outsiders to see it at the time. "I knew we had a lot of talent," Keeling said. "We had a great coaching staff, and they were enthusiastic and good, and I think they all felt very good that good things were going to happen. But we were in an eleven-team district. We were picked eleventh out of an eleven-team district."

Estacado wasted little time in proving those picks weren't worth the paper on which they were written. The Matadors opened the season by blanking Brownfield 14–0 and proceeded to shut out their first six opponents. Since they were in an eleven-team district, all of those games counted in the standings. In no time at all, Estacado went from an unknown factor to the front-runner in District 3-3A.

At the start, Keeling came up with a brilliant motivational tactic that kept his young team focused on the immediate task at hand. "We actually developed this ladder and put it in the dressing room," Keeling said. "It had fourteen rungs on it. We started out in Brownfield in the first game. We told them, 'If you don't win, you break the rung.' That ladder was a big deal to those kids. It kind of developed into a celebration deal. After every game, we'd go back to the dressing room, and it was kind of a ceremony. The kids did it. They put the new rung on the ladder. Each week we had a place up over the door that we put the rung of whoever we were playing that week. Each of those kids would hit that as they were going out every day. It was really on their mind."

The Matadors became one of those teams whose unbelievably stingy defense was almost overshadowed by a prolific offense. Like the Big Sandy and Daingerfield teams that would come after them in the 1970s and 1980s, Estacado set records for both points scored and the minuscule amount they allowed. Slaton scored on the Matadors in the seventh game, finally breaking the shutout streak, and the Matadors gave up a late long touchdown against San Angelo Lake View, a game Estacado won 73–6. That's all the points Estacado surrendered in their first ten games.

Going into the final week of the regular season, the Matadors had shattered expectations and established a 9–0 mark to set up a showdown with Sweetwater. But because this was before the playoffs were expanded to include teams other than district champions, the Matadors needed a win at Sweetwater to reach the postseason.

The Mustangs not only were undefeated coming into the game, at 7–0–1, but also were chomping at the bit to face Estacado. Keeling remembered a packed crowd and an electric environment at the Mustang Bowl. He didn't mention the hostility, though. I heard from at least two Matador players that they were pelted with rocks while walking into the stadium.

"You have to remember that us coming down to that area wasn't a good spot for us to be in," linebacker Fred White said. "In that time, it just wasn't a good place for people of color. It wasn't just a black team. We had a team of all races. It wasn't welcome down there. We went down, and that was probably one of the hard-hittingest games that you would ever imagine. We won on the scoreboard, but they beat us up pretty good."

Quarterback Kenneth Wallace recalled his introduction to that contest. "It was either the first or second play of the game, we had a little off-tackle play, a stretch play is what they call it now, where we stretch it out and give it to the tailback," he said. "Sometimes I would keep it, and sometimes I would fake it and pass it. You could tell that they had geared up for that play, so when we ran the stretch play to the left side, I actually handed it to the tailback. And after I handed it to the tailback, they had a defensive end, Aubrey McCain, he just slanted down inside, and I never saw him. And boom!—he hit me and I'm down for the count. I mean, I'm out and I'm hurting. Anyway, I could see the rest of the players standing over me saying, 'Come on, Ken. Get up, man. You're all right.' I went out for a play, and then I came back in the game."

Wallace said he went back in the game on the alert and ready for a slugfest. But the Matadors were equal to the fight, and justice was served late in the third quarter.

Estacado began a drive at the Sweetwater forty-three and plowed ahead behind running back James Mosley. Then Wallace kept around the left end for an eighteen-yard gain before being tackled at the Mustangs' twelve. A personal foul on the play moved it to the six, and Mosley scored from there.

Those were all the points the Estacado defense needed to grasp a victory.

"[Former Lubbock ISD athletic director] Pete Ragus always says that's the biggest game ever played in Lubbock," Keeling said. "That Sweetwater-Estacado game, because it was big and it meant we were going to the playoffs."

Estacado had a bye week during the final week of the regular season, which it used to prepare for the playoffs. The Matadors were set to play the winner of Wichita Falls Washington versus Brownwood. It was an easy bet that the defending state champion, Brownwood, would prevail, and so Keeling went to work game-planning for the Lions.

"I was so familiar with Brownwood and what they did, because Coach Wood was so great to me," Keeling said. "I used to go watch them work out when they were in the playoffs. I'd been there the year before. He was always so welcoming. I was familiar with what they did. We picked out those key plays that we knew we had to defend, and we worked really hard on those. And then we tried to have a really simple offensive game plan, and just used our speed and executed well."

Keeling's admiration and respect for Wood didn't keep him from playing hardball with the Brownwood legend. Estacado sought to amplify its advantage of having a week off before the playoffs by making Brownwood play on a short schedule on Thanksgiving Day.

"I knew Gordon was a tough negotiator," Keeling said. "Well, he wanted to play in Abilene real bad, and he did not want to play in Sweetwater, because we'd just won that big game there. He wanted to play on Saturday afternoon. We stuck with it. The bottom line is finally he said, 'Okay,' and he didn't really want to, but he said, 'We'll play on Thanksgiving Day if you'll play in Abilene.' I'm like [clap], 'Okay, let's go.'"

But Keeling didn't stop looking for angles that would help his team. At the last minute, he determined that his team needed longer spikes in their shoes, so he made that happen too.

The Matadors dug in on the snow-and-ice-covered field and walloped Brownwood. Some of the Estacado players were in tune with the esteemed reputation of their opponents, while others just played football. Either way, the Matadors were unintimidated and well prepared.

"The name 'Brownwood,' I'm being honest, didn't mean a whole lot to us," Wallace said. "Coach Keeling used to say that everybody that's in the playoffs is good. 'Cause I would always ask him. Every week I would ask him, 'Coach, is this team any good?' And he always would say, 'Yeah, this will be the best team we're going to play.' He would say to me every week—that we're play-ing a good team—and we go out and beat them by sixty points. So that's why I would always ask, 'Now, Coach, tell me the truth, is this team any good?'"

But Rose knew the stature that Wood and the Lions had established in a short time in Brownwood. "My brother and my father, everybody that loves football knew Gordon Wood and Brownwood," Rose said. "We knew his fame, and we thought it was really cool that we got to play them."

Brownwood won state championships in 1960, 1965, 1967, 1969, and 1970 (and tacked on two more under Wood in 1978 and 1981). But on that snowy afternoon in Abilene, the Lions were waylaid by the first-year varsity program from Lubbock.

Estacado running back Larry Miller scored on a twenty-three-yard run in the first quarter to give the Matadors the initial lead. Then Estacado unleashed a twenty-one-point barrage on Brownwood in the second quarter. Wallace fin-ished a fifty-six-yard drive with a seven-yard touchdown run early in the second quarter. Miller capped another march with a six-yard TD.

Already ahead by three touchdowns, White struck a crushing blow. "It's kind of like it's slow motion," he said. "The passer went back, and I just kind of dropped back, and when I looked up, I had the ball and headed in the right direction. That's pretty much what happened. You don't get many of those chances to pick off a pass and then run it back for a touchdown, so that was a pretty big deal. That was a momentum booster."

White's interception return covered forty yards and sent the Matadors into halftime ahead 28–0. There was no comeback for the Lions after intermis-sion. Miller and Frank Judie scored on short runs in the third quarter, and then Jesse Lethridge struck the final blow, a sixty-eight-yard run up the middle for a touchdown.

The Matadors defeated Brownwood 49–8. The throttling was so complete that Keeling didn't even have to give a postgame speech. Wood came into the Estacado locker room and delivered it himself. "He told them how great they were, how good they were as a team," Keeling recalled. "He congratulated them on how they conducted themselves on the field, and he told them, 'You're the best team in the state, and you're going to win the state championship.'"

Of course, Wood might have been beaten, but he could see clearly. Estacado went on to beat Kermit, Henderson, and Refugio in succession to finish 14–0 and win the state title.

Sitting in his living room in 2015, Keeling marveled at the accomplishments of his Matadors players after they graduated from Estacado. Almost to a man, he listed their success stories later in life. But the players know it's hard to top what they did as high school football players.

"When I reflect, we did something that was very, very special," Wallace said. "Didn't know it at that time. We thought that's just the way it was. Looking back, that was the highlight of most of our careers. That may have been the most special thing that many of the players and the coaches on that team ever accomplished in their lives. It's just hard to beat. I consider myself lucky."

Members of championship teams, I've found, tend to stay connected with one another through reunions and award ceremonies. That's certainly the case with the 1968 Matadors, though they also seem to have a kindred spirit that's stronger than most.

"It made a big impact on us," Rose said. "If I look at that year, the first integrated high school in Lubbock Independent School District, I don't think it really struck us that way, at least the ones that stayed there. Moody says education in his family was a nonfactor. You didn't go to school to learn. You went to school socially and to play football. His father didn't have an education. My father was a truck driver. Education to me was a way out and a way up. We learned from each other. I tried to be as good as him in sports, and he tried to be as good as me in grades, and he would be embarrassed if he didn't have the same grades, and I would be embarrassed—I knew I couldn't lift as much as him—if I didn't try as hard as he did. That was sort of our team attitude that sort of protected us in a bubble from whatever else was going on."

Rose graduated in 1969 and was one of the only Matadors that didn't return for the 1969 season. Estacado once again went undefeated until it met Brownwood in the playoffs. But this time, no cleats would be long or sharp enough to propel the Matadors past a determined Wood.

Keeling laughed about the rematch as he told me the story. "I'd see [Brownwood assistant coach] Morris Southall or those guys, and they were like, 'Hey, [Wood] is obsessed with beating Estacado in the playoffs.' He knew in his mind whoever won that game was going to win state again."

And that's what happened.

# 7

# MEXIA

## 1968

### *Blackcats Roll with the Changes*

If it were a movie, we would swear we had seen the scene before.

It begins with a panning shot of a 1960s-era gym, chock-full of white country boys lifting weights and climbing ropes in gray sweats, participating in calisthenics in all the ways high school boys did that in 1967.

In walks the coach, giving the grand tour to four black kids, and everyone freezes in place. There's silence, and everyone involved processes what's happening. No one is completely comfortable, but no one knows how to react.

But it wasn't a movie. That was the scene described to me by Bob McQueen and all the former players I spoke with from the Mexia Blackcats of that moment. It was the beginning of a great story, but not one that followed all the familiar twists and turns.

Ray Rhodes, who played seven seasons in the NFL for the New York Giants and San Francisco 49ers and then coached in the NFL for more than three decades, was one of the four new students at Mexia High School.

"The biggest thing was, it was all foreign to everybody," Rhodes said. "For the white kids, for the black kids, it was foreign. It was one of those moments where you were a little nervous about the whole thing."

Perhaps this story would fit with all the other sports stories during integration of the 1960s if it had a little more conflict. But from what I've gathered, it seemed that McQueen looked all his players, black and white, in the eyes and said, "This is how it's going to be," and everyone fell in line.

It was, after all, sort of McQueen's idea to get out in front of the game. Integration was coming in Texas in 1968, and Mexia had two schools at the time—Mexia High and the all-black Dunbar High School. McQueen, who was twenty-five when he arrived in Mexia as the Blackcats' head football coach in 1965, saw that the two schools would soon become one, and he embraced the change a year early.

In 1967, students were given the freedom to choose which school they would attend. Rhodes was going into his junior year, so McQueen made the pitch for him to choose Mexia.

"Raymond's father, Thetford Rhodes, was the assistant manager at the J. C. Penney store there, and on the side he made drapes," McQueen said. "We needed some curtains, and so I called Thetford and asked him if he would come out and measure our windows and do us some curtains. And told him I'd also like to talk to him about his son. So he came out and we sat down. He measured, and we sat down, and I talked to him about Raymond, because I knew he was really special. I talked to him about how if he just came in here his senior year, that there would be so much involved in just learning the system that he wouldn't be able to be everything he could be."

It made sense to Thetford Rhodes.

"Quite honestly, during that time, I didn't know what to make of it," Ray Rhodes said. "My dad said, 'Hey, you really don't have a choice. This is what you're going to do.'"

But Raymond wouldn't be making the move alone. When Rhodes walked into Mexia High School for the first time, his Dunbar teammates Willie Charles Dancer, Charlie Livingston, and Eugene Baker were with him. If Raymond was going to Mexia, they were going to follow him.

In the movies, this would be the scene where the black players have to prove they can hack it with the white kids, and then the white kids begin to change their minds about people of other races. From what they told me, the Mexia kids skipped all that drama. Rhodes and Dancer and Livingston and Baker fell right in with athletes such as running back Benjie Reed and quarterback Stephen Sims.

"We had no issues whatsoever," Sims said. "Those guys that came over were coming over from very successful programs at Dunbar High School. They had either played for or won the state championship in their black division [in basketball] and had gone deep into the playoffs with football. We knew who they were and had great respect for them before they came over."

But there was one major adjustment that had to be made. Rhodes said McQueen's expectations for what happened on the football field in practice and in games raised the standard for the new players.

Throughout his career as an NFL player and coach, Rhodes pointed to the hard-nosed grit he gleaned from his high school days, and that specifically meant playing through pain. "When I went over with Coach McQueen, the number one thing that he instilled in me was toughness," Rhodes said. "The difference between being hurt and being injured. Coach McQueen made sure that he got that point across to me early in my career. When I was at the black school, you'd get hit hard a little bit, and you lay on the ground. Coach McQueen did not play that. 'Nobody lays on my field. You get up, and you get off the field the best way that you can, but you're not going to lay on my field.'

"We had a little nose guard named Billy Archibald. He got his leg broken, and you could see that his leg was broken. He got up off that ground and hopped off the field. When I saw that, I said, 'You know what? Coach McQueen has instilled something special with this football team.'"

While Rhodes worked toward learning McQueen's style and system, his new teammates noticed he was bringing a new dimension to the Blackcats. Reed said that if there was any learning curve, the new players, and especially Rhodes, took it in stride as far as the white players knew. "I mean, Coach McQueen may have said that Raymond needed to learn the offense," Reed said. "Really, all that he had to teach somebody was just how to get the ball to Raymond."

When I spoke with Reed, now an attorney in Mexia, he rattled off Rhodes's attributes as if he were making an airtight case for the consummate team player. "He was an extremely gifted athlete," Reed said. "He encouraged the younger players to be good. He was very faithful to practice. He worked hard in practice. He more or less led by example. He wasn't loud. He made plays when plays were needed."

The Mexia players gelled quickly, which led to the Blackcats winning their district in 1967. Two victories early in the 1967 season over powerhouse Belton and area rival Teague proved to the Mexia players just how tough they could be. "We got behind Teague at halftime, like, 20–6, and we were going, 'My God, we're getting ready to get beat by Teague,'" Sims said. "We ended up winning 39–20, and when we came back that much in the second half to beat Teague, all the sudden that really was what began to instill some additional confidence. Not only can we beat a team that's well known like Belton, that's got a good program, but we can come back when we're down."

Since only the district champion made the playoffs, a format that didn't change until 1982, Mexia surged into the postseason, only to lose to Plano in the first round, the same fate it had suffered in 1966.

Before the 1968 season started, the Blackcats were elevated to 3A. McQueen said the enrollment count placed Mexia in the bigger classification by six students, meaning the Blackcats would face a steep challenge by having to compete in a new district. But looking back, that change set up the game that the coach and players pointed to as their defining moment at Mexia.

The Blackcats began the 1968 season by winning their first four games, so they took an undefeated record into battle versus Waco Jefferson Moore, which was ranked tenth in 3A at the time. It was also Moore's homecoming game, and the word on the street was that the Lions had never lost a homecoming.

Looking back through the newspaper archives, I found one of those hidden gems in the lead paragraph of the *Waco Tribune-Herald*'s game story by Alan Eskew. "The intercom system was in good working order Friday night at Municipal Stadium for the more than 8,000 fans on hand for the Moore-Mexia game," Eskew wrote, setting up one of the more gloriously bad puns I've ever encountered. "What was needed was an inner-calm system though."

For the Blackcats, perhaps the most difficult moment to overcome was the coin toss, when the Mexia captains stared up at giant Moore offensive lineman Walter Baisy. "We walk out to the middle of the field for the coin toss, and Walter Baisy had pads from his neck all the way down to his fingertips," Sims said. "And I said, 'That is the biggest, most intimidating guy I've ever seen in my life.' I think he was about six-four, maybe, at the time, about 240 pounds, and that was enormous back in the late sixties."

Mexia came out swinging anyway. After Moore went three-and-out to start the game, Blackcats Jon Phillips and Bennett Barham blocked the punt to set up Mexia at the Lions' four-yard line. Reed scored on a one-yard dive to put the Blackcats ahead 6–0.

Eskew employed a simile that rivaled his earlier pun. "Moore started the game like it had flunked out of chiropodist school—on the wrong foot," he wrote.

Moore found its rhythm, though, and pushed ahead 14–13 at halftime. In the locker room, the Mexia players knew they were in a more ferocious battle than any they had ever seen. McQueen said he wasn't sure whether Rhodes, who was beaten and bruised from a busy first half, would be able to go back in the game in the final two quarters.

Reed attempted to rally his defensive teammates, but since he hadn't entered the game on that side of the ball, he knew his words could fall flat. "In the locker room, there were some guys bleeding a little bit, as you will do," Reed said. "I remember saying, 'Come on, guys, y'all can play better than that. These guys aren't really that tough.' I thought to myself, 'My God! You haven't been in the game yet.'"

The Mexia defense was up to the challenge, though. The Blackcats shut out Moore in the second half, and Rhodes played a key role in pushing his team in front in the 8-3A clash.

Rhodes broke loose for a thirty-seven-yard run to spark Mexia's go-ahead touchdown drive. Blackcats fullback Jackie Hartnett finished it with a one-yard touchdown plunge. Sims passed to Dancer for the two-point conversion to give Mexia a 21–14 lead with 2:58 left in the third quarter.

Moore quickly put Mexia's back against the wall, and it was time for Sims to make another crucial play. Lions running back Rayford Wilkins eluded the Blackcats' defense for a fifty-seven-yard run to the Mexia ten. The Blackcats held their ground from there, and on fourth-and-goal, Sims stopped the drive cold. "[Moore quarterback Larry Rose] threw a ball over the middle, and I stumbled my way to find a way to intercept the pass," Sims said.

It took one more takeaway for the Mexia defense to keep Moore from making an equalizing touchdown. "With less than two minutes to go, a happy Levi Chambers climbed off a Moore fumble at the 50 and the Mexia fans started a victory chant," Eskew wrote.

McQueen said it was probably the best game Mexia played during his four-year run at the school. The Blackcats needed it to notch their third consecutive district title and playoff appearance. Corsicana defeated Mexia later in 8-3A play, creating a three-way tie between the Blackcats, Corsicana, and Moore.

Sims's father, R. Q. Sims, was the Mexia principal, and when coaches and administrators met to break the tie, he was chosen to pick a name out of a hat to name the playoff representative. Sims picked well for his school, since the Blackcats advanced. Long before Twitter could have spread the news like wildfire, the Blackcat players learned their fate in old-school fashion.

"I met Coach McQueen going down Hopkins Street in Mexia, and he says, 'Get ready to play next Friday,'" Reed said.

Mexia tied Lancaster in the bi-district game 9–9 and advanced to the area playoff on penetrations. Next up was a battle with Henderson, featuring dynamic quarterback Keith Bobo. Sims would later room with Bobo when they played together at SMU. This time, though, the Blackcats couldn't find a way to break through, and Henderson claimed a 10–7 victory on a late field goal. That meant that Henderson went on to play Mexia's old nemesis, Plano.

"I see Keith all the time. He comes to Dallas, and we go out and play golf, and I say, 'Keith, doggone it, you beat us on a forty-something-yard field goal,'" Sims said. "We wanted to play Plano so badly. He goes, 'Let me tell you something. You guys would have run all over Plano. You had a much better team than Plano.' Henderson beat 'em, like, 30–0. He said, 'You had one of the best teams that we ever played.'"

That's how much high school games resonate in the lives of the men who played in them. But more than anything that happened on the field, Rhodes and Sims described how playing together changed their lives forever. "Steve Sims was a calming factor, really, in integration during that time," Rhodes said. "He was unbelievable as far as being there to talk to people and help people through situations. I still think of Stephen today, about how he helped me out through that whole transition."

There came a point when Sims and his white teammates had to stand up to outside forces that threatened to alienate their black teammates. McQueen described to me how schools at the time would cancel their proms because they couldn't throw a white prom and a black prom. In the void, some communities would host "senior girls' dances" and invite only the white kids.

Not in Mexia.

"I told my mom, 'If Raymond Rhodes cannot go, I'm not going,'" Sims said. The Blackcats players stood up in united opposition to the act of exclusion, and it never came to pass.

Another thing Mexia's white and black players shared was the experience of playing college football. Reed went to Texas Tech, and Sims to SMU. Dancer led Baylor in receiving in 1972 and 1973.

Rhodes went to TCU for two seasons, where he played running back for the Horned Frogs. He then transferred to Tulsa and switched positions to wide receiver and defensive back. His career from high school through the NFL was marked by the ability to transition from one place to another. When I spoke with Rhodes, he left no doubt that everything he did in his career had its start in the conversation McQueen had with Thetford Rhodes. That's when a talented kid became a man on a mission.

"Coach McQueen would not let you quit," Rhodes said. "If you got an opportunity to try something, you go try it. Don't be afraid of it."

Early in 1980, Rhodes was traded from the New York Giants to Bill Walsh's San Francisco 49ers. But Rhodes wasn't sure whether he wanted to go across the country to start again or to retire instead. So he went back to his roots, visiting McQueen, who was by then the head coach at Temple. "He asked me what I thought," McQueen said. "I told him, 'Raymond, if you don't try it you'll always wonder. I think this guy that they've hired, this coach Bill Walsh, I think he's a pretty good coach.' Raymond ended up going over there and the deal was he was sort of a player-coach. They had brought in all these young DBs [defensive backs], and they needed some maturity to help them until they got ready to go."

That launched Rhodes's coaching career, and he smoothly made the move to full-time assistant coach in 1981. In 1995, Rhodes took the job as the Philadelphia Eagles' head coach, becoming the fourth African American head coach in NFL history and the first at the helm of the Eagles.

Rhodes earned NFL Coach of the Year honors in his first season after the Eagles rebounded from losing three of their first four games to finish 10–6 and make the playoffs. That's the kind of toughness in the face of adversity that can be attributed to deep roots.

It's definitely an oversimplification to write that Rhodes's career path was put in motion the day Thetford Rhodes went to the McQueen house to install new curtains. It's also naive to suggest that Rhodes and his black teammates didn't face adversity as part of the integration process. Rhodes just chose not to describe that to me.

The one thing that is clear is that everyone involved dug in and faced the challenges for the sake of playing football together. Only in hindsight can we see the difference it made.

"You're a seventeen-, eighteen-year-old kid, you don't think about all that stuff," Rhodes said. "All you're doing is playing football, something you love to do. And then you get older. You can see the people who really influenced your life. I know what Coach McQueen did for me, because he instilled a toughness in me that I did not have when I got there. This is the way football is played. You're going to go out and hit this team in the mouth, and that stuck with me."

# 8

# CELINA

## 1974

### *The Birth of the 10-1 Defense*

Maybe Celina epitomizes everything we think of when we think of Texas high school football, because the people in that community make a concerted effort to make it so.

Or maybe everything we think of when we think of Texas high school football comes from the way it's done in Celina.

Actually, there's much more evidence to support the latter proposition, and it's not just because their legendary coach, G. A. Moore, wore a cowboy hat on the sideline and still runs a cattle ranch right in the same little corner of Texas where he was born, raised, and coached teams to eight state titles. There's also the barbershop in the downtown square, where the barber, David Renteria, has decked his walls with posters commemorating the Bobcats' state championships. Renteria himself, wearing number eighteen, looks out from one of the posters as he and his teammates hoist the 1974 Class B state championship trophy.

But even before you drive into downtown Celina, you know you're in a football town. Just a blink of an eye away from the north end of the North Dallas Tollway, you make a left off Highway 289 onto Pecan Street, and the first thing you see, almost as if it's being showcased to the left side of the road, is the football stadium. In context, it's impressive; a perfect small-town stadium with the home bleachers and press box facing northeast and welcoming folks to town.

If all that's not enough, the billboard facing the road lists the football program's accomplishments, including eight state championships and more district titles and playoff appearances than it's possible to count during a casual drive by.

All of it points to Moore, who, as of this writing, is still the winningest football coach in Texas history, with 422 victories. But even he will tell you that passion for high school football in these parts predates him.

I met with Moore in the office–storage space in back of the Bobcat Kuntry Stop & Go on Pecan Street. It's another one of those small town staples where the owner, E. L. Marks, runs the counter and where Moore feels at home. He told me that though he went to school from first grade through high school graduation thirteen miles away in Pilot Point, his mother's family lived in Celina, and he grew up in both places.

Moore said he and his friends and teammates on his Pilot Point Bearcat teams believed they were the best around in football, basketball, and track. That's where he wanted to coach, and that dream came true in 1963. So began one of the more intriguing coaching careers in all of football. Moore ping-ponged back and forth between Pilot Point and Celina during the next five decades. He had three stints at Pilot Point and two at Celina.

After leading the Bearcats for eight seasons, Moore intended to leave coaching and go to seminary in the early 1970s. But needing to make some money first, he took a job as principal at Celina. That's where he first engaged with the town's fierce pride in its school. "Celina's got a Quarterback Club that's fantastic," Moore said. "They had it before I got here. I'd like to say, 'Hey, I started it.' I didn't start it. They were great when I got here."

And Moore remembers how its importance was stressed to him.

"One thing, when I came to Celina, something that impressed me," Moore said, "I met with the superintendent and the principal, and the superintendent told me, Mr. Sears, he said, 'Look, three things you will do.' He didn't say, 'I hope you'll do this.' He said, 'There's three things you will do. One of them, all the kids will say "yes, sir" and "no, sir" and "yes, ma'am" and "no, ma'am." You'll be responsible for that. The other thing is, you'll wear an orange shirt to school on Friday. The third thing is, you go to the Quarterback Club on Thursday morning. The leaders in this town, the people who made us what we are, are in the Quarterback Club.'"

Obviously, Moore took those responsibilities seriously, which probably had more than a little to do with him moving from the principal's office to the field house as the head football coach in 1972.

Moore took the reins from Gerald Browder, who had led the Bobcats to an 11–0–1 record and the regional championship in 1971. Browder's final year as Celina's head coach was also the final season that Class B schools didn't advance to a state title game. A regional championship was as far as Celina could go that season, so that's the baton Moore took from Browder. Moore pointed out that it's the only time in his career he took over a program that had won the year before.

Meanwhile, having seen their elder statesmen go as far as they could go, the freshmen of 1971 began to imagine winning a state title. "That's way out there, but that was our goal," said Steve Carey, who was a senior tight end and defensive end in 1974.

Celina lost one game in each of the 1972 and 1973 seasons, but that was enough to keep them out of the playoffs both years.

In '73, an eight-point loss to Prosper kept Celina out of the playoffs. But in 1974, Celina took sweet revenge with a 66–6 trouncing of Prosper in the final game of the regular season, finishing with a perfect 6–0 district record and a 9–1 regular season. Even the Bobcats' lone loss served as evidence of their prowess.

Celina faced Allen in the second game of the season at a time when Allen had triple the Bobcats' enrollment. But each was state ranked in its classification, and Celina came ready to hold its own.

Celina had a new weapon in its arsenal for the Allen game. For the first time in its history, the Bobcats deployed their now-famed 10-1 defense for an entire contest. The 10-1 lines up ten defenders with hands on the ground at the line of scrimmage. It is a man-to-man defense with heavy pursuit of the ballcarrier at the point of attack. It's the responsibility of one player, the man standing up behind the line, to run down anything that gets past the line. The Celina 10-1 defense caused frustration for opponents and won games for the Bobcats for five decades.

But it almost didn't make it out of the first quarter.

On the game's first offensive play, Allen running back Mark Beaty ran off right tackle and scooted fifty-nine yards for a touchdown. The Eagles added the extra point for a 7–0 lead. Celina linebacker Rex Glendenning, the player standing up behind the line, had failed to stay in position to be the safety net. "It only stung us one time the entire year," Glendenning said. "I was the only guy standing up, so I guess it was my fault. They kind of ran a bit of a cross-buck move and threw me into the line a little bit, and once Mark popped outside the tackle, the only person that had a chance to get him was me, standing up. But I took a step into the line."

Glendenning was the leader of the Bobcat defense. He went on to record more than twenty tackles in the state championship game later that season. He played college football for Hayden Fry at North Texas State University, where he joined forces with Beaty on the Mean Green defense.

Glendenning and Beaty, who were roommates for three years at NTSU, often reminisced about the Allen-Celina game. "He said, 'We got lucky and popped one,'" Glendenning said. "He remembered it pretty vividly, and so did I. We're still good friends, and he's a heck of a guy."

Beaty's touchdown run put Celina in a 7–0 hole. But before the Bobcats could attempt to turn around the scoreboard, they had to change their coach's mind about altering his defensive tactics.

"I said, 'Y'all want to go back?'" said Moore, recalling a democratic meeting on the sideline. "We ran a 26 defense and stunted a lot. They said, 'No, Coach. Let us run it. He won't do it no more.' They had three first downs the rest of the game. But they beat us 7–6."

Celina running back Randy Nelson scored on a twenty-five-yard run, but a costly penalty on the point after caused the Bobcats to fall short on their two-point conversion try, which would have boosted them in front of Allen.

Despite the disparity in the schools' sizes, Celina took the loss to Allen hard. Following the game, the team gathered in the end zone for a bull-in-the-ring drill that seemed to go on endlessly. Essentially a full-pads, no-holds-barred wrestling match between two players at a time, the bull-in-the-ring is controversial at the high school level in the twenty-first century. In the 1970s, though, it was just a way to teach a lesson and perhaps release frustration. "There was a lot of blood and snot on that corner of the end zone," Glendenning said. "We got beat, so they were trying to ingrain in us toughness. It was more of a reach-down-deep-in-your-gut. 'You guys have to toughen up and be a tougher team.' I don't know if they'd let you do that these days."

Whether it was the close call against Allen or the motivational session afterward, something ignited Celina. The Bobcats responded by thumping Princeton, another bigger school, in the next game, and then tore through their district competition.

Celina needed a win in the final week of the regular season versus Prosper to make the playoffs. "Prosper at that time was our big rivalry," Carey said. "I remember as a player sitting there in the locker room and hearing the caravan coming down the highway and people honking their horns from Prosper. They really thought they were going to win this game. I was scared to death of that game. I think that always helped. It always helped me."

By the final game of the 1974 regular season, Celina had progressed far beyond its rival, though. Carey told me the Bobcats scored just about every way a team could score in the first half and led Prosper 59–0 at halftime. Celina eventually claimed a 66–6 victory. More than just revenge for the previous year's loss, the Bobcats' win propelled them into the postseason. "It was from that point that we just really rolled, and people were shocked with what they were seeing us do offensively," Carey said. "It was crazy."

Three lopsided wins later, Celina earned the right to meet up with the Class B powerhouse Big Sandy in the state final. In 1973, Big Sandy had held its fourteen opponents to a combined fifteen points, including a 25–0 victory over Rule in the state championship game.

Celina and Big Sandy agreed to face off at Forester Field in Mesquite. The clash held the attention of high school football fans in Dallas–Fort Worth. In the lead-up to the game, the *McKinney Courier-Gazette* characterized it as yet another David-versus-Goliath tilt for the Bobcats. "Now the big one, the shootout between Big Sandy's Wildcats and the Bobcats Saturday afternoon," wrote *Courier-Gazette* sports editor Norman Wilson. "Again, the Bobcats are supposed to be the team on the short end of the score. According to scouting reports Big Sandy is a quicker team than Celina."

Wilson's story also points out that Moore had had his sights set on a championship matchup with Big Sandy from the outset of the playoffs. But the *McKinney Courier-Gazette*'s description of the Celina–Big Sandy game as a shootout proved anything but prescient.

Big Sandy had surrendered thirty-five points in thirteen games coming into its clash with Celina, and the Bobcats were unable to add to that total. But Celina's ten-man defensive front had developed into an iron curtain. The game that unfolded was possibly the greatest defensive clash in the history of Texas high school football. "I just remember a true, all-out, balls-to-the-wall gutsy defensive struggle," Glendenning said. "I think one of the reasons I ended up getting a couple of DI [Division I college] offers is by being able to have so many opportunities on defense and making twenty-eight or twenty-nine tackles."

The Wildcats intercepted four Celina passes, and the Bobcats answered by taking the ball away from Big Sandy six times. That proved vital for Celina, which didn't penetrate Big Sandy's thirty-five-yard line and amassed only half the yardage of the Big Sandy offense.

Celina successfully corralled a Big Sandy offense led by quarterback Gary Chalk and tailback David Overstreet. But the Wildcats' defense, led by middle linebacker Lovie Smith, clamped down on the Bobcats, holding them to seven first downs for the afternoon.

Carey showed me the scouting report from the game, which he had kept for more than forty years. Smith's name wasn't listed, just his number, the letters "MLB" (middle linebacker), and the brief description "GREAT."

The stalemate of a scoreless game threatened to be broken by a flurry of activity in the final 1:16 of the fourth quarter. Big Sandy intercepted two Celina passes, but those takeaways were mitigated by a Bobcat fumble recovery. Then Celina's Joe Wester intercepted a Chalk pass at the Bobcats' eight to stop Big Sandy's final chance to score.

Celina and Big Sandy tied 0–0 and split the state title.

At one point, Celina briefly believed it had come up with the difference-making play. "They did a quick pitchout to David Overstreet, and he fumbled," Moore recalled. "The ball hit the turf, and Randy Nelson caught it on the first bounce and ran seventy yards for a touchdown."

Alas, a fumble recovery couldn't be advanced at the time, so no touchdown. It's a play that has been relived many times from every possible angle. "They had a film," Moore said. "One of them was chasing him, and they quit after about thirty yards. Nelson said, 'They never would have caught me,' and somebody else said, 'Yeah, they would have caught you. They knew it wasn't going to count.'"

By sharing the state championship, though, Celina and Big Sandy have shared an even bigger place in Texas football lore. Of course, it helps that Moore went on to win more football games than anyone before him in the state, and that Lovie Smith went on to lead the Chicago Bears as their head coach for nine seasons, including taking them to Super Bowl XLI.

Celina met up with Big Sandy again in 2012 when Moore and Smith were inducted into the Texas Sports Hall of Fame as members of the same class.

Although it would be twenty-one years before Celina won its first outright state championship, that initial foray into Texas's ultimate contest spurred on an already-smoldering football hotbed. Carey later became a captain of the Quarterback Club, and he preaches the organization's impact on the Celina community and the entire region.

Glendenning's Rex Real Estate greets drivers as they cruise into Celina on 289. Celina and high school football are indivisible, and Glendenning points to his senior season as the time when that association became set in concrete. "It's absolutely the defining moment for Celina," he said. "Not that they didn't have some great teams before that. [Moore] brought such charisma and moral fortitude and will to win that basically engulfed the entire community. I would tell you, from that point on, that was basically the platform that launched the program onto the success that we've had over the past couple of decades."

Celina's streak of sixty-eight consecutive wins from 1998 to 2002, which netted four straight 2A Division II state titles, came at a time when the passing game was pushing its way to center stage in all of football. But having claimed its first state title in a 0–0 tie, the Bobcats' identity remained predicated on defense, to the delight of the community that adored them. "Defense wins championships," Glendenning said. "And that's what I always loved about Celina football, was how much pride we took on the defensive side of the ball."

That's meat-and-potatoes football at its finest, and it's a big part of the reason why the Bobcats are the quintessential Texas high school program. Plenty of towns have their flashes of greatness, but Celina has sustained it over decades. One could make the argument that without Moore, the Bobcats might never have reached the championship level, but without a place so dedicated to forming its community around its high school football team, Moore couldn't have won all those games.

While I was in town talking to Carey, who showed me around the football field and the high school, we discussed how the urban sprawl of North Dallas was encroaching on Celina's small-town aesthetic. Frisco, just fifteen miles south, had one high school at the turn of the twenty-first century. At the time of this writing, there are eight. If the same type of population explosion happens around Celina, the Bobcats could soon have a rival high school within their district. How that would affect the Celina tradition is hard to predict.

But like Texas high school football itself, it's a safe bet that the essence, the intangible quality that makes it special, will prevail.

"I told somebody yesterday I still think I have the best of both worlds," Carey said. "Celina has it. I'm not sure how to define what it is. My wife was the cheerleader sponsor for twenty-six years. As she and I talk about the 'it,' it really is everything involved. That's why Coach Moore was the best of anybody around. He was able to pull everybody together for a common cause."

# 9

# BIG SANDY

## 1974

### *The Wildcats Kiss Their Sisters*

As the Big Sandy players walked off the turf at Forester Field on a Saturday afternoon in December 1974, the Wildcats searched for how to feel.

In the distance, they could hear the crowd cheering. Maybe it was Celina celebrating, but who really knew? Who could really celebrate at the end of a 0–0 tie? For decades afterward, the game would be revered for its novelty as much as for the stars of the game represented on the field that day. Celina coach G. A. Moore went on to win more games than anyone before him. Big Sandy running back David Overstreet went from high school stardom to a leading role for the Oklahoma Sooners to a career in the Canadian Football League and the NFL. Wildcat linebacker Lovie Smith earned a formidable reputation for coaching defense and then became the Chicago Bears' head coach, leading them to the Super Bowl. Up and down each roster are the names of men who went from successful high school careers to flourish beyond that game.

But when the final whistle blew, it was hard to appreciate the game's significance.

Big Sandy had won the Class B state championship in 1973, and it had a two-season unbeaten streak going into the championship. On the field that day, the Wildcats felt as if they had enforced their will. All the statistics showed it, except the one stat that counted most. "We were kind of shell-shocked, really, not knowing what had happened," Big Sandy quarterback Gary Chalk remembered. "Ending in a tie, what did that mean? Coach [Jim] Norman had a son that was a senior on the team, named Jim Norman as well, and he said it was like kissing your sister. You got a kiss, but it was just your sister."

The clash between Big Sandy and Celina in 1974 pitted the number one Wildcats against the number two Bobcats. Looking back on it, it's one of the classic games in the history of Texas high school football, but it produced plenty of hype even at the time. It was the type of game that, going in, each team felt it would be lucky to go home with a victory. Chalk said despite Big Sandy's accolades and winning streak, the Wildcats didn't hear many people picking them to win the game.

Yet somehow, when it ended in a tie, the Big Sandy players had that sinking feeling. "Because we had been the underdog, we should've felt like a tie was a win for us, but we didn't," Chalk said. "We felt like we should've won, especially after we had dominated the game like we did."

It's easy to see from just the final stats why the Wildcats felt that they had left points on the field. Big Sandy doubled up Celina in rushing yards and first downs. But the Wildcats lost three fumbles and three interceptions. They partly made up for it by intercepting four Celina passes, but still couldn't break through for a score.

Celina defenders Joe Wester and Scot Tingle each intercepted Chalk passes inside the Bobcats' ten-yard line. Wester's interception at the eight turned away a Big Sandy chance in the final minute. The Wildcats also missed a twenty-seven-yard field goal late in the first half.

Meanwhile, the Big Sandy defense didn't let Celina drive any deeper than the Wildcats' thirty-six. Celina was well aware of Lovie Smith's prowess at middle linebacker; his number, 24, in the scouting report was underscored simply by the word "GREAT." But the whole Wildcat defense caused problems for the Bobcats: Larry Chalk, Tim Overstreet, Tony Newman, and Ricky Davis picked off passes. Chalk credited Davis, also the punter, with keeping the Bobcats backed up inside their own territory all day.

But Big Sandy's twenty-seven-game winning streak ended that day. The *Dallas Times Herald* sportswriter Kenny Hand noted in his game story that Celina coach G. A. Moore and Norman agreed before the game that a tie would result in a cochampionship.

So who really won is just a matter of opinion.

Smith spoke with me over the phone in the spring of 2015, taking time from a busy off-season in which his new team, the Tampa Bay Buccaneers, had the top overall pick in the NFL Draft. He made sure I knew how vital a role high school football had played in his life, and he expressed earnest admiration for Moore and the Celina team. But the competitor in him keeps wanting to tilt the outcome of the 1974 championship game. "Still to this day, it's still hard," Smith said. "I mean, how in the world can you let a state championship game end up in a 0–0 tie anyway?"

It's the only game in three seasons from 1973 to 1975 that Big Sandy didn't win, which of course makes it all the more memorable and debatable. "Oh, I'm sure Coach Moore's team and all the Celina guys would say, 'Hey, we should've won that game,'" Smith said. "But probably to a man, Big Sandy's people would say, 'Yeah, we should've won that game.'"

One footnote has been lost in the shuffle of history surrounding the 1974 Class B championship game. When the older generation of high school football fans talk about those Big Sandy teams, the two names they mention are Smith and David Overstreet. Smith said that any Class B team with Overstreet on it would have been special. But Overstreet didn't play a major role against Celina. Injured earlier in the season, he mainly served as a decoy. He's not mentioned in the *Dallas Morning News* or the *Dallas Times Herald* game stories.

Chalk told me he knew Overstreet's injury had shifted the pressure to him and backup running back John Jones, and they almost came up with the game-changing play. "I rolled out, and I believe it was [Celina linebacker] Rex Glendenning—I remember I was going to try to pass, and he jumped up, and I threw the ball too high and overthrew John Jones," Chalk said. "I believe John would've scored if I made a good throw."

Remembering and reliving those plays has long since lost its sting for Chalk. It helps that plenty of highlights were still to come for those Wildcats. Apparently, that strange feeling the Big Sandy players experienced while walking off the field after the championship game versus Celina motivated them the following season.

With that drive, and another year of age and experience, Big Sandy was fierce in 1975.

The Wildcats didn't just win games—they demolished opponents. Big Sandy averaged more than fifty-eight points a game and gave up only fifteen points all season. That figure includes the Wildcats' 26–2 state championship game victory over Groom, which, while still a blowout, brought down Big Sandy's scoring averages by its relative competitiveness.

Big Sandy posted eleven shutouts that season and never gave up more than seven points in a game. Chalk described to me both touchdowns that opponents scored that season, adding that one of them happened because a defensive back slipped down and missed a sure interception. "That's what Lovie likes to brag on, is the shutouts record," Chalk said. "And of course, I brag about the points."

Chalk told me he remembered the 1975 Wildcats being ranked fifth nationally among schools of all sizes, never mind that Big Sandy was in the smallest classification in Texas to play eleven-man football. He also remembered a rankings expert telling the Wildcats that they could've defeated any team in Texas that year in a one-game playoff.

When I asked Smith to compare all three teams, he said the 1974 squad was the weakest. Chalk, making the same comparison, gave a colorful and straightforward description of the differences between the 1973 team, which went 14–0, and the 1975 team, which accomplished the same feat.

"Bobby Mitchell on the '73 team scored all our touchdowns, kicked the extra points, sold popcorn at halftime, drove the bus back home," Chalk said. "He made a big difference, but if you take Bobby off that team, I don't know if that team would've been that good. I think the '75 team, not just because I started, [but because] we were just so much faster and so much smarter. Lovie started on the '73 team, but he was a sophomore. You put him as a senior on the '75 team. Overstreet was a freshman on the '73 team, that made him a junior in '75."

No doubt the 1975 Big Sandy team was talented and experienced, as well as hardened by the fire of fierce competition. The schedule clearly didn't challenge them much. No matter, though; the players kept challenging themselves in football and then after high school.

Smith graduated in 1976 and went to Tulsa, where he became a two-time all-American. He graduated in 1980 and returned to Big Sandy to begin his coaching career, but the high school ranks couldn't contain his mind for the game for long. Smith spent most of the 1980s and early 1990s building a coaching resume, serving as defensive back or linebacker coach at Tulsa, Wisconsin, Arizona State, Kentucky, Tennessee, and Ohio State. In 1996, Tony Dungy hired him to coach the Tampa Bay Buccaneers linebackers. The St. Louis Rams then lured Smith away to be their defensive coordinator in 2001, and the Bears made him their head coach in 2004.

"Proud is not even close to it," Chalk said about the emotions he's felt following his cousin through a successful coaching career. "Everywhere he's gone, we feel like we've been a part of that, because we're relatives as well. And Lovie and I have always been best friends. Everywhere he's gone, I've made it my business that we go by and visit with him and pat him on the back and keep pushing him forward. When he became the head coach of Chicago,

Chicago became our team. All of us wore the blue and orange. I threw all my Chicago Bears stuff away, and now I'm a Buccaneer."

When my conversation with Smith was coming to a close, I thanked him for taking time to speak with me. He told me plainly, "Everything I have, I owe to Texas high school football."

Earlier in the interview, he had drawn a direct line from his experience in Big Sandy to his philosophy as an NFL head coach. "Jim Norman, he ingrained, 'Hey, we're going to win based on what we do defensively,'" Smith said. "That's still my mindset. To build our football team in order to win a championship, you have to play great defense. And once you play great defense and special teams, and you get your offense going, too, then you have something special. I'm still trying to create the same type of environment [in Tampa Bay]. I think you can also create an environment where the expectations are for you to win each week. That's what we had then. The Celina game, when we tied them, that was a shock to us because of the expectations. We trained every day to win, and we expected to do that based on our work. That same mentality I still have to this day."

Smith's experience happened to apply directly to football. Chalk gleaned the same types of things from Norman and put them to work in building a career in the natural gas industry.

"I started out on a shovel out on the road, working on a crew. And because of that work ethic and that tenacity and perseverance and that championship mentality, it has allowed me to work my way up through the company, and now I'm a district director for that company," Chalk said. "There were days when I contemplated saying, 'Enough is enough.' Kind of like on a hot August day, practicing, 'I'm through. I'm not going to ever play again.' There were days when I drove home from work for different reasons, a mean boss or whatever, and I'd say, 'You know what? I'm not going back.' But then that next morning, you get back up and you lace your boots back up and you go back to work. I tell people that about Coach Jim Norman all the time, that [as far as] Xs and Os, he was not a G. A. Moore, but as far as motivating young men, he was a great motivator. He made you feel like you could conquer the world. I think that's what stays with the athlete that came through that era."

In his spare time, Chalk gave back to high school football by officiating for more than thirty years. He said he never saw a team that he thought would have outmatched his Wildcats, though he did acknowledge that the advent of seven-on-seven and year-round training have begun to change his mind on the subject.

It doesn't matter though. None of the modern teams will be able to play those Big Sandy Wildcats. So the Celina Bobcats are the only ones who can say for certain that they held their own with Big Sandy.

And looking back with forty years to think on it, the feeling is mutual. "I celebrate the '75 state championship probably the most because we were so dominant that year," Chalk said. "But I'm actually proudest of the '74 championship, because in all reality we probably should not have even been playing in the state championship game, and certainly we should not have tied Celina. We were very fortunate to get to that state championship, so I'm real proud of that team for those reasons."

# 10

# TEMPLE

## 1975

### *Bob McQueen Adds It Up*

—

Every football fan whose team has ever gone into the halftime locker room facing a deficit has had the same thought: "That ole coach better go in there and get them boys fired up."

We put our faith in the halftime speech.

We all imagine that this is when the coach, by being an inspirational leader, earns his paycheck. The problem, though, is that there are always two head coaches going into separate locker rooms at halftime. Which raises the question: How often is our guy the better orator? And how much does that really matter?

My feeling on the matter is that the halftime speech seldom comes into play. But it mattered on November 7, 1975, when the Temple Wildcats were trailing the top-ranked Bryan Vikings.

I sat down with longtime Temple coach Bob McQueen in his man cave adjacent to his Temple house one Friday during football season in 2014. McQueen won 243 games, lost 77, and tied 7 during his twenty-eight seasons at Temple High School. When I was on staff at the *Waco Tribune-Herald* in the mid-2000s, we selected McQueen as the Super Centex 50th Anniversary all-time team coach in 2005, an honor that McQueen was still blushing over when we met. McQueen's Temple teams won state titles in 1979 and 1992, and the Wildcats were annually a force in Texas high school football's largest-school division. When I surveyed Aledo coach Tim Buchanan about towns and people I needed to include in this book, he went directly to Bob McQueen from Temple.

So I asked McQueen where I should begin with Temple. What did he feel was the catalyst for the Wildcats during his era? McQueen quickly homed in on the Bryan game in 1975.

The Bryan Vikings held the top spot in the rankings in the largest classification at the time. They entered the Temple game with an 8–0 record and one of those star-player names that pops. Decades before Cedric Benson or Adrian Peterson or Johnathan Gray grabbed headlines and magazine covers as the nation's top-rated running back, Bryan had a big lightning-fast back named Curtis Dickey.

Going into the Bryan game, Temple was riding momentum, too. The Wildcats had reeled off seven straight wins after losing the season opener against San Antonio Churchill. Actually, even the loss to start the season didn't discourage the Wildcats much, given the circumstances. "Churchill was the hottest thing in San Antone," McQueen said. "We played 'em down there, and on the way down there our bus nearly turned over. It fishtailed. We started the game, and it started raining. And we were sort of shook up anyway, and we lost nine of eleven fumbles, and we lost to Churchill in a tough game. Well, then we won every game until we played Bryan."

Both Temple and Bryan had won their first five district games and were tied atop District 15-4A with two weeks left in the regular season. As I learned from the men who played for Brownwood in the 1960s, anytime Temple came to town, it was a big deal, and so the 1975 Vikings-Wildcats clash was moved to Kyle Field in College Station. "I don't know the real reason we played at Kyle Field," McQueen said. "But I would suspect strongly their normal stadium would not have held the crowd that showed up."

McQueen recalled the game attendance being estimated at 22,000. All the players I spoke with from the 1975 Temple team remembered specific details about the game and the crowd, though it had taken place almost forty years previously. "Before the game, as we're going into the stadium, I remember running around to get ready to warm up and just, this is going to sound odd, enjoying the moment so much," said Mark Jermstad, the Wildcats' quarterback. "This is what you live for. This is it right here."

But Dickey killed the Wildcats' buzz. The running back, who would go on to rush for 3,703 yards and 31 touchdowns at Texas A&M and then 800 yards and 11 touchdowns as a rookie for the Baltimore Colts, broke loose in the second quarter against Temple. Dickey scored on runs of forty-five and sixty-two yards and set up another touchdown with a forty-three-yard run. His brilliant running boosted Bryan to a 21–6 halftime lead, which seemed an even steeper hill for the Wildcats to climb after linebacker Lester Ward broke his foot on the final play of the first half.

Ward had been assigned to spy (that is, key on or cover directly) Dickey, a critical point of the Wildcats' defensive game plan. With a lump in their collective throat, the Wildcats limped into the halftime locker room. McQueen ran the factors through his football mind and delivered a message to his assistant coaches before they talked to the players. "I told the coaches as we were going in, 'Don't fuss at these kids, because they're playing their hearts out,'" McQueen said. "'Let's figure out a way to win this game.'"

While McQueen and his staff were putting together a plan to stop Dickey and score on the Vikings, the Wildcat players sat quietly, waiting for some kind of inspiration.

"It was a real unusual halftime," said Doug Streater, the Wildcats' tight end and linebacker. "Where normally the coaches would've been talking to the players, all the coaches left. There was a chalkboard up there, and Lester Ward kind of limped up to the chalkboard and wrote, 'Believe in one another.' That was really impressionable. Only the players were there when he did that."

Meanwhile, McQueen decided that the best motivation for his team would be to simply show them the way to a victory. He said he recalled the saying "Sixty minutes to play, a lifetime to remember," and that concept stirred an idea. "The kids, their heads were sort of down and everything," McQueen said. "I went up to the chalkboard, and I wrote 21-dash-6, which was the score. Then I put '+12,' which represented two touchdowns, and then '+4,' which represented two two-point plays. Drew a line, '21-dash-22. Twenty-four minutes to play and a lifetime to remember.'"

Knute Rockne told them to "Win one for the Gipper," and Grant Teaff ate a worm. McQueen used math, and it worked.

"What we needed more than anything at that moment was, 'Okay, guys, here's what we're going to go do,'" Jermstad said. "That's exactly what he gave us with the chalkboard stuff. We were going to win the game 22–21. What it did is, it settled us back down and refocused us."

Temple went back out for the second half with a purpose, but the first challenge was to stop Dickey. After running through the Wildcats in the second quarter, Dickey and the Vikings were determined to give Temple another dose and put away the game.

"They got the ball first and I didn't think we were ever going to stop them," McQueen said. But Lawrence Flowers, who would play a pivotal role the rest of the game, made a play that swung the momentum to the Wildcats. "Finally, they threw some kind of little ole screen to Dickey," McQueen said. "Larry is tougher than the back end of a shooting gallery. Larry hit Dickey and knocked him out of both shoes on the sideline."

That's the kind of tale that needs double-checking, so I asked Streater about the play. "His shoes are just sitting there like he'd untied 'em and put 'em right there," Streater said. "They had to help Dickey find the sideline at that point. Today they probably wouldn't have let him back in the game."

Temple held Bryan and got the ball back. The Wildcats turned to Flowers to power the ball down the field on the pitch sweep, then threw a curve at the Vikings with a reverse to get the ball to the Bryan three. From there, Temple notched its first touchdown and two-point conversion, cutting the Vikings' lead to 21–14.

But as the fourth quarter ticked away, the Wildcats were still looking for the go-ahead score. Their last chance began at their own five with a little more than two minutes remaining. Jermstad hit Jeff Davis for a thirty-nine-yard gain to dig the Wildcats out of the deep end of their own territory.

That's when McQueen played his ace in the hole. "Late in the ball game, we ran a pitch sweep, and Joe Matulich was our quarterback coach, and Joe said, 'Coach, the throwback is there when you want it,'" McQueen recalled.

Standing in his man cave almost forty years after that game, McQueen diagrammed and then acted out the intricacies of the double-handoff play. Using sleight of hand, the quarterback pitches to his left, then twirls to his right to take a handoff from the running back he just pitched to. In this case, Jermstad pitched to running back Charles Young, then took the handoff from Young and found Flowers, lost behind the defense, over the middle.

"Jermstad lofted a perfect pass to Flowers, who raced untouched into the end zone," wrote Bill Knight in the *Temple Daily Telegram*'s game story.

Jermstad's fifty-nine-yard touchdown pass to Flowers drew Temple to within a point at 21–20. The Wildcats still needed the second prescribed two-point play, and for that they turned to their fastest player. Charles Young would go on to Houston on a track-and-field scholarship. There he helped the Cougars win the 1982 national championship in the 4 × 100-meter relay with a time of 38.53, which was still the school record in 2014.

McQueen had the ball placed on the left hash mark in order to give the Wildcats plenty of room to the right on the pitch sweep. There were twenty other players on the field, but the deciding play came down to a race between Young and Dickey, in the game at defensive back, to the front-right pylon.

"The Temple speedster kicked in his afterburners," wrote Knight, "and out-raced none other than the most talked about football player in the US, Curtis Dickey, to the flag for two points and the 22–21 lead."

Just the way McQueen had chalked it up.

"Then we held on for dear life, because we left a little bit too much time," McQueen said. "We finally got 'em stopped and won the game. That was our defining moment."

Jermstad said the Temple fans went berserk, and the Wildcats celebrated all night. "It was probably an hour and a half ride from Bryan back to Temple, and you didn't want it to end," Jermstad said. "It was such a feeling of satisfaction. Well, we get to [the town of] Rogers, and a bunch of police cars are waiting for us. They escort us from Rogers all the way to Temple. We get to the field house, and as far as you can see in the parking lot there's people waiting to greet us. It was unreal. We get off the bus, and people are going nuts. It was a great night, probably one of the greatest nights in my life."

In the short term, the effect of Temple's victory over top-ranked Bryan was muted by a 31–13 loss to Killeen on the final night of the regular season. A coin flip would decide which of the tri-champs—Temple, Bryan, or Killeen—would represent the district in the playoffs. Killeen won, leaving both the Kyle Field combatants home for the postseason.

In the long term, though, Temple began to see itself as a contender of the highest order. "That game taught us how to win big," McQueen said. "The next year, we were 13-1-1, and we played in the state championship game."

For the record, Temple had reached the highest level of Texas high school football before McQueen arrived as coach. Wildcats teams lost in the state title game in 1940, 1941, 1951, and 1952. With the championship-game loss in 1976, Temple had the unique distinction of losing five title games before breaking through. But a legacy of winning on the biggest stage had to start somewhere, and it was clear that McQueen believed the seeds of Temple's state championships in 1979 and 1992 were planted on that night in 1975 at Kyle Field.

Jermstad said he attended a playoff game during the 1976 run and witnessed how much the win over Bryan meant to the program. "I went to the Sherman game the next year, and they were behind, like, 26–14," Jermstad said. "I'm in the stands, and people start chanting, 'Remember Bryan.' Well, I mean, when you hear that, you go, 'That mattered. That's a big deal.'"

11

---

# MIDLAND

## 1983

### *Lee Rebels Pull Off Historic Double*

Spike Dykes looked out the window of the Midland Lee bus and knew he was seeing something special.

Dykes had been around the block a time or two before he guided the Rebels into the regional final that Saturday. He had coached on Darrell Royal's staff at Texas and Emory Bellard's at Mississippi State. He had made so many stops at high schools around the state, ate chicken-fried steak at so many diners, and stopped at Dairy Queen on so many scouting and recruiting trips that he could probably draw a map of every highway in the state on a ketchup-smudged napkin.

By the time Dykes arrived in Midland in 1980 as the head coach at Lee, he already had head-coaching experience at Coahoma, Big Spring, Belton, and Alice, along with forays into the college coaching ranks. If ever there was a man designed for the rocky road of coaching, it was Dykes.

Never a schemer or a screamer, Dykes plodded along the coaching road, winning friends and influencing people by believing in them. He was going to roll with his buddies because they were why he got into the business in the first place. "Somebody said, 'Why did you coach?'" Dykes recalled. "It's simple. My high school coaches and my junior high coaches had more fun, and they were the greatest guys I've ever seen in my life. After being around them, I said, 'Golly, it's like stealing if I could ever be a coach and have as much fun as they had.'"

Perhaps that's why Dykes never seemed to be aching to take a bigger, better job. That day on that bus going from Midland to Lubbock, Dykes had his team and his fellow coaches with him, so he was exactly where he wanted to be.

And when he looked out the window and saw Lee Rebel flags lining Highway 87, they reminded him that this Midland Lee game against Odessa Permian had everyone's attention. "It was amazing," Dykes said. "The funny thing about it, [Permian went] to Lubbock through Andrews and Seminole, and we go through Lamesa. All along the route there were Rebel flags, all along their route there were the Mojo flags. It was a heck of a deal, it really was. It was a big deal. That was probably the most fun game I was ever around."

At that point, Lee football existed mostly in the shadow of Permian. The Panthers had won three state titles, and the Rebels none. It took Lee eight attempts before it defeated Permian for the first time, in 1968, and the Panthers began 1983 with a 19–3 lead in the all-time series.

Even when Lee defeated Permian 20–7 earlier in district play in 1983 it was regarded as a fluke. But for the first time in history, the Rebels would get a chance in the same season to prove it was no fluke.

The UIL had expanded the playoffs in 1982. Before then, a team had to win its district championship to qualify for the postseason, leaving some of those who tied for a title sitting at home. By allowing the runner-up from each district in all conferences to keep playing, the UIL opened the door for dramatic rematches, like the one that took place at Texas Tech's Jones Stadium on December 2, 1983.

Even with the expansion, Lee was almost left at home. "We were lucky, because the last game of the year Odessa High beat San Angelo," Tyrone Thurman remembered. "San Angelo would have made it. It would have been Odessa Permian and San Angelo."

Thurman, who went on to Texas Tech stardom as one of the Red Raiders' famed Mighty Mite wide receivers, was part of a three-headed Lee backfield monster that also included Walter Jones and Isaac Garnett. Thurman's diminutive five-three stature allowed him to hide behind bigger players and then turn on the jets to race past them. He earned all-American honors as a punt returner for the Red Raiders.

I met Thurman at a coffee shop on a Sunday night during the 2014 football season. He explained the Rebels' winding road to the playoffs in 1983. Lee lost to San Angelo Central early in district play and then defeated Permian. But a freak loss to Abilene Cooper, on a night when the Rebels' bus blew a tire on the way to the game, put the Rebels in the precarious position of needing to defeat Midland on the final night of the regular season, and to get some help from Odessa.

Two seasons earlier, Lee would have been packing up the pads after the tenth game. As it stood, the Rebels were only getting started. The second-place Rebels tore through Amarillo and El Paso Irvin in the first two playoff games. Lee won each game by at least three touchdowns. Then came the first real battle, when the Rebels fought past Fort Worth Trimble Tech 23–6 at TCU's Amon G. Carter Stadium. "The hardest game we ever played, it wasn't the state championship game, it was the game against Trimble Tech," Thurman said. "We played against James Gray and them. They ran the ball well, and they had a lot of speed."

By defeating Trimble Tech, the Rebels became the school's first team to win eleven games in a season. More importantly, they set up a rematch that made West Texas football fans drool. "And if you want history, Lee will face Odessa Permian for the second time this season next weekend at a date and site to be determined today," wrote *Midland Reporter-Telegram* assistant sports editor Terry Williamson. "That matchup will surely be the biggest athletic event ever staged in Permian Basin football history.

"Not even past state championships by Permian, Abilene High, San Angelo and Odessa High will match up to this encounter."

Even before the dust settled in the previous round of the playoffs, the hype and hyperbole were building for the Panther-Rebel showdown. It was the kind of game that had every high school football fan from Dalhart to Brownsville talking. The district that included the Midland, Odessa, San Angelo, and Abilene schools was referred to in those days as the Little Southwest Conference. But the SWC never had a championship game, and this Permian-Lee game amounted to that.

Thurman said that he and his teammates inside the Rebels' field house knew the temperature of the matchup. The Lee players had come up through two middle schools, but both those schools had had success against the Odessa middle schools in seventh, eighth, and ninth grades. "Growing up in Midland, we had the west side and we had the east side," Thurman said. "The east side had some good players, and the west side had good players. Once we got together at Midland Lee, we knew we could beat Permian. That one game we wanted was to play Odessa Permian."

Thurman was a junior on a senior-laden roster in 1983. Senior middle linebacker Michael Johnson, who also went on to play at Texas Tech, couldn't wait to get one more shot at the Panthers.

Johnson had sprained a knee after being chop-blocked early in Lee's first matchup with Permian that season. He feared the worst, but the injury sidelined him for only a couple of games. After the Trimble Tech win, Johnson felt as if Christmas had come early. "To get another opportunity to play Permian was just unfathomable," Johnson said. "I just could not believe that's who we were going to be facing again in the playoffs. That was going to be my last opportunity to play Permian again. Our rivalry probably was one of the biggest rivalries in high school football, not just in Texas but nationwide. Just to be able to get that second opportunity, I was chomping at the bit, foaming at the mouth."

Coach Dykes and the Lee players didn't need to see the decorations along the highway in order to feel the intensity, but they were a reminder that the Rebels were headed to a historic, first-ever meeting between Lee and Permian in the playoffs. "They had Panther paws on the ground when they were driving," Thurman said. "We had a whole bunch of people on the side of the road with their Rebel flags. That was fun. It was different because it was the first time ever and we didn't know what to expect."

Dykes said the rematch took place at Jones Stadium because there wasn't a ballpark big enough in the Midland-Odessa area to accommodate the expected crowd. The game story in the *Reporter-Telegram* estimated the crowd that afternoon at 32,000. "When we left Midland to travel to Lubbock, half the city was coming with us," Johnson said. "It was pretty unbelievable to look up in the stands and see a sea of maroon and white, and of course, Odessa Permian was well-traveled with their Mojo."

In most stories of this kind, the stage would now be set for a phenomenal football game, one decided by a dramatic play in the fourth quarter. Instead, Midland Lee controlled the contest with a suffocating defense and a running game that benefited from at least one really good bounce. Early in the first quarter, Thurman started right, preparing to take the pitch from quarterback Jeff Motley. But Thurman bobbled it, spelling possible disaster. "I missed it," Thurman said. "It hit me in my chest, and the ball bounced, and it took a bounce right back into my hand, and I scored a touchdown on it."

The *Reporter-Telegram* story pointed out that the Permian defense froze when the ball hit the turf. That gave Thurman the opening he needed. After he gathered the ball on the fly, he skirted the right end for a twenty-four-yard touchdown. Always ready to deliver a one-liner that reporters would lap up, Dykes joked that Thurman's play worked exactly as designed. "We work on that play every day in practice," he said. "He [Thurman] is a heck of a basketball player. We call it 'dribble sweep.'"

Thurman added another touchdown in the third quarter on a three-yard run, and kicker Craig Kamradt nailed two extra points and a twenty-yard field goal for the Rebels' twenty points.

Turns out, that was nineteen more than they needed.

The Lee defense smothered Permian in the rematch, shutting out the Panthers for the first time in Lee's history. The Rebels dropped Permian quarterback Rex Lamberti five times for losses totaling thirty-six yards. "We wanted to keep the pressure on them and hit 'em in the mouth and not give 'em any confidence whatsoever to get them going," Johnson said.

Permian rushed for a net total of twelve yards in the game. The *Reporter-Telegram* described Lee's effort as annihilation: "Panthers weren't just being tackled or blocked, they were being driven into the ground."

For all the doubting high school football fans in the area, the continuation headline in the Sunday *Reporter-Telegram* the next day put the issue to rest: "Lee proves first time no fluke."

By defeating the rival Panthers, Lee moved into the state semifinal round to face another of the state's perennial powers: the Plano Wildcats. By virtue of a lucky home-and-home flip, the Rebels faced Plano at the brand-new Ratliff Stadium in Odessa. "If you think about it, back in the day it was always you heard about Permian from West Texas," Thurman said. "But you also heard about Plano down in the Metroplex. It was so overwhelming that we had a chance to play Permian and we also had a chance to play Plano."

Johnson remembered wanting to guard against a letdown after the big win over Permian. But the Rebels were up to the task. Lee defeated Plano 35–14 to climb to the state final against Converse Judson.

Thurman told me he and his teammates were more concerned about facing Converse Judson's semifinal opponent, Houston Yates. This was before Converse Judson won the first of its six state championships. But the Rockets ended Lee's bid for a state title by winning the final 25–21.

Despite coming up five points short of a state championship, the Lee Rebels emerged from the 1983 season as a program to be reckoned with in West Texas. Since then, Lee has been in the playoffs twenty-four times, winning eight district championships and a three-peat of state titles in 1998, 1999, and 2000. The Rebels even claim to have won a national championship in 1999.

Before the end of the decade, Dykes was leading Texas Tech to bowl games with a few of his Lee players, including Thurman and Johnson, as key cogs on his Red Raider teams. Always one to roll with the punches, Dykes took some convincing to leave the Lee post to go back to the college ranks. "After that [Permian] game, we went home, and Jerry Moore called me and asked me to come to Texas Tech and be the defensive coordinator," Dykes said. "I said, 'Jerry, I'm not going to do that. I'm here at Midland and we're doing good and having a good time.'

"And so anyway, after the [Converse Judson] game was over, he called me and said, 'I really hate it you lost the game. I just wish you'd change your mind and come on up here.' I said, 'I'll just take the job then.' I was down in the dumps and just lost, and that's the best thing I ever did."

I went to Texas Tech during the first four years of the Big 12 conference, when Dykes led the Red Raiders to a .594 winning percentage in the new conference in his last four seasons as a head coach. Mike Leach took over in 2000 and raised Texas Tech's national profile, though he couldn't improve on Dykes's record, going .588 in Big 12 games.

By the time Dykes was done at Texas Tech, he'd earned a place in the hearts of Texas football fans from both his high school and college coaching days. He showed me a room in his Horseshoe Bay house dedicated to memorabilia collected through the years, from a portrait of Darrell Royal to drawings by the wonderfully entertaining cartoonist Dirk West.

Dykes's legacy, including the way he raised the level of the Lee program, shows that it's not so much where you go as how you get there. "It seemed like I was always the bridesmaid, never the bride," Dykes said. "We had the best team in the state when we lost [in the 1983 state championship game]. We just got outcoached. Converse Judson did a better job than we did, but we sure should've won the state there."

# 12

# DAINGERFIELD

## 1983

*The Tigers' Amazing Shutout Streak*

The more that football evolves into a touchdown-a-minute, video-game-like experience meant to thrill viewers with dynamic offenses around every corner, the more the Daingerfield Tigers' record is safe.

Those who have heard of the 1983 Daingerfield team, and especially those who watched them play, won't be surprised to find their story here. Those who are reading about them for the first time will find the whole thing a little unbelievable.

I was part of the latter group.

Once I began writing about the most memorable players and teams and moments in Texas high school football history, I received a ton of tips. Everyone I told about the project had an idea for me. Of course, I also sought out advice. Two of the men I asked were Bill Lane, a longtime Baylor assistant coach who guided the 1968 Daingerfield Tigers to the Class 2A state championship, and David Smoak, a Tyler and Waco radio personality. Both of them told me about the 1983 Daingerfield team and the minuscule amount of points the Tigers gave up on their way to the 3A state title.

I took those opinions to heart and was probably already sold on the idea of adding Daingerfield to the list. But then, while researching the 1983 Midland Lee Rebels, I ran across a jaw-dropping sentence in the *Midland Reporter-Telegram* microfilms from December 18, 1983. The headline "Daingerfield Drubs Sweeny," stopped me, and this sentence floored me: "The 13th consecutive shutout for Daingerfield allowed the Tigers, 16–0, to join Everette, Md., in the record books," stated the Associated Press game story.

That's when I saw Bigfoot. The "oh my gosh!" moment was followed quickly by a call to Troup High School to speak with Dennis Alexander, the Dainger-field coach from 1976 to 1988. Alexander led the Tigers to a pair of state cham-pionships, winning in 1983 and 1985, wrapped around a state finals appearance in 1984. At the end of the 2013 season, he was in fourth place on Texas's all-time coaching victories list, with 322 wins in forty seasons as a head coach.

That accounts for a lot of types of teams in a lot of places, but it was clear the 1983 Tigers never stray far from Alexander's mind. "People would be a little amazed," he said. "Certainly, that was a great team, but there's been teams that I've seen, probably before, but certainly in the last thirty years, that had great talent, that win big, that dominate, but still can't play with the intensity to have thirteen shutouts in a row and give up eight points in sixteen games. The other remarkable thing was, if you go back and get the stats, it wasn't a deal where you gave up 200 yards and shut 'em out. It was, like, one or two first downs a game, practically no rushing. It was total domination. The kids fed on it."

I was more than a little amazed—eight points in sixteen games is a record guarded by astronomical odds against it ever being broken. For the sake of comparison, I did a brief survey of the twenty teams that played in eleven-man state championship games in 2014. The Mason Punchers had given up 121 points going into their 1A Division I title game, the fewest points allowed by any of the state finals combatants. The Katy Tigers entered the 6A Division II championship game with the most shutouts, five, and they had given up 132 points in their other ten games.

Again, those were statistically the best defenses in terms of points allowed of the teams playing for state championships. Perhaps that's why Eric Everett, who played safety for Daingerfield and went on to Texas Tech and five seasons in the NFL, knows his team's record is safe. "The way football is played now, that will never be done," he said.

After reading articles, including an excellent one by Smoak, and interview-ing the players and head coach, I understood clearly that the Tigers had brought a high level of talent to the field at every position. But it was Everett who put Daingerfield's domination in simple terms. Because opposing offenses couldn't run on the Tigers, they were forced to try to beat the Daingerfield secondary. "I had ten interceptions," Everett said. "I think I led the state that year. Johnny Hendrix had eight. He returned at least two of them, that I know of, for touch-downs. I'm pretty sure Rodney [Mims] had, like, six, and I think Mark Austin had five. Just from us—not counting some of the other people when they got in the game—just us guys in the secondary had about twenty-nine interceptions."

The Tigers knew going into the season that they had an experienced defense, with ten seniors coming back on that side of the ball. Alexander said linebacker Ladd Freeman led the defense, and he was joined up front by Guy Searcy, Mark Rowe, Randy Woods, and Tom Lipham. Daingerfield's success would be predicated on its defense, especially since the Tigers had a much younger group on offense.

Senior Doug Pittman and Everett took turns running the offense at quarterback during preseason practices until Pittman showed in scrimmages that he was ready to direct the offense, allowing Everett to focus on starting at free safety.

The Tigers rolled into the 1983 season with high expectations, though perhaps not the mind-set to set unbreakable records. Daingerfield, which never has to go far to test its mettle in the rich football territory of Northeast Texas, opened the season with a 10–6 victory over 4A Carthage. The Bulldogs' second-half touchdown would be the only points the Tigers' defense gave up all season.

"I think Alexander jinxed us when we played Carthage," Everett said, only half joking. "We went in at halftime. It was a tough game. We were moving up and down the field. We just kept turning it over. We kept fumbling or [doing] something that would keep us from scoring. At halftime, he said we might have to shut 'em out to win. And we did up until right at the end of the fourth quarter. They did a little trick play, which kind of caught us off guard a little bit. I know for a fact that if we had tackled them outside of the end zone, they never would have got in, I promise you that."

The next week, Daingerfield shut out Gilmer, then finished nondistrict play with 4A Kilgore. With Pittman ready to punt deep in the Tigers' end of the field, the snap sailed over his head and into the end zone. Pittman scooped it and ran out of the back of the end zone for a safety.

Little did they know those would be the final points allowed that season.

The Tigers closest district game was a 27–0 win over Linden-Kildare in the district opener. It would be a while before they began to notice just how menacing their defense had become. For one thing, a deep stable of running backs, led by Tony Evans, scored points in rapid succession. Daingerfield finished the season with 631 points on offense, a huge number that will nonetheless forever be in the shadow of the eight points allowed.

In fact, it didn't occur to the Tigers what they were doing as they plowed through district play. "We never even thought about what was really going on," Evans said. "We were just going out every Friday, just lining up, playing ball. We never even thought about the magnitude of what was going on until probably in the playoffs. Then it was like, 'Man! We done had ten, eleven straight shutouts!' That's when it became noticeable that this is something special that's going on now."

By the time the playoffs began, Daingerfield had notched a seven-game shutout streak, and the Tigers kept it going in the first round with a 43–0 victory over Clarksville. Next up was the area-round game versus Robinson in Rockwall. The Rockets proved to be Daingerfield's toughest playoff foe and threatened to end the shutout streak.

Though Robinson gained only three first downs the entire game, it reached the Tigers' four-yard line and attempted a twenty-one-yard field goal from there. But Robinson kicker Mike Andrie never put toe to ball, since a high snap forced holder Kevin Hoffman to try a desperation pass, which fell incomplete. Daingerfield defeated Robinson 22–0 after holding the Rockets to fifty-eight yards of total offense, according to the *Waco Tribune-Herald* game story. Freeman posted all the points the Tigers needed to win when he kicked a thirty-nine-yard field goal in the first quarter.

After rolling through two more playoff opponents, Daingerfield's iron-wall defensive streak reached eleven going into the state semifinal versus Post. The Antelopes produced a defensive play that all the Tigers I interviewed remembered as the closest anyone came to putting a blemish on the Tigers' blank canvas.

Post's Daniel Gonzalez intercepted a pass in the flat and took off for the Daingerfield end zone with no one in front of him. It was up to Evans to make a touchdown-saving tackle. "We had the streak in jeopardy," Evans said. "I went and caught the guy on about the ten-, twelve-yard line. From that point the defense took over." Everett said Post lost yards on four consecutive plays. Alexander remembered a couple of sacks. Either way, the Antelopes didn't move in for a touchdown, and were even pushed out of field goal range.

That meant Daingerfield had only one more game between it and tying the national record for consecutive shutouts. Of course, that wasn't the carrot the Tigers were chasing. In fact, Everett claims he only ever had one thing on his mind. "I don't remember ever thinking about it," he said. "My main thing was win the game. I think our thing was, we're going to dominate them and they're going to have a tough time. They're not going to get much if anything. I think that was our mind-set, and shutouts just came."

Just three seasons before Daingerfield shut down opposing offenses at an amazing rate, neighboring Pittsburg had set the bar pretty high. The Pirates posted twelve shutouts on their way to the 3A state championship. I asked

Alexander whether he felt pressure not only to win the state title, but also to do it by blanking the opponent once more.

I received a friendly but emphatic lecture on priorities. "No," Alexander said. "If you're a coach in Texas, and you spent your playing time and everything you've done, and you're a serious coach, and you get a chance to be in that situation, you don't want to blow it. With the run we'd had, if you lose that game, you're going to feel unsuccessful as the coach. As a lot of places go, and Daingerfield is one of them, when you lose, the coach is responsible. The first goal was to win."

But it didn't take long to take care of that goal in the championship game versus Sweeny at Baylor Stadium. Pittman threw touchdown passes of sixteen yards to Herman West and nineteen to Everett. Austin recovered a Sweeny fumble at the Bulldogs' four, setting up Danny Mitchell's four-yard touchdown run. That barrage of points gave the Tigers a 21–0 lead with seven minutes left before halftime.

In today's wide-open game, a 21–0 deficit in the second quarter would be a punch in the gut, but no reason to give up hope. Facing a team that had given up eight points all season, the Sweeny players no doubt felt that they were looking straight up at Mount Everest.

"After we got into the game and could see the dominance beginning to happen, then yeah," said Alexander, pointing out that the Tigers' thoughts turned to finishing the shutout streak. "We could see the win coming, and you kind of gain momentum, and the other team, no matter how good they are, it kind of begins to wear on them, and we kind of took control."

Daingerfield defeated Sweeny 42–0. John Werner, who covered the game for the *Waco Tribune-Herald*, underscored the Tigers' dominance in the second paragraph of his game story. "The Daingerfield defense was an offense in itself," Werner wrote. "While holding Sweeny to just 100 yards, the Tigers forced five turnovers and even outscored Sweeny's offense. Mark Austin's 39-yard interception return for a TD in the third period gave the Tigers a 35–0 lead. It was four more TD's than they actually needed."

Although they weren't playing in the state's largest classification, Daingerfield's defensive prowess earned its players plenty of attention. The senior-laden defense and the junior-heavy offense led to two waves of Tigers ascending into the college ranks. "Everybody on that team got scholarships to play football somewhere on a full ride," Everett said. "And then the next year, all the guys that were behind us, they all got scholarships too. Baylor, Tulsa, Kansas State, quite a few went to Stephen F. Austin."

As mentioned, the Tigers returned to the state title game in 1984 and won state again in 1985. Although Alexander moved on after the 1988 season, the Daingerfield tradition of excellence continued as the Tigers won 2A state championships in 2008, 2009, and 2010.

Everett went to Texas Tech, where he became a teammate of several players from Midland Lee's 1983 state-finalist team, as well as the guy who hammered the Rebels in that championship game, Converse Judson running back Chris Pryor. "I remember watching their tape of their state championship game," Everett said. "I think I watched about five minutes, and I told them all, 'There's no way y'all would have beat us. No way.'"

The bigger-school guys might not have believed Everett's claim or given it much attention. When football players start boasting about their high school glory days, it can be one big-fish story after another. But in Everett's case, the feat on the field speaks louder than any amount of bravado. The Daingerfield Tigers' amazing 1983 season is as close to mythology as it gets in Texas high school football. It's one of those legends you truly have to see to believe.

# 13

## CORPUS CHRISTI

### 1985

### *Calallen Builds a Winner*

Phil Danaher threw caution out the window very early in his tenure at Corpus Christi Calallen. The way he figured, if it was going to be short-lived, then so be it. "Who wants to stay if it's going to be short?" Danaher said. "I want to be associated with winners."

In the 1984 season, five games into Danaher's tenure at Calallen, the Wildcats had won three and tied one, but they were getting shellacked by Gregory-Portland in the early stages of the second half. Danaher wasn't going to back down, though. Faced with fourth down and two or three yards to go multiple times, deep in his own territory, the Calallen coach elected to go for it. So Danaher doesn't blame Gregory-Portland coach Ray Akins for hanging a 69–0 loss on his Wildcats.

If anything, it proved to be exactly what Danaher needed in order to teach his players as well as the Calallen community what he expected. "When I went in Monday to booster club, what do you tell a group of parents that you just got your butt kicked 69–0?" Danaher asked me when I spoke to him in the winter of 2015 in the Calallen field house. "I guess the Good Lord whispered in my ear, and I looked at them all, and I knew they were kind of edgy. 'I've got two questions for y'all. The first question: when your son got home, how many of y'all said, "That's okay. That's Gregory-Portland"? If you said that, you put Gregory-Portland on a pedestal higher. We're not going to make excuses when we get beat. It doesn't matter who they are.

"'The second question: how many of y'all, when Johnny got home, said, "Johnny, I was disappointed in the way you played. Not only did you let down your teammates, your coaches, yourself, but also us the community, the school." When you take that approach, then we'll start knocking those pedestals down one at a time.' That Monday I told the booster club, 'Your boys, when they go home tonight, they're going to tell you they're sore. We're going to do sixty-nine push-ups before we start. It doesn't matter whether it's football, off-season, tiddlywinks, we're going to do sixty-nine push-ups.' When they stand up, I say, 'What's that for, boys?' 'We're never getting beat that bad again, Coach.'"

In a sense, Danaher gave the Calallen booster club an ultimatum: jump on board or fire me. I met Danaher a little more than thirty years after that conversation took place. By then, he had compiled a 408–102–4 career record in forty-one seasons, including thirty-one as the Wildcats' head coach. At the time of this writing, he needed nineteen wins to pass G. A. Moore for the most career wins in Texas high school football history.

Obviously, those booster club members liked the gumption and grit that Danaher put on display at that Monday meeting. Soon after, it began to show up on the scoreboard. But there were some growing pains along the way for the Wildcats players.

The sixty-nine-push-up rule was not an idle threat. "We did sixty-nine push-ups every damn Monday," former Calallen offensive and defensive lineman Eric Schmidt remembered. "Nobody looked forward to those push-ups. I'm sure I cheated going through those push-ups. There's no way I could've done sixty-nine in a row. In my mind, it built that disdain for Gregory-Portland even more."

Nor were those push-ups solely for the purpose of psychologically motivating the Wildcat players. One of the first things Danaher noticed on Calallen's game film of 1983 was that while many of the Wildcats players passed the eye test at first glance as big, strong athletes, they were getting beaten at the point of attack. When Danaher walked into the weight room, he saw outdated workout equipment, and not the kind that proved to be quaint but effective.

"My offensive line coach came with me, and we were watching film one day," Danaher remembered. "I had to come in my office and do something because I was the athletic director also. All the sudden, I hear, 'Hey, Coach, get in here. I've watched this film. I know what it is. Watch when they make contact. They come off the ball good, but when they hit, their feet quit, and that's it. They don't have strength in their legs.'"

Danaher went to work overhauling both the off-season strength-and-conditioning program as well as the equipment in the field house. When I interviewed him, Danaher took great pride in showing me around the field house, which had the latest generation of equipment as well as meticulously organized equipment rooms. We talked about blueprints that had been finalized for a new field house to serve all of Calallen's sports.

In the decades after that first season, Danaher's vision synced with the Calallen community's values to launch the Wildcats program among the elite. The wheel started turning with a 5–4–1 season in 1984, their first winning campaign since the late 1970s. Then in 1985, the Wildcats demolished their first three foes by an average of more than four touchdowns a game. In the fourth game, Laredo Nixon handed Calallen its first loss of the season, 7–6, on a muddy track. Then came time for the rematch with Gregory-Portland to open district play.

"If that was a made-for-TV movie, we would have beat the hell out of [Gregory-Portland] the next year," said Schmidt, further complaining about the sixty-nine-push-up rule following the memorable loss in 1984. "We cut the deficit by half, which, looking back, was the steps towards dominating Gregory-Portland like Phil did." Gregory-Portland defeated the Wildcats 33–0.

Hung over the next week, Calallen slogged through a lackluster first half versus Rockport. "It was 14–14 at half, and I remember Phil saying, 'You guys are better than this team; the fact that it's 14–14 is crazy,'" Schmidt said. "We went out and won that game, like, 28– or 35–14. That's what helped us believe we could."

Calallen needed to win its regular-season finale, versus Beeville, to get into the postseason. The Trojans entered with a 4–0–1 district record, having tied Gregory-Portland, and expected to grab a share of the district title by winning on their home field.

Instead, Calallen's rise to power took a major step forward. Wildcat running back James Brown ran for a touchdown and threw for another one on a halfback pass to wide receiver Robert Rosas for a seventy-six-yard strike. Calallen claimed a 17–10 victory and went to the playoffs for the first time since 1956.

In his game story, the *Corpus Christi Caller-Times* sportswriter Tom Kleckner recorded a priceless excerpt from Danaher's postgame speech. "Gentlemen, let this be a lesson to you," Danaher said. "If you want something bad enough, go get it."

Calallen's playoff berth ignited a long-awaited flare-up of football pride. From the vantage point of the second decade of the 2000s, when the Wildcats have been riding a streak of thirty consecutive seasons of making the playoffs, including sixteen straight campaigns of ten or more wins, it seems almost unfathomable that there was a time when Calallen had a futile, dilapidated football program.

Schmidt saw firsthand how the win in Beeville stirred deep emotions in the Wildcats' fans, whose thirst for a winner on the football field had gone unquenched for almost thirty years. "Another thing I remember about that game, my father was never much of an affectionate man," Schmidt said. "But he hugged me after that football game. He came down on the football field. That was really the pinnacle, if you want to see what a change in Calallen football was. Fans were coming out of the stands, and we're going to the playoffs."

After I interviewed Danaher, it wasn't difficult to track down the quarterback from the 1985 Wildcats. Dr. Sam Hartman practiced family medicine diagonally across Northwest Boulevard from Calallen's Wildcat Stadium. His office was in a clinic next door to the hospital where he was born.

Hartman has had a front-row seat for the rise of Calallen football, which he helped ignite. He said he remembered going through other towns when he was a kid and seeing the local store windows painted with bright colors, celebrating the high school football team. But that had never been the case in his hometown. Not until the Wildcats stamped their ticket to the playoffs with the win over Beeville. "It was amazing," Hartman said. "It was absolutely amazing. The Dairy Queen was painted up 'Go Calallen! Go Wildcats!' People were asking me for my autograph. It was really wild and crazy. There was such a hunger for it."

The Wildcats finished the regular season with eight wins and just the two back-to-back losses to Laredo Nixon and Gregory-Portland. I've seen a few high school football teams that broke a long playoff drought for their school and then, satisfied, exited the playoffs in the first round. But that's not where Danaher, a bulldog of a man in physical appearance and attitude, wanted to stop.

Calallen opened the playoffs with a home game versus Mercedes. The Wildcats claimed a 33–26 victory as Brown rushed for 170 yards and scored the clinching touchdown on a fifty-nine-yard run late in the third quarter. Running back Jeff Walker gained 111 yards on the ground and scored a pair of touchdowns to help power the Wildcats' offense.

Not only did Calallen advance, but the stars were so aligned that, remarkably, they played their first two playoff games at home. Perhaps it was because Calallen was playing its inaugural season in a sparkling new stadium, or because the Wildcats had not yet earned a reputation as a playoff-savvy football team, but Mercedes and then San Antonio Southwest both agreed to flip a coin for home field in those playoff games.

Calallen won both flips, and that resulted in a little more spark to get the Wildcats' fire going. In the week leading to the Saturday-afternoon game, Southwest probably didn't lose too much sleep about going to Corpus Christi to play Calallen. For one thing, the Dragons came in with an unblemished 11–0 mark. And they were led by one of the most prolific passers in Texas high school football history.

Future Brigham Young University Heisman-winning quarterback Ty Detmer entered the Calallen game having passed for 3,154 yards and thirty-two touchdowns as a junior. He would finish his junior season with the highest passing-yards total in Texas high school football history at that time.

Detmer had a shot at a national record for passing, which the Calallen coaching staff all but conceded. "Ty came into that game needing 327 yards or something like that to set the national record in passing," Danaher said. "We told our kids going into it, he's going to get his 327 yards. It's going to happen. He was good, and their receivers were real good. 'Boys, we're just going to have to outscore 'em and keep the ball out of their hands.' At one time, if you got up to go to the restroom, you missed five touchdowns."

In anticipation of the playoff clash, Calallen fans bought up the available tickets so quickly that the school brought in extra bleachers for the contest. Football fever had arrived in the Gulf Coast community. "I'd been to a few college games before that, and I remember walking out on that field and thinking, 'This is a college game,'" Hartman said. "This is the biggest game I've ever played, right here. I had relatives come in town that had never seen me play before. To this day, I get people coming to me and say, 'Sammy, I've seen every Calallen playoff game since they made the playoffs, but that Southwest game, that's the one I'll never forget.'"

The clash of offensive styles lived up to the hype and then some. According to the *Caller-Times*, Calallen rolled up 458 yards of offense, mostly on the ground; Brown, Walker, and Andy Caceres all rushed for more than 120. Detmer threw for 417 yards and four touchdowns to finish the season with 3,571 yards and thirty-six touchdowns.

Danaher's claim that getting up to use the restroom might cause a fan to miss five touchdowns wasn't necessarily hyperbole. At one point, the Wildcats and Dragons combined to produce five touchdowns in less than six minutes of game time. "[Detmer] would just throw that ball down the field, and somebody would come up with it," Schmidt said. "I remember a few times we'd get pressure, and it's third-and-long, and he throws this ball down the field. And one of his receivers goes up and gets it, and it's, like, 'Oh, shit, another first down. Now I've got to rush the passer again.' I think we had a lot of confidence defensively because offensively we could do whatever we wanted."

Schmidt and the Wildcats defensive front did get after Detmer, sacking him five times and rushing him into three interceptions, a huge factor in helping Calallen prevail. Brown gave Calallen a 20–6 lead in the second quarter when he ran forty-one yards for a touchdown. But after rushing for 131 yards in a little more than a quarter of action, Brown went down with a knee injury that ended his season.

Caceres and Walker picked up the slack and drove the Wildcats' prolific running game. The Calallen blockers were opening up gigantic holes, allowing the Wildcats to control the game by keeping Detmer on the sideline. Caceres scored on a thirty-nine-yard run with 3:26 left in the third quarter to put Calallen ahead 35–12.

Although video-game-like passing offenses weren't the norm in the mid-1980s, Danaher knew enough about the "Southwest Airlines" attack not to relax. "We told our kids early in the week that whenever we got three touchdowns up, we couldn't let up, and if they got three up, not to worry," Danaher told the *Caller-Times* after the game.

Danaher was correct in his thinking. Calallen won the game 55–28, which seems like a blowout. But if the Wildcats had failed to keep scoring after going ahead 35–12 in the third, they could have easily been caught up in an avalanche of Southwest scoring.

Hartman evidently stayed so focused that he didn't even watch the scoreboard. "What was the score anyway?" Hartman asked *Caller-Times* reporter Kleckner in a postgame interview. "Good Lord! That's a basketball game." The answer was not given for effect. "I honestly lost count of the score," Hartman told me more than twenty-nine years later. "I just knew we were ahead, and I didn't care what the score was."

By defeating Southwest, Calallen moved on to the third round of the playoffs, which could have meant a rematch with their district rival. Instead, New Braunfels knocked Gregory-Portland out of the playoffs 28–21. The Unicorns awaited Calallen in the third round at San Antonio's Alamo Stadium.

With Brown sidelined by a knee injury, New Braunfels controlled the Wildcats offense, forcing six turnovers. The Unicorns claimed a 27–10 win. Still, Calallen had shown what was possible and set the bar high. As of this writing, the Wildcats have upheld that standard ever since. Calallen now represents the elite of the elite programs in South Texas.

In the rest of the state, the Wildcats might be known more for how many times they have come painfully close to a championship. La Marque defeated Calallen in the state semifinals in every season from 1993 to 1997, and then the Cougars did it again in 2010. As of 2015, Calallen had advanced to the penultimate game of the season ten times and compiled a 1–9 record in those games. In 2005, the Wildcats broke through to the 4A Division II state championship game. Lewisville Hebron defeated them 28–0 for the title.

It's possible, perhaps even likely, that Danaher will pass Moore as the winningest football coach in Texas history sometime in 2016 or 2017. When and if that happens, there's sure to be ample debate about where Danaher belongs among the Texas coaching elite. Gordon Wood won nine state titles, and Moore claimed eight. But Danaher created a cultural change in the Corpus Christi area the likes of which has rarely been seen anywhere in the state. Calallen's name rings out now.

And the coach can trace that change of attitude inside the community to the Sunday morning following the Southwest game and a conversation with a football mom. "Gatha Jones, whose son Troy was a wide receiver, goes to church, still does, with me," Danaher said. "Right before half, we threw a pass, and we hit Troy in the end zone, right in the hands, and he dropped it. I said, 'Wow. That would've really gave us a good cushion at halftime.' So the next day at church, I saw Gatha. I said, 'Gatha, what'd you say to Troy about dropping that ball?' She looked at me and she said, 'I told him if he ever dropped another touchdown pass like that, not to bother to come home.' I said, 'We're there. Our expectations are high.'"

# 14

# WEST ORANGE

## 1986–1987

### *Kevin Smith Leads Stark to Title*

Kevin Smith began as a West Orange–Stark Mustang and, though West Orange–Stark didn't begin with Kevin Smith, the Mustangs' identity has been built on his teams.

Come to think of it, for any Texan, looking back at Smith's football career creates a sense of awe and pride: the assurance that that's what a football player from our state looks like.

It doesn't matter how often he played for your team or against your team. Smith wore the West Orange–Stark, Texas A&M, and Dallas Cowboy uniforms, so there's a damn good chance he played for your team at one time or another. And when he wore those uniforms, those teams won.

Smith's WO-S squads claimed two state titles.

His Aggie teams compiled a 34–14–1 record and a Southwest Conference title in 1991, when he earned consensus first-team all-American honors as a senior.

Smith's Cowboys teams won three Super Bowls.

So you look at him and marvel at how great a player he became and how he played a key role on some amazing football teams. That's true, and Smith praises the high level of football players around him from high school on up to the NFL.

But the thing about a player like Smith, the thing that makes us want to hold him up as the Texan ideal, was that he was going to have his say in the outcome. Everybody hates to lose, but not everybody has that many chances to do something about it.

Smith's WO-S team was locked in a battle with Jasper in the middle of the 1987 season. The Mustangs and Bulldogs tangled frequently and for high stakes in those days. They split two meetings in 1986, when WO-S went on to win the 4A state title. In their 1987 district clash, Smith made a mistake that could've sunk the Mustangs.

Early in the fourth quarter, WO-S marched into Jasper territory and set up kicker Russell Turkel with a field goal try from the sixteen-yard line. But Smith, holding for the kicker, let the snap fly past him. "The center snapped the ball. I didn't see it," Smith said. "The ball rolled, they kicked the ball around, and we chased it." The Bulldogs finally fell on it and took over at the WO-S forty-eight.

The Mustangs had their back against the wall in Jasper's stadium. The WO-S players nicknamed it the "Alamo" both because of the brick facade and because, as former Mustang and Smith compadre Russell Botley told me, "that's what it was like when you went up there: you're going to the Alamo to go to war."

But Jasper couldn't strike a final, fatal blow. Bulldog kicker Terrance Watts attempted a forty-eight-yard field goal, but didn't have the leg.

Given a second chance, Smith seized the moment. WO-S quarterback Dewayne Evans lined up the Mustangs on their own thirty-two. They didn't gain a yard on first down, so Evans, who came into the game in the second half after having missed most of the previous three games with a wrist injury, went over the top of the Bulldogs' defense. "I ran a little hook-and-go, and the quarterback threw the ball up in the air, and some kind of way I got a hold of it," Smith said.

Smith's description of the key play when I spoke with him in 2015 was either humble, faded by the years, or both. "Smith timed his jump perfectly between two Jasper defenders, plucked the ball out of the air and raced 59 yards to the Jasper 9," *Beaumont Enterprise* reporter Chris Jenkins wrote in the game story.

Smith's catch put West Orange–Stark in point-blank range of a game-winning score. It wouldn't come easy though. Mustangs coach Dan Hooks didn't necessarily want to put the outcome on the kicker's foot again, but Jasper's defense offered no other choice. "I tell you how good they were on defense," Hooks said. "We had first-and-goal on about the nine and second-and-goal on about the seven. We had third-and-goal on about the nine, and we end up kicking a field goal. We couldn't move it an inch."

The second time around, everything worked according to plan, from the snap to Smith to Turkel's boot. "We end up kicking a field goal with maybe twenty seconds left," Smith said. "Three to zero—that was the separation of both teams that night. We were number one and they were number two at the time."

Big-fish stories can sometimes embellish the details of such classic contests. In this case, Smith didn't miss it by much. Jenkins's game story reported that WO-S, the defending state champion, was number one, while Jasper held the number three spot in the 4A state poll. That's not the only detail Jenkins's story captured brilliantly.

The Beaumont sportswriter, in the tradition of hardworking and passionate writers who follow the best teams' every move, knew Hooks had taken extra steps to get his team ready for the Jasper showdown. A week earlier, the Mustangs had stomped Port Arthur Lincoln 52–0, giving the WO-S coach time to work on important details. "Hooks had his kickers attempting field goals on first and third downs in the rout over the Bumblebees," Jenkins wrote.

That's the way it went, then. The coach knew his kicker needed the work, because three points could prove vital. And while Smith made a crucial play on offense versus Jasper, he and everyone else knew the emphasis was defense. Smith told me that in those days the offensive coordinator might take his pick of athletes at quarterback and running back, but the Mustangs' defensive coordinator, Cornel Thompson, was going to get everybody else.

"The better players, the more athletic players were going to play defense, because you have to defend the triple option," Smith said. "You had to defend the veer, and that was offenses back then. You had to have some real talented guys." It was an era that fit Smith perfectly. He was a key cog in the glory days of Texas A&M's "Wrecking Crew" and went on to help resurrect the Cowboys' "Doomsday Defense."

But before he played for those famous squads, Smith had to earn his first silver helmet. Although WO-S didn't reach the pinnacle until 1986, the Mustangs began building a winner in the 5A ranks in the late 1970s. Hooks, who had been defensive coordinator under Steve McCarty, took over as WO-S's head coach before the 1982 season. Playing in a rough-and-tumble 5A district on the Texas Gulf Coast, the Mustangs had to fight every year to make the playoffs. In 1985, Botley's senior season, they broke through by winning their first eleven games and then advanced to the third round of the playoffs, finishing 11–1–1.

One tradition that helped WO-S motivate its players from middle school on up was the chance to wear the silver varsity helmet. Freshman and JV teams wore a solid-white hat while working toward the rite of passage of wearing silver.

"When we first came to West Orange, we had a silver hat for our kids, and it just grew and grew and grew," Hooks said. "I remember one time I was going to change it to go to that West Virginia blue. 'No! No!'"

Another way Hooks set the bar high was to put his football players through spring drills almost as soon as they returned from Christmas break. Smith played basketball as well as football in high school, which meant intense double duty. But having watched just about every WO-S game from the time he was in elementary school, he had his heart set on making the varsity football team. As a sophomore, it was time for Smith to show up or shut up. "I was on varsity in basketball, and Coach said, 'We've got spring ball, and you haven't earned that silver helmet yet,'" Smith remembered. "My biggest goal as a kid—I didn't care how much I played or if I ever played—my goal was to get that silver helmet and play on the West Orange–Stark varsity."

The Mustangs made the playoffs in basketball during Smith's sophomore season, so it wasn't as if he could slack off in one sport to accommodate the other. It became one of those good problems, since Smith had to find an extra 100 percent every day to excel at both.

Smith played pro football at five-eleven and 180–190 pounds. But as a Mustang sophomore toggling between two demanding teams, he was a much scrawnier 135. "Game day, I had to go through the spring practice," Smith said. "It wasn't up for discussion. If you want to wear that silver helmet, you better be over there at practice. Then I'd go straight to basketball."

Those grueling, cold days of spring practice early in 1986 paid off for Smith and all the Mustangs. WO-S lost two regular season games during the 1986 campaign, falling 14–0 to 5A Aldine MacArthur and losing 21–8 to rival Jasper in district. But the Mustangs found their rhythm, giving up a total of only twenty points during a five-game winning streak that led to a rematch with Jasper in the state quarterfinals.

The district rivals chose Sam Houston State's Bearkat Stadium for the rematch, and that's where WO-S overcame three early turnovers with stingy defense and some creative solutions on offense.

Mustangs offensive guard Desmond Smith pulled off a fumblerooski and fumbled twenty-one yards for a touchdown that sliced Jasper's lead to 9–7 in the second quarter. In the second half, WO-S quarterback James Reed took the pitch on a double reverse and then threw to running back Brian Cleveland for a forty-two-yard hookup that set up the go-ahead score.

WO-S prevailed 21–15 in the all-important second meeting with Jasper. "It was a thriller, and we knew whoever won it was going to advance and do good in the playoffs," Hooks said. "It was a big win for us. All the community was there. I'll never forget it."

Hooks won 283 games, lost 75 and tied 2 in thirty years at WO-S, the only place he was ever the head coach. For him to say that whoever won that second Mustangs-Bulldogs game was going to "advance and do good in the playoffs" is a classic old-ball-coach understatement.

The Mustangs won both the state semifinal over New Braunfels and the state championship game versus McKinney in the Astrodome by double dig-its to claim the school's first football state title. Pressed for the impact of that championship, Hooks became a little more ornamental. "Oh Lord, that was a big deal because [WO-S] had been to the playoffs a time or two here, but they never advanced very far," Hooks said. "The community went crazy, and we had parades and I don't know what all. We had all kinds of recognition. The kids were deserving. I still think about it today, and the community does too."

Having reached the top, the WO-S players and coaches used the momentum instead of basking in the glow of the championship. The Mustangs came back in 1987 with a perfect regular season. Along with the 3–0 victory over Jasper, WO-S defeated Aldine Nimitz 7–6, and Aldine MacArthur 6–3. WO-S shattered everyone else that the regular season or the playoffs had to offer. Other than the three low-scoring battle royals, the Mustangs' closest game was their 17–7 victory over Rockwall in the state championship game.

Smith saved his best for his final high school game and the watching eyes of the Texas A&M coaching staff. Playing at Kyle Field, Smith made a leaping interception on the second play of the game, then caught a ten-yard touch-down pass from quarterback Tremain Lewis to give the Mustangs a 7–0 first-quarter lead.

Smith finished with five catches for fifty-five yards and helped the WO-S defense bottle up Rockwall. R. C. Slocum, at the time Texas A&M's defensive coordinator, looked on and knew Smith was ready for the next level. "He's told me before that was their determining factor in them recruiting me, because of that game," Smith said. "That was the thing that pushed everything over the edge for me. Once they came in with Coach Slocum, I was all in."

It was at once the top of the mountain and a jumping-off point. *Beaumont Enterprise* sportswriters Jenkins and Dwain Price each interviewed Smith and captured his elation at having helped WO-S win its second straight state title. Price built his sidebar around Smith's emotions. "I'm crying because I'm happy," Smith told Price. "This is the end of my high school career, and in two years we went 28-and-two and won two state championships. I can use a lot of adjectives to express my feelings right now, but I would be here all night."

I spoke with Smith early in 2015, just weeks after he watched WO-S play in the state championship game versus Gilmer. Since claiming back-to-back titles in 1986–1987, WO-S has returned to the state final four times, finally winning its third state championship in 2015 when the Mustangs defeated Celina, 22–3, in the final at NRG Stadium. Smith said that watching those teams advance through the playoffs to that level provides kids with opportunities and motivation that elevate an entire community.

He clearly took full advantage of it, since he won titles at higher levels, including Super Bowls. He said that's part of the reason he stays in close communication and involvement with the West Orange community through Botley, who still worked for the school when I talked with them on the phone.

It's debatable whether WO-S would have won a state title without Smith. But it's obvious there wouldn't be a Kevin Smith without the Mustangs. "My goal was always to wear that silver helmet with that mustang on the side," Smith said. "I didn't dream about A&M. I never had a thought about playing professional football. My ultimate goal in life was to put that silver helmet on and play on Friday nights for West Orange–Stark."

# 15

## IDALOU

### 1988

*South Plains Superman*

The intriguing thing about Superman is that on most days he's just Clark Kent. He's just a guy with two first names. He's just a guy that you might nod to as you pass him on the way to the bathroom at the office. He's just a guy that goes to church with some friends of yours. He would never talk about the fact that he can fly or has X-ray vision, so you'd never know. And of course, it would greatly embarrass him if you wrote a chapter in a book revealing that he was actually Superman.

But what the heck.

I was dining at a Rosa's Cafe in Waco one day in the mid-2000s when some friends introduced me to a family they knew from church. The reason my friends introduced me to Tracy and Kyna Saul was because I had gone to Texas Tech and that's where they went to college. Furthermore, I'm a lifelong Red Raider, since my parents met while they were at Tech. So that's the moment I realized that the man sitting in the booth was actually Superman.

Tracy Saul earned the nickname the "Natural" while at Tech, where he started at safety for the Red Raiders as a true freshman and intercepted eight passes that season. By the end of his career as a Red Raider, Saul had set the Southwest Conference record with twenty-five career interceptions. He earned consensus all-SWC honors all four years, making him one of just four players to accomplish that feat. The Texas Tech football team made good use of this athlete who could do it all. In addition, he played basketball for the Red Raiders for a spell, though the hoops team probably didn't deploy him to his full potential.

The folks in Idalou figure Saul was perhaps a better basketball player than he was on the gridiron. He averaged better than thirty points as a senior. On the same day that he committed to signing with Spike Dykes's Red Raiders, he dropped fifty-five points on the New Deal Lions as Idalou won 100–27.

Russ Reagan came to Idalou as an assistant coach during Saul's career and stayed through the Wildcats' dream school year, 2010–2011, when they won the Class 2A Division II state championship in football and the 2A title in basketball. But when I asked him for a comparison between Saul and members of those teams, he demurred.

When I changed the subject to Saul's senior year, 1988–1989, Reagan began with the basketball game versus New Deal. "He didn't miss," Reagan said. "That's the way it was. The only time that I remember him missing in that game was a half-court shot at halftime, and then the last shot at the end of the game. It was unreal. It was ridiculous."

Saul's high school teammate Cliff Alexander went on to win a Western Athletic Conference championship in the 400-meter hurdles while at Air Force in 1992, a SWC title in the event while at Rice in 1995, and he finished fourth at the Olympic Trials in 1996. But he said playing on the Wildcats' 1988 football team was his most fun season. And he still marvels at Saul's ability on the basketball court. "You couldn't foul the guy hard enough to make him miss the shot," Alexander said. "He would go in and almost draw the contact. And he was so strong at the basket. He would want you to foul him, because it was a three-point play every time. He wouldn't miss the free throw. I always thought he was a better basketball player than he was a football player, because one person could take over a basketball game."

Of course, when you're five-ten and Dykes and Grant Teaff and Ken Hatfield are coming to your basketball games because they want you to play football, you play football.

By the time Saul committed to the Red Raiders and scored fifty-five on the court on the same day, he had proved himself on the football field. For the 1988 season, he was the *Lubbock Avalanche-Journal*'s 2A South Plains Player of the Year, despite having missed three games with a broken hand.

Saul played quarterback and safety on a Wildcat team that went 10–0 in the regular season. That was merely the fulfillment of potential. Wildcat coach Eddie Hooper had led the team to the 3A playoffs in 1987 and had plenty of experience and speed coming back. "We knew it going into the season that we should be pretty good," Hooper said. "We were 7–4 and in the playoffs the year before. Dropping down [to a lower classification], we had confidence that we could do a good job, and a lot of those kids were back."

Idalou proved itself early in the season by sweeping a slate of 3A nondistrict opponents. Never one to hog credit, of course, Saul pointed to a group of players, including Alexander, who played cornerback and wide receiver, linebacker Chad Farris and running back Tommy Cook as key cogs for the Wildcats. "If you've got one guy that will go out and work, everybody else falls right along with it," Saul said. "We had some really good coaches, but we had a lot of great families and great kids. We had a lot of good kids that went out and knew how to work hard."

In many of the stories in this book, that's the description of a state-champion football team. But Idalou's story is about the one that got away and how it escaped them.

The Wildcats had ascended to 11–0 and the second round of the playoffs when they met the Quanah Indians on a frigid night at Shotwell Stadium in Abilene. The *Lubbock Avalanche-Journal* account of the game put the temperature in the low forties with winds that gusted up to thirty mph. Facing those unfriendly conditions, the Wildcats and Indians pitted their best runners against each other. Quanah handed the ball to running back Setrick Dickens, and Saul consistently tucked and ran on option plays in Idalou's veer attack.

Dickens, who finished 1988 with 350 points, rushed for 151 yards and scored three touchdowns on that brutally cold night. Saul, meanwhile, gained 143 yards on twenty carries.

Still, Saul knew when to give it up, and so it was Wildcat running back Ricky Westbrook who matched Dickens's three touchdowns. Westbrook's final score, on a two-yard run, cut Quanah's lead to 25–20 on the first play of the fourth quarter.

Dickens and Saul would see each other again when Dickens played for TCU and Saul was at Texas Tech. Their final collision in the fourth quarter that night at Shotwell Stadium more or less decided the playoff contest. "They were going into the wind, and they were running a short crossing pattern to Setrick, bringing him out of the backfield and running a crossing pattern, and he catches it," Saul said. "I hit him, and he fumbles, and I recover the fumble, so we've now got the ball."

Saul's fumble recovery gave the Wildcats possession at the Quanah forty-seven with more than four minutes left in the fourth quarter. Only there was one major problem: the toll the fumble-forcing hit took on Saul. "I got hit when I hit him," Saul said. "When I hit him, he goes back, and his knee comes up and hits me right in the groin area. I knew something was wrong when I got hit."

Saul went to the sideline and briefly went to his knees before assistant coach Bryan Huseman insisted that the quarterback was needed on the field. Though Saul made it back into the game, he couldn't run the option keepers that Idalou needed to carry it into the end zone. Instead, Saul's fourth-and-ten pass from the Indians' thirty, intended for Alexander, was broken up by Dickens.

The Wildcats' first loss in twelve games ended their season. Quanah went on to the 2A state championship game, losing to Corrigan-Camden.

But Saul had more pressing matters to attend to before he could make the trip home from Abilene. One of his testicles, which took the brunt of the collision with Dickens, swelled to the size of a softball.

"We didn't have a trainer at the school, but Tech at the time sent out their trainers to go help at the local high schools," Saul said. "Well, we had a girl that was our trainer. The coaches, I showed them in the locker room, and they were like, 'Oh!' They said, 'You've got to let her see it,' and I'm like, 'Uh-uh, I'm not letting her see it.' They take me to the hospital. Everything was fine. It was just one of those things."

Saul, who with Kyna has two daughters, laughs shyly about the story now. At his twentieth reunion, he said he and his teammates reminisced about the Quanah game and what might have been. Reagan said he went to the hospital with Saul and drove him home later that night. Although Saul went back in the game after the injury, the Wildcats could see their leader was off balance. "I knew at the time that he stripped the ball that something had happened," Reagan said. "He's going to do everything possible to keep from letting the team know he's hurt. I knew he wasn't right. That's one of those things, but it's hard to get a kid out that's that dedicated to what he's doing."

Most football players, especially ones on an eleven-win football team, don't want to think about basketball season arriving in November. But Saul was hit by a double whammy, because the injury in the Quanah game kept him out of the first month of basketball season.

As I sat in a cafe in Waco with Saul, he took the most pleasure in remembering the atmosphere around high school sports in West Texas in the late 1980s. He said the guys he played against on Friday night would meet up at Texas Tech football games on Saturday afternoon and rehash the action. "We were so intertwined," Saul said. "Friday night, we would play Post and then the next day, Saturday, we'd all be at the Tech game sitting up in the grass, talking about the ball game. It didn't matter if it was Post or Brownfield or Denver City, we all seemed to congregate at the Tech ball games, sitting up there in the grass. I think it's what's so unique about that area out there.

"You go into basketball, and at that point you're seeing each other every Tuesday and Friday night. You get into track, and you're seeing each other every Saturday. It was one big group. To this day, I miss being out in that area."

Following his Texas Tech career, Saul signed as a free agent with the Chicago Bears, making it until a late-August cut. He coached for a year in the Lubbock area before going to work for a sporting goods company. Saul is in the Texas High School Football Hall of Fame and the Southwest Conference Hall of Fame, but if you ask a coach in Texas these days, they're likely to know him from his friendly presence at the annual massive coaching convention known as Coaching School.

Sounds like another mild-mannered civilian working for the *Daily Planet*, doesn't it?

Speaking with Alexander about athletes he's known during his career, the track standout compared Saul favorably with Rice's Bert Emanuel and Larry Izzo, both of whom had extended NFL careers. Alexander said he often wonders what Saul could have done if he'd made that late-August cut.

I raised an alternative: what if Saul had been a receiver in a spread offense? "You read my mind," Alexander said. "[Wes] Welker. [Danny] Amendola. I'm certain that Tracy is a more gifted athlete than either. Just a tick away in so many ways."

But even if Saul sometimes ponders what might have been, he doesn't betray it. In casual conversation at a Mexican food restaurant, or in an interview specifically about his high school career, it's obvious this is a man without regrets. He seems to hold on to the times shared with teammates, and even with opponents, as the value of those days.

Because he played a few years before the invention of YouTube, it's difficult to find video on the Internet of the Natural from Idalou. There's a grainy video from his Texas Tech career, which finishes with a fantastic interception against Houston: Saul stretched out to intercept a pass, one-handed with his left hand, and then, before hitting the ground on the diving catch, he tucked the ball under his right arm.

Even though he's Clark Kent traveling around Texas as a mild-mannered sporting goods salesman, that's the Superman side of Tracy Saul that folks from Idalou remember.

# 16

## WHITE DEER

### 1988

*Bucks Ride Swinging Gate to Glory*

The White Deer Bucks seniors knew they had a football team ready to accomplish lofty goals during the 1988 season.

Bart Thomas had been playing ball with Tommy Martinez and T. W. Lowe and Bryan Waitman and Brady Burns and the rest of their crew of buddies for a long time. In fact, most of them had played together from elementary school through their junior year by the time they were getting ready for the fall of 1988.

The older they got, the more they won. The more they won, the more their confidence grew. And the more their confidence grew, the more chips they put on the table. "We returned ten starters both ways from the year before," Thomas said. "That's what let us know we were going to be pretty good. We just had everybody coming back."

The season before, White Deer had scratched out a 7–3 record in Class 2A. So when the Bucks were reclassified to 1A, and had most of their team coming back, they knew what they were working toward.

The Bucks were ready for a high bar and willing to work to clear it. "We had the work ethic to make it happen," Lowe said. "It was a very dedicated team, a very close team. I think that's what made it work: the way the team played together."

But the state is full of senior-laden ball clubs willing to put in the extra work and sweat and blood to win a state title. In the end, White Deer needed that something extra to put them over the top. It came in the form of a pugnacious freshman and a gutsy call.

The freshman was Thomas's kid brother, Zach. Growing up in the country in the Panhandle, Bart and Zach Thomas spent their early days finding boyish ways to pass the long summer days. They would, on occasion, leave in the early morning for a hike to the nearest ghost town and return just before or just after sunset. On other days, they would practice amateur acrobatics at the swimming hole. "We grew up in the middle of nowhere with nothing else to do," Bart Thomas said. "We'd put the trampoline beside the pool and do some of the craziest stuff you'd ever see. Most parents would not allow that, but we grew up a little backwoods. We were a different breed."

Like any younger brother, as soon as Zach Thomas was agile enough to toddle around, he followed his older brother's every step, attempting to mirror everything Bart did. The age gap between them meant that when Bart was a senior ready for one last glory ride, Zach was desperate to play a role for the Bucks. "I was that little kid underneath that didn't want to be annoying them when we were growing up," Zach said. "They're all hanging together, and you really couldn't ever be part of the group. When I got to step in on the football field, though, they welcomed me with open arms. But that's only because of my play. But I had to earn it. That was one thing that really drove me, because I wanted to earn the respect."

It didn't take Zach long to make it clear that he could be a dynamic part of the White Deer varsity team. Although he spent the first couple of games of the season on the junior varsity and playing cornet in the band on Friday nights, it was obvious it wasn't doing anyone any good for him to play sub-varsity football.

"It was pathetic," Bart said. "He started out on freshman team the first game, and he just went crazy. I think he had 80 percent of the tackles, so they put him on JV. The next two games, he dominated. During practice, he dominated our starting center. They put him at nose just for the scout team, and he just dominated. I couldn't get the ball and hand it off half the time. He was five-nine, 185, as a freshman, and fast."

When I spoke with Buck running back Bryan Waitman, he could still feel the bruises of having to deal with the freshman during practice. After all, practice is sometimes about repetition to perfect a play, making it a drudgery for Waitman. "Somebody kept messing up, and we had to run that play, like, three or four times in a row, and I would have to block Zach," Waitman said. "I wouldn't let him know this, but he was killing me. He would hit so hard. It was just unbelievable a freshman could hit that hard."

Just like the seniors, White Deer coach Windy Williams knew in the spring that his Bucks were going to be good. He didn't want to bring the freshman

Thomas up. He didn't believe in having a freshman on the varsity. But sometimes personal principles have to be tossed out when faced with overwhelming reason. "I was saying, 'We're going to have a heck of a JV football team with him on it,'" Williams said. "I've never started a freshman before or since. We had a conversation with their father [Steve Thomas], and he said, 'It seems like you need him.' From then on, he kept on growing and growing as a player. He had a knack for the ball."

Zach Thomas finished a thirteen-year NFL career with more than 1,100 tackles and seventeen interceptions. That followed a Texas Tech career during which he twice earned all-American honors, totaled 390 career tackles, and made one of the most memorable interceptions in Red Raider history when his pick-six boosted Texas Tech to a 14–7 win over Texas A&M in 1995.

Yeah, Zach Thomas had a knack for the football. Even after joining the Bucks midway through the nondistrict schedule, he led the varsity in tackles as a freshman. "We knew Zach had the potential to go play in the NFL when he started playing with us," Lowe said. "He did have a certain level of intensity. His instinctive ability to find the football, being right there as that middle linebacker and to help lead that defense at a young age was just phenomenal."

Given the senior leadership on that team, I asked Bart whether he felt as though his younger brother had really made an impact or whether the Bucks might have won a state title anyway. "He ended up being the leading tackler for the season, so I think he made a pretty big difference," Bart Thomas said. "Once the playoffs got here, he was very important. He was the leading tackler about every game in the playoffs."

After fighting through a nondistrict schedule packed with 2A opponents, White Deer tore through its 1A district schedule. The Bucks earned a bye in the first round of the playoffs and then commenced the drive for the state title game. A 21–20 victory over Garden City proved the toughest test before White Deer met Flatonia in the final at the Mustang Bowl in Sweetwater.

Williams had a sense of White Deer's tradition in football. For a town that maxed out at around 3,000 people before the Great Depression and had dwindled to around 1,100 by the late 1980s, White Deer has the amazing legacy of producing three consensus all-Americans. Jim Weatherall earned all-American honors at Oklahoma in 1950 and 1951, Carl McAdams did the same with the Sooners in 1967, and Zach Thomas was an all-American at Texas Tech in 1994 and 1995. Williams also knew that White Deer had won its only state championship while playing in the Mustang Bowl in Sweetwater, and that the 1958 team began the game with a straight dive that resulted in a fifty-eight-yard touchdown.

So when White Deer took the ball for the first time against Flatonia, Williams dialed up a straight dive. "We ran it because they had," Williams said. It worked. Waitman took the handoff and went up the middle for fifty-two yards to the Flatonia thirteen. That set up Bart Thomas's ten-yard touchdown pass to Lowe, giving the Bucks a 6–0 lead after a blocked extra point. The missed point would play a huge role, but not in the Bucks' demise.

Flatonia won the middle portion of the game and surged ahead 13–6 late in the third quarter. As the clock wound down on the fourth quarter, it was time for White Deer to make a gutsy call. Bart Thomas ran right on a quarterback keeper on fourth-and-five from the Flatonia thirty. He stretched out as he went to the ground and reached just far enough for a drive-saving first down. Again, it was Thomas going right for the touchdown, this time on a seven-yard run that cut the Bulldogs' lead to 13–12.

Going through his normal routine as the kicker as well as the quarterback, Thomas took his flat-toe shoe from the sideline and began the wardrobe change that would allow him to tie the game with a straight-on punch through the goal posts. Meanwhile, Williams had done some quick figuring on the sideline. "We had three moves off our kicking game," Williams said. "We had a PAT [point after touchdown], which was called 'Patty.' We had a fake field goal, which was called 'Sally,' and we had the honey play, which was a swinging-gate kind of deal. We had already tried the fake field goal and had it smacked earlier in the game. The next call was going to be the honey play. Bart's tying his shoe and we give the signal."

All season long, White Deer had lined up for extra points in the swinging-gate formation, with most of the team setting up left while Martinez, the holder, and Bart Thomas lined up in the middle of the field. Only once all season had they run the swinging gate, though, and it failed on that occasion. But Martinez took the signal from Williams and felt his gut leap. "He made the call," Martinez remembered. "Okay, I've got to walk over here now in front of these guys who are basically two, maybe three yards away, pick it up as quickly as I can, and toss it over to T. W. without anybody intercepting it or knocking it down. For me, that's where the nervousness is at. Picking it up without dropping it and getting it over to T. W."

If Martinez was nervous, imagine how Lowe felt as he waited for the throw and the run that could decide a state championship. But he concentrated on the defense's reaction. "You could look over at the defense and see there was some chaos going on," Lowe said. "They slid over into position, but I don't think they were really confident in how to cover it. Tommy had a great throw over to me. There was just a mess of bodies on the ground there, and I saw a little gap."

Zach Thomas told me that his brother did an excellent job of carrying out the fake as he knelt down to put on his kicking shoe. I told Zach that if Bart was faking it, he had done the top method-acting job of all time. "I never knew it," Bart Thomas said. "I was putting my flat-toe shoe on and had my head down. I heard the crowd going crazy, and I looked up and Tommy Martinez threw it to T. W. Lowe, and he scored by about a foot."

White Deer successfully executed a swinging-gate pass for a two-point conversion to take the lead in the state championship game with 2:07 remaining in the fourth quarter. If that happened in a college football national championship game, it would be the play of the century.

With the 14–13 lead, White Deer had a new set of concerns. Flatonia still had time to score, especially since Bulldogs kicker Wesley Scott was known to have a strong leg and had already made two field goals. Another Scott make would be enough for Flatonia to steal the game back from White Deer.

So Waitman stepped in from his linebacker position and locked it up. "I don't want to play too light on that interception," Lowe said. "That interception was as big as the two-point conversion to me. It was exciting to score that touchdown and take the lead, but quite honestly, we knew we had to stop those guys. When we scored, we said, 'Yes, we got 'em, but now we got to hold 'em.' When Bryan picked that ball off, that was it. That's when you know it was game over."

That's the tale of an unforgettable state championship game. But I'm not sure I would have included this story in this collection if it weren't for the Thomas brothers. Bart and Zach Thomas went on to stardom at Texas Tech and in 1993 became the first brothers to earn all-SWC honors in the same season in the history of the conference.

As I interviewed the members of the 1988 White Deer team, each one pointed to the work ethic and professionalism instilled in them while playing high school football. When they won the state championship, Williams encouraged them to take that title and build on it. "I said, 'Don't let this define you as a person,'" Williams said. "This is not a culmination of something that you tried to do. This is the beginning of something that you tried to do."

The pugnacious freshman took the words to heart. Zach Thomas's football path took him to Pampa High School for his junior and senior seasons, then Texas Tech, where his college career eventually landed him in the SWC Hall of Fame. The Miami Dolphins drafted Thomas in the fifth round, and he went on to play twelve seasons for the fish, then one final season in Dallas.

No one would say that state championship season defined Zach Thomas. But he still thinks of it as the peak of his football career. Thomas didn't make the play that won the game on the scoreboard or the play that sealed the victory. He was merely part of the effort, but it was still as good as it ever got. "I will say, and I'm not just saying this, that was the best moment of my life when it came to championships and winning football," Thomas said. "After that, I really saw how hard it is to really win a championship. I never sniffed it again all the way into the NFL. What's important, what I look back at, it doesn't matter what level it is, if you got high-character guys on your team, you got a chance, and that was that team right there. It was the best moment of my football career. That's what you play for. There's not a better feeling than that."

# 17

# ROCKPORT-FULTON

## 1992

### *Dat Nguyen's Pirates Raid Homecoming*

When Dat Nguyen became a big-name linebacker at Texas A&M, he wasn't the type of big name folks were used to. His name, for one thing, stood out on the roster. But then, to most folks, and especially to Texas A&M fans, it didn't matter where he was from or that he was an anomaly. As long as he could blow up ballcarriers, he could have been from the moon.

Except it does matter.

Not because Nguyen came from a family of Vietnamese refugees, but because he came from Rockport-Fulton. He came from a community and a school that was divided by much more than a hyphen. "Everybody—Asian, Mexican, white, black—everyone was at each other's throats," said Jeff Aguilar, describing the town where he grew up with Hung Nguyen and his younger brother, Dat.

In his book *Dat: Tackling Life and the NFL*, Nguyen describes how his family and other Vietnamese living in the Texas Gulf Coast town of Rockport experienced racial tension and discrimination. Some seafood markets wouldn't deal with Vietnamese fishermen. When a white family friend named Jimmy Hattenbach picked Dat for his youth soccer team, the coach faced blacklisting by those in the community who weren't comfortable with the new Asian presence. Nguyen's mother warned him when he began school to stick with his people and not trust the whites.

Nguyen detailed the awkward nature of being different in a small Texas town. He gave a compelling account of how soccer, basketball, and football blurred racial lines. But to him, he was just a kid playing games. "The community did change," Nguyen said. "No doubt about that, but I don't think you realize it until you sit back and think about it. It was so fast. You're a bunch of kids, and that's the last thing you worry about."

I met Nguyen in San Antonio near the North Star Mall, where his sports-radio talk show was doing a remote broadcast the day of game six of the Spurs versus Dallas Mavericks first-round playoff series in 2014. We were supposed to meet at a sports bar called Slacker's, but it was closed at noon when we arrived. So, much more appropriately, we walked across the shopping center to a Vietnamese restaurant.

Nguyen seemed to enjoy conversing with the owner, who was waiting on our table. He spoke in Vietnamese as he ordered a mountain of food. Just as a person doesn't forget his or her native tongue, a man doesn't forget how to eat like a football player. In between slurps of noodles, Nguyen and I talked through his high school career. When I first asked him about a moment when he knew he could perform at a high level, he demurred. He would like to deflect all personal attention to his team, which makes him like most football players I've met.

Don't let that fool you, though. Nguyen's teammates knew he was different. "Dat was the focus, but it never got to his head," said Aguilar, who was a year ahead of Nguyen but played beside him at linebacker for two seasons. "You knew he was special because he could take over a game defensively."

As Nguyen and I delved into his high school football career, two specific games came to light. The Rockport-Fulton Pirates finished 9–1–2 in 1992. The highlight of the season came when the Pirates tied mighty Sinton, 7–7, to win Rockport-Fulton's first district championship in twenty years. Nguyen clearly remembers the packed stands, where fans of all races meshed together, and how they rushed the field after Rockport-Fulton won the game by virtue of penetrations and, in doing so, claimed the district title. "Everybody and their dogs that was a fan of Rockport was out there on the field," Nguyen said. "It was one of those moments."

But Nguyen quickly realized that the game behind the game had happened two weeks earlier when the Pirates traveled to play the Taft Greyhounds. Rockport-Fulton took a five-game winning streak and their hopes of winning a championship with them, but the Pirates had fallen in a deep hole, 22–7, by halftime. The locker room was deathly quiet at the break, and the Pirates were reeling.

Then Rockport-Fulton defensive coordinator Mike Coleman unleashed a tongue-lashing that did its job. "Coach Coleman came in and used some expletives," Aguilar said. "He just hyped us up and got us going."

The Pirates had made the playoffs the previous season, but hadn't earned much respect in the process. Rockport-Fulton was playing its third homecoming game of the season when it went to Taft, and homecoming opponents are supposed to be patsies, or at least that's how the Pirates received the gesture. That is, they took it personally. "[Coleman] said, 'We've already won three homecomings. What's one more?'" Aguilar remembered. "People were leaving the stands because they thought we had already lost."

Words have to be accompanied by actions, though, and it seemed the Greyhounds were going to retain the upper hand in action. Taft took the ball to start the second half and marched deep into Pirate territory. "We were like, 'Oh man, if they score, it will be over,'" Nguyen said.

Facing third-and-three inside the Rockport-Fulton five, Nguyen made the play that shifted momentum. Nguyen launched himself over the Greyhounds' offensive line to meet the quarterback just as he was handing to the running back. A decade later, Oklahoma's Roy Williams would make a similar play, launching himself over the line into Texas quarterback Chris Simms. Both plays netted the same result—a defensive touchdown. "It was like what you saw with Texas and Oklahoma," Aguilar said. "Dat was able to beat a lot of blocks and be very disruptive in the backfield."

Dat Nguyen knocked the ball loose, and his cousin Van Nguyen scooped it and ran ninety-five yards for a touchdown. If there were any doubts that the Pirates had grabbed the momentum, Dat Nguyen erased them on the next Taft possession. This time he blew up a screen play and forced another fumble, which Rockport-Fulton corralled at the Taft forty.

The *Rockport Pilot* told the story succinctly from there. It took exactly one play for the Pirates' offense to cash in on the turnover. Rockport-Fulton running back Daniel Vasquez broke loose for a forty-yard touchdown, leaving the Greyhounds in his wake on the way to the score with 4:45 to go in the third quarter. The Pirates had failed to add the extra point on Van Nguyen's touchdown, and their attempt to make up for it with a two-point conversion on Vasquez's TD run went awry as well. Rockport-Fulton still trailed the Greyhounds 22–19, but the Pirates had the momentum. Rockport-Fulton scored once more in the third quarter, converting yet another Taft fumble into another Vasquez touchdown, this one from two yards out.

That's all Rockport-Fulton needed to notch its sixth straight win. "That game was really the bigger game than Sinton," Nguyen said. "I can remember it gave us confidence more than cockiness or arrogance."

The week after coming back to defeat Taft, the Pirates rocked Odem 34–6, setting up the showdown with Sinton. Rockport-Fulton took an early 7–0 lead, which it held at halftime. But silence once again prevailed in the Pirates' locker room as they awaited Sinton's charge. Sinton had won at least twelve games and advanced at least four rounds into the playoffs during the previous two seasons, and Nguyen said their coach, Gary Davenport, was a legend in South Texas.

Again it fell to defensive coordinator Coleman to make an impression. After speaking with Aguilar and Nguyen separately about the scene in the locker room, it's clear to me how it unfolded. Coleman hopped up on one of those tall boxes used in grueling up-down training. That gave the coach the height he needed to reach the motivational posters tacked up around the locker room. "'You see this right here? All these goals? That doesn't mean crap,'" Nguyen quoted Coleman's rant more than twenty years later. "He tore that thing down and so we were like, 'Oh man!' All of us guys got chills."

Rockport-Fulton needed every bit of the motivation. Sinton tied the game with 9:19 left in the fourth quarter. Then with 3:59 remaining, Sinton took the ball and marched into Rockport-Fulton territory. On a fourth down from the Rockport-Fulton eighteen, Sinton tried to win the race to the corner, but Nguyen was ready. "Sinton's Ross Partlow ran a sweep on fourth down late in the game," Aguilar recalled. "Dat just lit him up. Just blew him up, and that's what won the game for us."

Rockport-Fulton had the edge in penetrations and therefore claimed the District 30-3A championship. But karma would play its hand in the second round of the playoffs when the Pirates tied Port Isabel 21–21 and lost on penetrations.

The next season, with his brother and Aguilar gone, Nguyen led Rockport-Fulton to an 8–3 season. Meanwhile, interest from college programs began to increase. Michigan coach Gary Moeller traveled to Rockport to recruit Nguyen, which made a dramatic impression on the Vietnamese family. "He's going to play on national TV, and he's at your house," Nguyen said. "It was awesome, but you couldn't believe it. It never even crossed your mind junior year or senior year. I thought I might go to [Texas A&M] Kingsville and have a chance to play. Sam Houston was one of my unofficial visits. That was the only places I thought I could go."

Texas A&M stepped in and it proved to be a perfect fit. Nguyen helped the Aggies transition from the Southwest Conference to the Big 12 by starting fifty-one consecutive games and racking up 517 career tackles. He's the only player in Texas A&M history to lead the Aggies in tackles for four straight seasons.

The Dallas Cowboys selected Nguyen in the third round of the 1999 NFL draft, and he became the first Vietnamese American to play in the NFL. He played six seasons, all in Dallas, and was selected second-team All-Pro in 2003.

It's impossible to know the impact that one moment can really have on a team or an individual's career. As with so many of these stories, I wonder how Nguyen's career might have been different if Taft had scored that touchdown when they were going in, early in the third quarter. If one little thing had changed, how would that have changed the story for Nguyen and Rockport-Fulton and Texas A&M and the Cowboys?

It's clear, though, that it helped define a diverse community on the Texas Gulf Coast. "People were so supportive," Nguyen said. "I can remember— Asian people don't really go [to football games]. My parents went to two games my whole high school career; they went to parents night. But there would be a whole section of Vietnamese people, fifty to a hundred people. I was just like, 'Oh, this!' I talk about that all the time. The community shut down to go watch the games. It was amazing, and it was fun. That's what's so cool about it."

# 18

# CONVERSE

## 1992–1993

### *Judson Rockets Blast Off*

By the end of his sophomore season, Jerod Douglas had seen enough Converse Judson highlight videos that ended with gloomy scenes and tear-streaked faces. Clint Rutledge was just tired of seeing the expression on his father's face that told the story of another close-but-no-cigar finish.

They were both ready to do something about it. That was the motivation when Clint Rutledge, Rockets' coach D.W. Rutledge's son, called a late-night class meeting just outside Darrell K Royal–Texas Memorial Stadium in Austin. The Rockets had just fallen to Sugar Land Dulles 27–26 in the Class 5A state semifinals. "After that game, I can still picture, we're standing outside the bus, everybody has gotten dressed," Clint Rutledge said. "They're loading their stuff. Just the sophomores, we met, and I looked at each one of them, and I said, 'I am sick to death of seeing this look on my dad's face. We're not going to do this again. From here on out we're winning it.'"

Perhaps 99 out of 100 high school football teams would have looked at a trip to the state semifinals as the culmination of a fantastic season. Clearly, that wasn't the case for Converse Judson. It would have been acceptable at some point, perhaps in the late 1970s or early 1980s, but by 1991, the Rockets were aiming at the absolute height of accomplishment, and nothing else would satisfy. Converse Judson won its first state championship in 1983 and claimed another one, though under odd circumstances, in 1988. The Rockets lost the 1988 state final against Dallas Carter 31–14. But when it was ruled that the

Cowboys had used an ineligible player, the Rockets were awarded their second state crown.

Either way, though, by the early 1990s making the penultimate game of the season just wasn't good enough. "We watched those highlights with the team crying, and we were, like, 'This can't be us,'" Douglas said. "We don't want to have a great highlight film, and then the last minute of it or last two minutes is everybody on the team, fans, cheerleaders, everybody, crying. Let's go ahead and see if we can finish the deal. It added just a little bit more focus. We were definitely a focused group, and well coached, because obviously Coach Rutledge was a legend, along with his staff. That can only carry you so far, and I think the team kind of picked up the rest. We didn't want that highlight film to end with a sad song at the end."

The Rockets players' internal motivation burned hot, matching the fever pitch of the community.

Growing up with high school football, I've always known the name "Converse Judson." But I didn't fully understand the fervor of that community for its football team until I spoke with Clint Rutledge. "It really was like a college atmosphere at those games," he said.

When a small-town high school football program starts winning and gains a relatively massive fan following, folks like to say the last one to leave town on Friday night has to turn out all the lights.

It's true, it happens.

But when a big school gains that kind of all-encompassing following, well, things graduate from folksy to legendary. It's difficult to imagine the kinds of crowds that showed up to watch the Judson Rockets when they ruled the state's largest classification.

Not for Clint Rutledge, though. He was right there in the middle of it. "Judson was starting to reach its peak in popularity. I would say the peak was actually '92 and '93, when we were playing, because of our tailback, Jerod Douglas," he said. "It was really starting to gain a lot of momentum. At that point, there were people who would camp out to get season tickets. Before playoff games, they were camping out to get tickets. The crowd was there an hour and a half before kickoff."

By then, the Judson Rocket Nation had been growing for more than a decade. D. W. Rutledge joined then–head coach Frank Arnold at Judson in 1980, and they quickly established the Rockets' identity. Through discipline, stingy defense, and a top-notch rushing attack, Judson ascended to the top of

Texas's biggest division. Driven by running back Chris Pryor's 2,800 rushing yards, a single-season 5A state record, the Rockets defeated Midland Lee 25–21 for the 5A title in 1983.

Following the championship season, Arnold stepped into the athletic director's role, and Rutledge took over as the head football coach. He knew it was the type of place for a coach to stick. "I think the diversity is as good as any as I've seen," D. W. Rutledge said. "The kids got along so well. It was a blue-collar community, and good mammas and daddies in it that really supported their kids. It was economically and culturally very diverse."

Rutledge compiled a record of 197–32–5 at Judson, his only head-coaching job, which he held for seventeen seasons.

He became the executive director of the Texas High School Coaches Association in 2004, and that's where I caught up with him late in 2014. Rather than regale me with details of his battle decisions during the season, Rutledge was far more inclined to talk about the processes that led to success in the fall. He said his staff felt that the foundation for each team was established in the first two months of the year during classroom and boot-camp training. When I asked about the back-to-back state championships, he began with how the players responded in the off-season, immediately following the 1991 state-semifinal loss. "We talked a lot about character development and set goals and set individual goals," Rutledge said. "That really was the first phase, and you could see that in them during that classroom phase."

The Rockets rolled into the 1992 season, winning each of their first three games by at least twenty-seven points. They were talented and committed, but it took a loss to cause the reaction that ignited their launch for the rest of the season. The Temple Wildcats came into Judson Stadium and, with an estimated crowd of 13,000 watching, stormed back from a 21–7 third-quarter deficit to defeat the Rockets 37–21. On defense, the Rockets lost key linebacker Chad Scott to a concussion severe enough that Clint Rutledge recalled Scott didn't know where he was or who his teammates were. With Scott out, Douglas said the Rockets faltered on both sides of the ball as the Wildcats surged to a victory.

It served as an attention grabber. "From that point on, we knew we were going to win state," Douglas said. "There's no way—we're never letting this feeling happen again. It was so crazy how confident we got after that loss. We never thought they were better than us, and we were just upset. That was the fuel that sparked it."

Douglas rushed for 251 yards and a pair of touchdowns in the loss to Temple. He said it was the first time in his high school career that he gained more than 200, which made the loss even worse, because he couldn't celebrate the accomplishment.

Judson knew what it had in Douglas by his junior season, and Douglas knew he was in the perfect program. He moved to the San Antonio area with his family from Miami, Florida, where he grew up playing football all day with his friends. A football junkie by early elementary school, he said he could name every running back in the NFL at five years old. Douglas knew the sevens in his multiplication table far ahead of time from counting touchdowns in the schoolyard. "I was determined to play running back," Douglas said. "It was just a goal of mine to emulate my heroes like Barry Sanders and Emmitt Smith and Tony Dorsett and Marcus Allen and all those people. I was always trying to copy their moves because they made it so that must work."

With the confidence gained from his first 200-yard game in high school, Douglas blasted off into the ether. He finished his junior season with 2,966 rushing yards, breaking the 5A single-season record previously held by Pryor.

And as Douglas reached full speed, the rest of the Judson team followed on his heels. From the Temple game forward, the Rockets blazed through the rest of the regular season and playoffs all the way to the state final. Judson's only game decided by less than two touchdowns for the rest of the season was a 21–18 win over San Antonio Churchill.

The ascent continued when Judson ripped through Euless Trinity in the state final at Memorial Stadium. A photo by *San Antonio Express-News* photographer Rick Hunter shows Douglas running through the tackle of a Trinity defender as the Judson running back is stiff-arming the Trojan player's helmet. It seems a fitting illustration of Judson's 52–0 triumph. Douglas ran for 239 yards and two touchdowns.

Rocket quarterback Aaron Carter threw touchdown passes to Brandon Ercoline and Andra Johnson. Rutledge scored on a forty-one-yard run on the first play of the fourth quarter to make it 45–0. Meanwhile, the Rockets' defense shut down Trinity, holding the Trojans to seven first downs, 120 rushing yards, and zero passing yards.

Along with Douglas's season rushing record, Judson's 52–0 victory tied the largest winning margin in a state championship game. "It was kind of like all of that frustration from '88, '89, '90, '91, all of that frustration was just unloaded on Trinity," Clint Rutledge said. "It just exploded. It was time to finally win."

Douglas paved the way for the kind of all-smiles highlight film he wanted to watch. But the Rockets' juniors were only halfway through the ride. The idea was to never have that season-ending sadness again, which meant Judson had to keep it going in 1993.

The Rockets had to bring up some younger, less-experienced players to make up for key losses. Three of the five starters on the offensive line were gone, and perhaps the biggest hole, Douglas said, was left by Eric Brown, who played just about everywhere on the defensive side. Brown went on to play at Mississippi State and seven seasons in the NFL, claiming a Super Bowl ring as a rookie with the Denver Broncos.

Motivation wasn't a problem for the Rockets, but it helped to have a rematch with Temple on the schedule early in the 1993 season. The Wildcats had won the 5A Division II state title in 1992, allowing them to claim the mythical "over-all" 5A title, since they had defeated Division I champ Judson along the way.

"On their interview, they're saying, 'We're really the number one team because we beat Judson early in the year,'" Douglas said. "It was like, 'Okay, we've got them on the schedule early in the year next year.' We whupped them pretty good on their home field." The Rockets evened the score by trouncing Temple 28–0. Douglas rushed for 186 yards, and Judson quarterbacks Terry Hale and Rutledge each threw two touchdown passes, taking advantage of Temple sneaking up its safeties to stop Douglas.

With the wind of the win over Temple in its sails, Judson's 1993 regular season looked much the same as the previous year's had. Douglas pointed out that the Rockets had to replace a lot of parts, but they worked just fine. The biggest difference between Judson ripping through district and the early rounds of the playoffs in 1992, and the same run in 1993, is that the Rockets didn't even struggle with powerhouse Churchill the second time around. Judson smashed Churchill 35–14, which was still its closest game until the state semifinals.

But oh, that semifinal matchup versus Aldine Eisenhower.

A decade of competing at the highest level had taught Judson where the big hurdles were placed, and the hurdles didn't get any bigger than playing a Houston-area foe in the state semifinals. Dulles had knocked out the Rockets in 1991, and Aldine High School had done the same two years earlier. On their way to the state championship in 1992, the Rockets had survived with a 38–20 victory over Eisenhower in the semifinals.

The Eagles were out for revenge, and early on it looked as if it would be theirs. Rutledge took a shot to the ribs late in the first quarter, ending the game for him. Eisenhower took a 13–0 lead, thanks in part to a freak play. "I think our fullback [Josh Appleby] blocked a guy," Douglas said. "He blocked him so good that his leg flipped up and kicked the ball out of my hands. He kicked it so far that the cornerback picked it up and ran it in for a touchdown. It was 13–0, and then we were like, 'Oh my God! What is going on right now?'"

Douglas finished his senior season with 2,266 rushing yards and thirty-three touchdowns. A *Parade* All-American, he compiled 6,188 yards and eighty-five TDs in his Judson career. He went on to Baylor, where he gained 2,811 yards in his college career and earned all-Southwest Conference honors in 1995.

But he was never better than the rest of that afternoon against Eisenhower. With Rutledge out of commission and a massive Eagle defense clamoring from across the line of scrimmage, Douglas fought his way to 218 rushing yards and four touchdowns on twenty-three carries. Stats are just stats, though. There was a whole lot more going on than a great running back compiling numbers. "Jerod, after he fumbled that one, he ended up having an incredible game," Clint Rutledge said. "Kind of like Michael Jordan in a basketball game, he just took over."

Quarterbacks coach Mike Miller, who later became Judson's athletic director, marveled from the press box at Douglas's determination. "He turned it up into another gear and kind of carried us past that game," Miller said.

Douglas began digging the Rockets out of a 13–0 hole by returning a punt fifty-two yards for a touchdown to make it 13–7. After he scored on runs of nineteen, four, and sixty-one yards, Judson led 27–19.

But Eisenhower tied the game early in the fourth quarter when quarterback Clarence Cruse scored on a seven-yard run and added the two-point conversion with another run. With the game tied late in the fourth quarter, the head coaches met at midfield to make sure everyone was on the same page. It was still a few years before overtime arrived in Texas high school football, so in the event of a tie, the winner would be decided by penetrations. If that stat was tied, it would go to first downs. The Rockets had the edge in penetrations, 6–4, but Eisenhower had more first downs.

The Eagles needed two late penetrations or a deciding score. Rocket defensive back Paul Booker made sure they didn't get either when he intercepted a Cruse pass with twenty-three seconds left to secure the victory. "As soon as the ball was in the air, I was so scared. I knew I had to catch it," Booker told the *Express-News*. "I tried to take it all the way back because I didn't want a tie. But this is as good as a win, so we'll take it."

More than twenty years later, Douglas echoed Booker's sentiment when I spoke with him early in 2015. "I tell you what, that felt better than any win in my high school career," Douglas said.

The next week, Judson finished it with a 36–13 victory over Plano. Douglas scored on an eight-yard run, and Rutledge connected with Doug Maziur for a forty-six-yard touchdown, giving Judson a 12–0 lead just eight minutes into the game. Plano made a run, drawing within 15–13 at halftime. But Douglas owned the second half, scoring on runs of one, seventeen, and sixty-nine yards. He gained 244 rushing yards, five more than in the championship game the year before. By the time Douglas had scored the eighty-fifth touchdown of his high school career, it was all over but the crying.

After two years of staying committed to keeping tears out of their highlight film, the Rockets broke down in the wake of their second straight state title. And they weren't just tears of joy.

It was a bittersweet finish. "Our group of seniors, after the game, we were excited that we won the state championship game, but you would have thought that we lost by the way it was in the locker room afterwards," Clint Rutledge said. "We were wanting to go on and win the state championship game because that allowed us to play the longest together."

# 19

# TYLER

## 1994

*John Tyler's Lions Knew How to Finish*

Supposedly, there are at least two sides to every story.

At least two sides of the 1994 John Tyler Lions' story are well known. Television and the Internet made sure of that awhile ago. And some of those details will be rehashed and reexplored in this chapter. But before that, consider where the Tyler Lions came from before they won the 1994 5A Division II state championship, before they played perhaps the most famous game in Texas high school football history, before they even made the playoffs.

In the early weeks of the 1994 season, Tyler was just a team that had yet to prove itself. Despite missing the playoffs in 1993, the Lions felt that it was their time, their chance to win the school's first state championship since Earl Campbell had led Tyler to the promised land in 1973.

The Tyler seniors had felt like that for some time, since they had merged into one team coming out of the middle-school feeder programs. "When we combined the schools, when we came together as freshmen, we had said we were going to win state," Tyler quarterback Morris Anderson said. "Because the coaches, when they scout the middle school teams before they come over, they were looking at this class as being pretty special."

But by the third game of the season, these Lions had not yet shown much. They had scratched out a 14–6 win over a solid DFW-area opponent, Fort Worth O. D. Wyatt, and rolled over a hapless one, defeating Dallas Maceo Smith 56–13.

Then came gut-check time for the Lions when Dallas Kimball grabbed a 28–21 lead with a little more than eight minutes left in the fourth quarter. Knights running back Marquez Lewis broke a fourth-quarter tie with an eleven-yard touchdown run, and suddenly Tyler, which had led late in the third quarter, had to rally late on the road if it were going to notch its third win of the young season.

There comes a time when a team has to figure out whether it can win despite adversity. Facing that test, Tyler turned to its warhorse. The Lions deployed a stable of running backs, but the player who most liked to run through the trenches had a unique skill set that allowed him to play defensive tackle and running back. Trailing by a touchdown in the fourth quarter, Tyler gave the ball to fullback Marc Broyles. "We lined it up in the same formation and ran the same play seven times in a row," Tyler coach Allen Wilson said. "Marc ran over us, he ran over them, he ran over everybody that got in the way."

Broyles's hard running helped Tyler drive from its own thirty-three into Kimball territory to the twenty-four before the Knights finally stopped the momentum with a tackle for a two-yard loss. On second-and-twelve from the Kimball twenty-four, the Lions answered with some misdirection. "After running the cut back so many times, I kind of faked the cut back and rolled out," Anderson said. "I know it had to be a post pattern, because that's usually what Brian [Giddens] runs. I threw it into the end zone, and he was wide open to the point that all he had to do was catch the ball. It wasn't a dramatic catch. We pounded it so much that when we run that play, it usually comes wide open."

Anderson's twenty-four-yard touchdown pass to Giddens created a decision for the Tyler sideline, since the Lions had cut the Knights' lead to 28–27. Wilson never hesitated. He was going to go for the two-point conversion and the win. But the way the Lions were going to get there caused some debate. "Coach was like, 'We're going to give the ball to [Michael] Price,'" Anderson recalled. "It was going to go to the tailback, and we were going to let Marc lead block, and so forth. I was like, 'Coach, we're not going to do that. We're going to have to give the ball to Marc because he did get us to this point.' He was driving it. They couldn't stop Marc."

Wilson told me he never had any problem with letting the players have a say in play calling. He said it's part of coaching to listen to the players because they know better than anyone what's happening on the field. So Wilson yielded to his quarterback, and Anderson handed the ball to Broyles again.

When I spoke with Broyles, the one play he remembered more vividly than any other in the game was the two-point run. "[Keith Buckner] was the pulling guard. We ran our normal 7 Cut Back," Broyles said. "Buck was pulling, but he wasn't running fast enough in the hole, and I kind of ran up his back a little bit."

It worked. Broyles went over Buckner and into the end zone to put Tyler ahead by a point with a little less than four minutes remaining. "They knew it was coming, we knew it was coming, and they couldn't stop it," Wilson said. "You have to have something you believe in. We believed in that. Marc said give me the ball. From that point on, I said, 'This is not a bad football team.'"

On Kimball's next possession, Anderson, who, according to the *Tyler Courier-Times-Telegraph*, was playing defense for the first time all season, intercepted a pass to close out the Lions' victory.

The win served as a catalyst. The next week, Tyler pummeled Jacksonville, an area rival and a stalwart program, 41–21. None of the Lions' next three opponents came within four touchdowns of defeating them.

Then came a showdown with Lufkin. Tyler's 7–0 record had earned it a spot in the state rankings in the nine slot. Lufkin's record was not pristine, but the Panthers were plenty potent behind tailback Denvis Manns. By the end of the 1994 season, Manns had powered his way to 2,000 rushing yards. He went on to New Mexico State, where he rushed for more than 1,000 yards in four straight seasons. "We looked at him on video, and nobody could tackle the sucker," Wilson said about Manns. "I'm saying, 'These defensive teams are not very good. When we play 'em, we're going to get this sucker stopped.' And after that game, I'm saying, 'We can't tackle him either.' He was running through us like we wasn't even out there."

Manns finished the game versus Tyler with 104 rushing yards on twenty-two carries, but his biggest play came on a screen pass in the fourth quarter. Lufkin quarterback Jason Carter lofted the ball to Manns, who took off to score from forty-five yards out, giving the Panthers a 30–25 lead with 2:52 to play. Lufkin attempted to tack on a two-point conversion to extend its lead to seven, but when Manns took a pitch on a designed throwback pass, Broyles sacked him.

Nonetheless, the Lufkin sideline whooped and cheered after pushing ahead late in the fourth quarter. As I sat with Wilson at a Cracker Barrel south of Dallas late in the spring of 2015, he laughed heartily as he remembered the transformation on the opposite sideline during those closing minutes.

Manns's touchdown caused the third lead change in the fourth quarter. But having come back a few weeks earlier against Kimball, Tyler had been prepped for this challenge. Anderson came out throwing, and the Lions offense worked seamlessly and quickly. On the first offensive play of the ensuing drive, Anderson called the same play with which he'd hit Giddens for the crucial touchdown against Kimball. But this time Anderson rolled to his right and found a receiver on the right flank. "It pretty much opened up to where the flat came open real quick," Anderson said. "So I dumped it over their heads to my boy Jessie Taylor. In the rain for him to make the great catch, have to turn a little bit to catch it, and actually on the soggy field, I have to give him a lot of credit.

"But the credit also goes to Kendrick Austin, one of our receivers, who made a key block. And if you go back and watch the film, you can actually see him block two people. He laid out two people to free Jessie up for the go-ahead touchdown."

Taylor went sixty-four yards for the score, deflating the Lufkin sideline. "You could see on video. They're jumping up and down, celebrating 'cause they had just scored," Wilson said. "And then when he's running the ball back, they started looking, and all those heads start coming down."

More importantly than the Panthers' reaction, Wilson was gaining valuable insight into his own squad. "You've always got to wonder what happens to kids at closeout time, crucial times of the ball games when you're trailing, when you think you have a chance," Wilson said. "Kimball told us as long as there's time on that clock, we've got a chance to win the game. We did it against Kimball and came back and did it against Lufkin. We was going to do it against Plano East. We just didn't know how."

Mention the 1994 Lions to any fan of Texas high school football, and they will go right to the famous game. After coming back to defeat Lufkin, Tyler won four more games to close out a perfect regular season, and then reached the third round of the playoffs. The Lions won three more games after the Plano East game at Texas Stadium to go 16–0 and claim the 5A Division II state championship.

But all anybody ever wants to talk about is the end of the third-round game against Plano East. Broyles and David Warren each returned a fumble for a touchdown to seemingly ice the game for the Lions, who led 41–17 with 3:03 left. The rest is the stuff of high school football lore.

Plano East scored a touchdown on a twenty-one-yard pass from Jeff Whitley to Terrance Green, and then the magic started to happen. To hear it retold, Tyler was in cruise control, and its players were socializing in the stands while time remained in the fourth quarter. Having had plenty of time to consider all that went on in those now fantastical few minutes, Wilson sees things quite differently.

"The big myth is that when we were up 41–17, all our kids were not engaged in the game," Wilson said. "They started taking their pads off on the sideline and started talking smack. Marc Broyles got hurt, so we took his pads off, and he sat over there looking at his shoulder. That's when all this stuff started happening. Everybody likes to tell that part of it—now they get inspired and here they come. The thing that did happen, [Plano East coach Scott Phillips] put his second-string running back in the game. They started making some substitutions. They thought that game was over, and then he went and scored. You didn't think very much about it, but that kind of led to that whole onside-kick thing."

Plano East built up a frenetic level of momentum by recovering three onside kicks and scoring twenty-seven points in two minutes and eighteen seconds of game time. The last two of the three kicks were mishandled by Tyler's Roderick Dunn. The Panthers went ahead when Whitley hit Robert Woods for a twenty-three-yard touchdown with twenty-four seconds left. The Plano East fans roared and celebrated as if they had just won the state title, and their jubilation was justified. Had the Panthers prevailed, theirs would be the greatest comeback in Texas high school football history.

But on the other sideline, the Lions knew they had been in dire situations before. Anderson remembered feeling in his gut that his team had lost, but he also recalled telling a sportswriter who had found his way to the sideline that the Lions would prevail. "I told him it's not over," Anderson said. "Even when they went ahead, there was something about our team that we always believed. I told him when they scored, it's not over. You will never in your lifetime see a game like that again."

Plano East opted to kick deep when Tyler brought nine players up to the line of scrimmage. Dunn caught the kick at the three and took off on a run that would break the Panthers' hearts. He slipped through four Panthers defenders at the twenty, and astute Plano East fans could see what was happening. Dunn knew it too. "When I was at about the forty-five-yard line, that's when I saw the lane open up," Dunn told the *Courier-Times-Telegraph*. "I think it was Marc Broyles who threw a great block on the kicker [Terrance Green]. After that, I was gone."

Dunn's ninety-seven-yard touchdown return snatched a 48–44 victory from the jaws of defeat. The game still stirs myriad emotions. Watching the ESPN documentary *Good Gosh O'Mighty* after having spoken with key players on the Tyler side, and even having seen the decisive return dozens of times, it still gave me goose bumps.

For Wilson, though, the important feelings it ignited for him and the Lions were anger and fear: the coach's anger and the players' fear. "I really got on 'em," Wilson said. "We got in that dressing room, it was almost like we had lost. You can't say we were great and almost give the game away. From my perspective, we did all the things wrong and were just lucky to win. I got after 'em pretty hard. I chewed ass the whole week. I could use that. Coaches always look for 'What can I use to keep the kids engaged?' If that game had ended up 41–17, we might have got beat the next week."

Tyler pounded Lake Highlands 27–7 the next week. The Lions defeated Arlington 45–20 in the semifinals, and Austin Westlake 35–24 for the title.

As I watched the documentary on the Plano East–Tyler game, I saw a dichotomy between the Lions team portrayed on film and the one that won sixteen games. If the Lions were unfocused, undisciplined, and lucky to win that third-round thriller, then how did they survive all the tough battles along the way like the Kimball and Lufkin games?

They couldn't have. That's why the Plano East game doesn't define the 1994 Tyler team. "Everybody wants to talk about Plano East," Anderson said. "A lot of us don't even care to talk about Plano East. I guess that's probably why they don't like to get our story, because the way we view that Plano East game is totally different than the way Plano East views it."

Anderson told me the three toughest games the Lions played that season were their wins over Kimball, Lufkin, and Waco High (in the first round of the playoffs). Although the Waco game lacked the drama of the others, I heard enough about it from everyone I spoke with from Tyler to convince me it was the war of the year. At the time, Wilson told *Waco Tribune-Herald* sportswriter Mickey Humphrey, "This was our toughest game of the year."

Price scored on a seventy-yard run in the fourth quarter, catching the ball on a toss sweep and finding a seam down the sideline to go all the way. The touchdown put Tyler ahead 19–7 with just under ten minutes left. That was enough breathing room for Tyler to escape Waco. But it was one of those games where neither the box score nor the game story captures the action. "One of the backers told me from the get-go, 'It's going to be like hell from the beginning to the end,'" Anderson remembered. "That's what he looked me dead in my eyes and told me. I said, 'Okay, let's go.' They came with it."

Tyler might be known for cavalierly celebrating a little too early in one game, but that's not necessarily who they were. When they rode away from the Waco game late on a Friday night, they were victorious and quiet. "After the game, all the kids, all they did was get on the bus," Wilson said. "They never said a word. They just got on the bus and went to sleep." That side of the 1994 John Tyler Lions wasn't captured on film to survive in the mythology of Texas high school football, but hearing the whole story, it's the side that resonates.

The 1946 Odessa Bronchos went 14–0 and won the state championship, defeating San Antonio Jefferson 21–14 in the final at Memorial Stadium in Austin. Texas Sports Hall of Fame photo.

Brownwood coach Gordon Wood (*right*) and assistant Kenneth West (*left*) discuss strategy with quarterback Marvin Rathke (15) during the 1981 playoffs. Wood retired following the 1985 season, having won a Texas-record 396 games and nine state championships. Texas Sports Hall of Fame photo.

Warren McVea takes a pitch and looks upfield during a 1963 game for the Brackenridge Eagles. McVea, who went on to become the first African American player at the University of Houston, rushed for 1,332 yards in eleven games as a senior at San Antonio Brackenridge. Texas Sports Hall of Fame photo.

Estacado's Joe Rose (50), Frank Judie (31, *seated*), and others watch from the sideline during a game from the Matadors' historic 1968 state-championship season. Photo courtesy of Joe Rose.

Above: Estacado quarterback Kenneth Wallace (12) sprints to his right, looking for running room as Frank Judie (31) makes a lead block. Joe Rose (50), Larry Miller (44), and William Hall (74) watch from behind the play. Photo courtesy of Joe Rose.

Left: Celina coach G. A. Moore directs pregame drills while wearing his signature cowboy hat. Moore won a state-record 422 games while coaching at Bryson, Pilot Point, Celina, Sherman, and Aubrey. Texas Sports Hall of Fame photo.

Big Sandy quarterback Gary Chalk (14) and Coach Jim Norman walk off the field after the Wildcats' 26–2 victory over Groom for the 1975 state championship. Big Sandy won the 1973 Class B state title and tied Celina for the 1974 championship before ending its three-year run with the win over Groom. Photograph by Geoff Winningham, from the collection of Gary Chalk.

Temple coach Bob McQueen raises his arms in victory. McQueen led the Wildcats to two state championships as they claimed the 4A crown in 1979 and the 5A Division II title in 1992. Texas Sports Hall of Fame photo.

Idalou's Tracy Saul dodges a tackle in a game versus Slaton during his junior season. Saul led Idalou to a perfect regular season and an 11–1 campaign as a senior in 1988. Texas Sports Hall of Fame photo.

Converse Judson coach D. W. Rutledge pumps his fist in celebration on the Rockets sideline. Rutledge posted a record of 197 wins, 32 losses, and 5 ties, and won 4 state titles in 17 seasons as Judson's head coach. Texas High School Football Hall of Fame photo.

Sealy coach T. J. Mills holds up the 1994 Class 3A state championship trophy as the Tigers celebrate a 36–15 victory over Atlanta in the final. Mills's Sealy teams won four straight state championships, 1994–1997. Courtesy of the *Columbus (TX) Banner Press*.

Wortham's Leonard Davis poses for an individual photo during his sophomore year. Davis, who played four seasons of varsity football, helped the Bulldogs build from a winless season in his freshman year to an 11–1 record during his senior campaign in 1996. Davis family photo.

Waco University's LaDainian Tomlinson raises his helmet during the school song following a victory at Paul Tyson Field. Tomlinson, who was deployed mostly as a blocker until his senior season, rushed for 2,554 yards and 39 touchdowns in 1996. Rod Aydelotte, *Waco Tribune-Herald*.

Waco University running back LaDainian Tomlinson escapes the grasp of Gregory-Portland defenders during the Trojans' 51–28 playoff victory. Tomlinson led University to a 12–2 record and the Class 4A state quarterfinals during his senior season in 1996. Rod Aydelotte, *Waco Tribune-Herald*.

Kliff Kingsbury's high school career was a family affair. His father, Tim Kingsbury, was New Braunfels's head coach, and his mother, Sally Kingsbury, taught at the high school. Kingsbury has credited Sally, who died in 2005, with keeping his emotions stable during the peaks and valleys of playing quarterback. Kingsbury family photo.

Mart's all-purpose back Quan Cosby strides into the end zone for a kickoff-return touchdown that began the second half of the Panthers' 1999 state championship victory over Boyd. Duane A. Laverty, *Waco Tribune-Herald*.

Ennis head coach Sam Harrell celebrates the 2001 4A Division II state championship with his team at the Astrodome. Harrell led the Lions to state titles in 2000, 2001, and 2004. He and his son Graham Harrell, Ennis's quarterback in 2001, were inducted simultaneously into the Texas High School Football Hall of Fame in 2013. Texas Sports Hall of Fame photo.

Copperas Cove's Robert Griffin III eyes a defender during the Bulldawgs' first-round playoff game versus Waxahachie. Griffin led the Bulldawgs as they came back from two touchdowns behind in the fourth quarter to defeat the Indians. Duane A. Laverty, *Waco Tribune-Herald*.

Aledo running back Johnathan Gray (32) and his father James Gray, a standout at Fort Worth Trimble Tech High School and an all-American running back at Texas Tech, celebrate the Bearcats' 2010 state championship victory at AT&T Stadium in Arlington, Texas. Gray family photo.

# 20

# SEALY

## 1994

### *Tigers' Dynasty Rises Up*

T. J. Mills was a football coach if there ever was one. He looked the part, with a round, bulldog-tough face and a linebacker's build. He thrived in the role, gaining a reputation as one of the most competitive SOBs in a profession known for its competitive SOBs. Because he wanted to win with every ounce of his being, he would grind like a coach, watching film and preparing like few others. He talked like a coach, and he probably even smelled like a coach most days.

Of course, to do all that, a man better back it up. Mills did. In twenty-three years as a head coach, Mills won 195 and lost just 78. As of this writing, that ranked him in the mid-eighties all-time in Texas. But those numbers, while impressive, camouflage Mills's true claim to fame. In a four-year span of the 1990s, Mills's Sealy Tigers were almost unbeatable as they put together one of the most dominant runs of any dynasty in the state's thick book of legends.

By 1993, a sophomore named Brad Burttschell knew enough about the Sealy Tigers' coach to be more than a little nervous. "It was almost a fear factor whenever you were a young kid," Burttschell said. "That was the thing that I remember going into high school, coming in as a young sophomore on a senior- and junior-oriented team. 'How am I going to get the respect of not only the players but Coach Mills, this hard-nosed coach, being a skinny little sophomore kid that it's his first time putting varsity pads on?'"

That's the thing about those bulldog coaches, though. From Bob Knight to Bill Belichick to T. J. Mills, the ones with the bark to strike fear in opponents and the media also seem to have the most loyal disciples. There's a reason it happens that way. "From day one that I sat down with him, he had more confidence in me than I probably did," Burttschell said. "I think by his confidence and belief in what I could do for them, that made me a better player, because you kind of brushed off the fear of 'Am I good enough to be here?' You just saw the head coach. He's got your back 100 percent."

While Burttschell saw a different side of his head coach, Mills and his coaching staff were seeing something special brewing in the Tigers' program.

I missed out on meeting Mills, who died of a heart attack in the spring of 2015 at age sixty. But a few weeks later, I had the chance to sit down at the Millses' house with the coach's wife, Becky Mills; Mark Faldyn, a longtime Mills assistant coach; Leroy Zapalac, a former Sealy booster club president, and Herb Kollatschny, a Sealy sportswriter.

Faldyn said a playoff run in 1993 told the Tigers' coaches that they might be a tweak away from reaching the top of the mountain. "We went and watched [Southlake] Carroll play after losing out to Waco Robinson," Faldyn said. "They were doing some spread stuff. It wasn't shotgun; it was just spread, and it was putting defenses in a bind. Before that time, we always, when we had to prepare for games, we had to see what the defense was going to give us. About that time, things started turning, I guess offensive coaches started saying, 'We're not going to take this anymore. We're going to start telling defenses how to line up to us.' We kept our plays, and we found different formations, different variations of how we could get our plays adjusted to what we wanted the defense to line up, and that started it. They took to it."

Faldyn gave me a stack of highlight films from the 1990s, but I needed to watch only one of them to see how the 1994 Tigers ripped through opponents. To the tune of "Eye of the Tiger," "Johnny B. Goode," and similar songs, Sealy running back Fred Smith sliced open and ran away from defenses, Burttschell threw over the top, and the Tigers dominated virtually everyone on their regular-season schedule. Sealy opened the campaign with a 27–8 victory over Luling, but the Tigers were only beginning to gain steam. Luling turned out to be the only opponent in the regular season to come within three touchdowns of the Tigers.

The video included well-placed *Star Wars*–style scrolling quotations from newspaper articles in which Kollatschny succinctly framed the climax of the first ten games. Sealy faced fellow district front-runners Columbus, La Grange, and Bellville in a three-game stretch to decide the district champion and the playoff qualifiers. So much for the drama, though. Sealy stretched out a 35–14 win over Columbus, then walloped La Grange 27–3 and Bellville 55–3. "Before you know it, we're undefeated," Faldyn said. "Gosh, we're 8–0, we're 9–0, then we're 11–0, we're 12–0, then 13–0. It just kept on, and it kept getting better."

Faldyn found it difficult to identify a moment or game when Sealy turned the corner from a playoff contender to a team on a mission to win the state's top prize. He said each week was a new task of figuring out how to win the game at hand.

At the same time, the Tigers' players were doing more than gaining confidence; they were beginning to feel a little bit invincible. "It was such a machine type of approach that you kind of forgot how to lose," Burttschell said. "You expected to win each game."

In the record books and on the highlight reel, it's easy to see what made the Sealy machine run. The Tigers had a punishing defense, led by linebackers Steven Newsome, Paul Martinez, and Mario Tarver, that routinely separated ballcarriers from the ball. Offensively, they had a plethora of weapons, especially with Burttschell operating the option to near perfection and running back Chris Tate serving as the ideal option-pitch catcher. There was no doubt, though, that Sealy was going to go as far as Smith would carry them.

That turned out to be a long way.

Sealy played Groesbeck in the thirteenth game of the season at College Station's Kyle Field. That night, Smith passed the school's career-rushing-yards record holder, a back by the name of Eric Dickerson, who rushed for 5,877 yards and led the Tigers to the state championship in 1978. Dickerson, who was inducted into the Pro Football Hall of Fame in 1999, attended the game at Kyle Field to see the Tigers win and Smith break the record. By that point in the season, Smith had run for 2,195 yards and forty-one touchdowns.

Smith finished his career with 6,588 yards. But unlike Dickerson, Smith didn't go on to fame and fortune in college and the NFL. I wanted to interview Smith, but failed, despite extensive effort, to find even a link to him. The Sealy coaches and players I talked to remembered him playing college football somewhere in Arkansas, but they couldn't definitively say where. I searched the athletics websites of multiple Arkansas universities but couldn't find Smith. His name pops up most often on websites featuring Texas high school football record holders. But because he has such a common name, he is a difficult man to find. Smith's story as a player mostly exists in the memory of Sealy players, coaches, and fans of that era. "He bounced off of people and he'd stay on his feet," Faldyn remembered. "Fred wasn't very fast. If you lined him up in the 100 meters, he might get sixth. But if you put pads on him, he would win that 100-meter race. He was really strong."

As of this writing, Smith is not in the Texas High School Football Hall of Fame. To his teammates, that's a blatant oversight. "Fred honestly is a high school player that probably doesn't get the credit that he deserves," Burttschell said. "Look at Fred Smith's numbers. If you're truly looking at a high school career, there's not many people that have numbers that stack up to his." Burttschell's point is particularly poignant because both players were key cogs in a championship run and the quarterback readily deferred to the other guy in the backfield. "When you knew you had to get it in somebody's hands, it felt pretty good to know he was back there behind you," Burttschell said.

Most of the time, running Smith up the middle and taking the option around the end proved enough strategy on offense to baffle opposing defenses into submission. But there's always that one game a team just has to survive. For Sealy, that game came in a downpour on the second time around against an old rival. The Tigers had pulled away from Columbus a few weeks earlier, which almost guaranteed that the rematch would not be as easy when the two teams met in the state quarterfinals. To make it much more difficult, unpredictable late-fall weather dealt both teams a tricky hand.

The Tigers and Cardinals agreed to play at Rhodes Stadium in Katy. Little did they know, the Friday-night game would be drenched with rain throughout. "We wanted the Dome, but we couldn't get in there," Mills told *Houston Chronicle* sportswriter Scott Kaiser. "We would have loved to have been there, because this was unbelievable. I've never been in a game where it rained the whole ball game."

Kaiser reported that Sealy fumbled ten times and lost six of them. Columbus gave up four turnovers; neither team managed to grip the ball very well.

But the conditions couldn't keep away the masses of fans who had become invested in Columbus and Sealy by that point of the postseason. The *Chronicle* story noted that a standing-room-only crowd filled the stadium, which seated almost ten thousand. The fans saw Columbus take the early momentum when brothers Matt and Aaron Schobel connected for a fifty-one-yard touchdown pass in the second quarter. The Schobel brothers both went on to play in the NFL, Aaron as a defensive end for the Buffalo Bills and Matt as a tight end for the Cincinnati Bengals and Philadelphia Eagles. Against Sealy, Matt played quarterback, and Aaron lined up at tight end and at outside linebacker–defensive end.

Columbus had the lead headed into halftime, and then Burttschell came up with one of the most crucial plays of the Tigers' season. Burttschell told me he's now a close friend of the Schobels, and they regularly play golf and tell old football stories together. A few plays from that rainy night get replayed pretty often. "We were on their forty-yard line," Burttschell remembered. "We kind of spread 'em out. We sent the tight end and a wide receiver both on a deep route down the right side of the field, and I rolled right. What kills those guys from Columbus is Aaron Schobel was one defensive end, the other defensive end was Andrel Waddle, and he had a distinguished career. They'll tell me today [that] they decided to run more of a prevent type of deal. Rather than bringing pressure, they dropped. I rolled right and basically had all the time in the world."

As he did so many times that season, Burttschell lofted a pass over the top of the defense, this one on target for tight end Jarrod Novicke. "He caught it over his head, right over the goal line, and tumbled into the end zone," Zapalac said, describing the play as if it happened the night before.

Sealy shut out Columbus in the second half, and Newsome made an all-important pickup in the third quarter when he recovered a Matt Schobel fumble at the Sealy forty-three. The takeaway stopped a Columbus drive and ignited the Tigers' game-winning march.

Burttschell hit Novicke for a twenty-six-yard gain into Columbus territory to build momentum, and Smith finished the drive with a ten-yard touchdown run. The point-after kick missed, but it didn't matter much. Neither team scored again on the drenched field. Sealy hung on to a 12–6 victory.

"Brad Burttschell always tells me this story," Zapalac said. "He plays golf with them, and when they're sitting, drinking a beer, and football comes up, both Schobel boys will start talking about it, and they'll say, 'And I'll tell you what. I can't believe y'all won that effin' game.'"

At the moment, though, there was little time for Sealy to bask in the glory of the win. After drying out and meeting with the players on Saturday morning, the Tigers' coaching staff headed out in a van the next afternoon to scout their next opponent, making the 200-mile drive to Kingsville to watch Bandera play Port Isabel in another state quarterfinal.

After Port Isabel claimed a 24–11 victory, Tarpons coach Tony Villarreal had a trick up his sleeve when he set out for a meeting with the Sealy coaches at a K-Bob's Steakhouse. "We brought our film—everybody brings their film—and you sit down," Faldyn said. "We get through talking, and we go, 'Okay, film exchange.' T. J. grabs the deal and puts it out. [Villarreal] goes, 'I don't want no film. We're not exchanging film.' Oh my God, you could've heard a pin drop. We as a coaching staff standing behind him, everybody's going, 'Crap, this roof isn't tall enough, 'cause he's fixing to blow this damn roof off this building.'"

The assistant coaches cautiously looked at one another while Mills stared down his counterpart. "They think that he's in shock," Faldyn said. "He's not. He's trying to hold it together. He goes, 'Well, I think that's pretty chickenshit, because you told me over the phone—you specifically told me over the phone we would trade film here. But that's all right,' and he looks at him, 'because we're going to whip your ass.'"

With that, Mills wheeled and began working on plan B. They would call on the head coach of the team that had just fallen to Port Isabel, banking on the assumption that the Bandera coach was sore enough to turn over his video library. Faldyn said, "He turns around and he goes, 'Let's go.' We get in the van, and he goes, 'Get on the phone. We're going to Bandera.' We get that film."

Mills and company learned that a coach in Sinton, friendly to their cause, had film available as well. So after going north into the Hill Country for the Bandera tapes, they circled back for the Gulf Coast. "Sunday morning, we come home, we pull into the driveway next to the office," Faldyn said. "I think it's six o'clock, and everybody looks at each other, 'Let's go to work.'"

Going the extra miles likely played a role in the semifinal game, but so did playing on a dry field again. Sealy returned to its modus operandi: Smith rushed for 233 yards and scored a pair of touchdowns. Burttschell threw touchdown passes of forty-six and sixty-two yards to Jaron Dabney.

The fans from the Rio Grande Valley made up more than half of the fourteen thousand in attendance that Saturday evening at Texas A&M–Kingsville's Javelina Stadium. Zapalac told me that when he and his wife arrived for the game, two hours early, the stands were filling up, and that it was already apparent that Tarpon fans were spilling into the metal bleachers that had been assigned to the Tigers.

Port Isabel gave its crowd some hope by taking an early one-touchdown lead, but then Sealy took over and held up Mills's words from a week earlier. The Tigers scored thirty-four straight points to overwhelm the Tarpons. Sealy claimed a 34–13 victory and created a wave of momentum going into the state championship game.

The Tigers finished their 16–0 parade the next week with a 36–15 win over the Atlanta Rabbits at the Astrodome. Smith broke another Dickerson record, rushing for 313 yards in the championship game, passing up the 296 yards that Dickerson ran for in the 1978 final. Smith also passed Dickerson's Sealy single-season record in the process, finishing the 1994 campaign with 2,836 yards, 194 better than Dickerson's best high school season.

Sealy was just getting started.

Mills and the Tigers added state championships in 1995, 1996, and 1997, going 63–1 during that span and winning twenty-four consecutive playoff games. As of this writing, only Sealy, Celina, and Lake Travis have won four consecutive state titles.

When Mills died suddenly in 2015, the Sealy faithful packed the school's auditorium for a Friday-night memorial service. Players from Sealy as well as other Mills coaching stops eulogized the coach. Burttschell told me he remembered wishing the coach could have been in the audience. "For some people, it took him passing to get past that reputation and really realize how much good he did and how many accomplishments he had," Burttschell said.

But the quarterback's lasting memory, the one that epitomizes what the coach did for his players, comes from the days before the 1995 season was about to start. "The one thing I'll remember from Coach forever: when we won the first year and [*Dave Campbell's*] *Texas Football* came out the next year, I think there was a big debate over whether we should be preseason number one or whether Cuero should be preseason number one," Burttschell said. "I'll always remember him telling the reporter, basically, 'We've got sixteen in a row, we've got seven coming back on offense, eight coming back on defense, we've got an all-state running back . . . and then we've got the trophy. So you tell me who should be number one.' As a player, reading that and seeing that from your coach, that's what gives you that extra step to want to perform for a guy like that."

# 21

# GALENA PARK

## 1994

## *North Shore Lays Its Foundation*

Writing about sports, perhaps writing in general, sometimes means picking a person or place and diving in to see what stories are there to explore.

Cory Redding of Galena Park North Shore represented an ideal combination of a person and a place for this project. Redding came out of high school with the trajectory of a can't-miss college prospect. As a senior at North Shore, Redding earned national recognition as the USA Today Defensive Player of the Year after he posted 215 tackles, including twenty-two for losses, as a senior. A six-five, 235-pound linebacker with 4.5 speed, Redding was college ready at eighteen and joined then-second-year Texas coach Mack Brown's first great recruiting class. Texas landed both Redding and the USA Today Offensive Player of the Year, quarterback Chris Simms.

And while Simms would battle with Major Applewhite in Brown's first quarterback controversy as the Horns' coach, Redding was an impact player from the start. He played in every game during his Texas career, including thirty-five consecutive starts. When I caught up with Redding at Indianapolis Colts camp in the summer of 2014, he was entering his twelfth NFL season. His career trajectory was what every kid dreams about while pushing through hot and humid two-a-days in August. But I had no idea where Redding would want to go when he began talking about playing at North Shore.

The first words out of Redding's mouth sent me down one of the more enlightening roads of this entire project. "David Aymond changed the whole culture from what was there before to what is there now," Redding said. "He brought in that discipline, the structure, zero-tolerance kind of attitude. All he wanted out of his players was the max. Whatever your max was, you had to give it to him, whether it was conditioning, hitting, tackling, no matter what."

When Aymond applied for the job in the spring of 1994, North Shore had played thirty-two seasons of football, but had never made the playoffs. A native of Louisiana, where he was a sharecropper's kid, Aymond came to Texas in his mid- to late forties, having already made his way in life as a coach. After transforming his own life, he began doing the same to the Houston high school football landscape. He had just turned Aldine Nimitz into a winner when he looked around the Houston area and decided he could do even more at North Shore.

After speaking with Redding, it took me a few months to catch up with Aymond, who retired as North Shore's coach after the 2013 season. We met for lunch at Papa's Bar-B-Q in downtown Houston. Over brisket and sausage, Aymond described how he and Galena Park athletic director Ed Warken had many long meetings before Warken finally hired Aymond as North Shore's coach. "He had a lot of questions, and I had a lot of questions," Aymond said. "I would have complete autonomy, and he would do his best to provide me with whatever I needed. I'm talking about evaluating present staff, making recommendations. I wanted to know what the principal was like, what all the players were like. What's the landscape?"

As with most head-football-coach vacancies, there were politics to maneuver around, but Warken could see this was a battle he needed to fight. "I just got a very good feeling about the structure and discipline, and yet he was a coach the kids could talk to and enjoyed being around," Warken said. "There's no doubt he wanted this job badly."

Aymond began implementing his holistic system from the moment he stepped on campus. He emphasized that everything would be scrutinized, from off-season workouts to daily grade sheets. The results on Friday night, though Aymond told me those were essential to making his system work, were the last piece of the puzzle, not the first. After meeting with the team, he went a step beyond and alerted the faculty that it was on the hook to help with the development of the football program. "I spoke to the faculty about how the climate and the culture was going to change," Aymond said. "I believe you have to create a culture. It's not about a season, an off-season. It's about a culture."

For example, the weight room wouldn't just be made available for athletes who wanted to put in extra work. Aymond might not have made it a requirement to spend extra hours in the weight room, but he preached it like hellfire and brimstone. "No, no, no," Aymond said as we discussed the idea of a casual approach to work ethic. "It needs to be a little more emphatic than that. It has to do with what we're going to get done and the reason we're going to do that. Preparation is one thing, but there's nothing like preparation with a purpose. The only way you can truly prepare is with a purpose. You have to make them aware of what the consequences are going to be when they're not there."

The Mustangs' coaches began closely watching the football players' performance in the classroom. Aymond and his assistants came up with grade sheets so that each player, upon arriving at midday study hall, would turn in a grade sheet that showed updates from the previous twenty-four hours' course work from all classes. The player would then pick up a new blank one to be turned in at the next study hall the next day.

To make it work, all of Aymond's assistants had to be on board, because the grade sheets applied to every athlete in the program, varsity, JV, and three freshman teams. Then Aymond took the grade sheets to the middle-school level to incorporate future Mustangs high school players into the system.

Cedric Cormier was an early adapter of the Aymond way. He was a freshman when Aymond arrived in the spring of 1994, and he became the Mustangs' quarterback as a sophomore. Cormier, who went on to play wide receiver at Colorado, was the wide receivers coach at the University of Nevada–Las Vegas when I spoke with him early in 2015. He said he had watched North Shore play when he was in middle school, and he burned with desire to be one of the players who would help turn the program into a winner.

That meant doing what Aymond was asking. "Every single day we had to turn in grade checks," Cormier said. "Every single day. He took roll every day. Everyone would sit in single-file lines, Indian style. It was going to be structured, and you were going to have to be fast to play for him."

Aymond told me about the details of his system as we ate barbecue. We sat down just after eleven and talked through the lunch hour. The busy restaurant filled up around us, but I was caught in the vortex of Aymond's enthusiasm. He told me the buy-in wasn't one-sided. He said he tried to immerse himself in the culture of his athletes, even listening to rap to stay engaged. I listed a few of my favorite hip-hop artists, and he nodded. Aymond said that later in his career he began following all his players on Twitter.

The former North Shore coach admitted to being a bit obsessive in everything he does. He described how he's jumped into fly-fishing since his retirement in the same way. When it came to football fundamentals, Aymond's intense attention to details was turned up a couple of levels. We spent the bulk of our time talking about the little things in practice that made a difference on

Friday nights. He talked about the value of the best players on offense consistently practicing against the best players on defense, the need to teach four-minute as well as two-minute offenses and defenses, the way to use film to inform practice, the process of critiquing practice, and even the best way to distribute water.

Most enlighteningly, he gave me the inside juice on how to tell a good tackler from a player who's going to be sprawled on the turf while the ballcarrier runs away. "What's the width of their feet compared to their shoulder width?" Aymond said. "You ever try to see a guy set his feet and get in a good hitting position? Check the width of his feet. If his feet are wider than shoulder width, he's not going to do it, because he's going to lunge because he's got no base. It can't be narrower than shoulder width. Your feet need to stay parallel, not one turned, and so all of that's critical. Sideline tackling, when a player is near the sideline, that sideline's another defensive player for you. How do they learn to take the proper angle? If you're on the hash and if I've got the ball and I'm coming down the sideline, how do you know what angle to take? Because I could plant on that right foot and I could divert. You've got to come under control."

And Aymond explained that when a coach stops a drill could affect how well his defense makes stops on Friday night. "You can take a tackling drill and you can stop it at lockup," he said. "If [the player] knows that I'm going to blow the whistle at lockup, you know what he's going to do? He's going to lock up, because he wants the drill to stop. They're tired, they've been working hard, but they know coach blows the whistle when I lock up on that offensive player. So now you've got a better tackler."

Pretty quickly, the new North Shore way took hold. Instead of being a bunch of cast-aside football players at a basketball school, the Mustangs, under Aymond's training, were becoming an army of athletes with specific skills. Cormier could see it happening around him. "The cream's going to always rise to the top," Cormier said. "If you're not focused, you stick out like a sore thumb there. You will definitely get weeded out. That's part of coach's goal. Coach Aymond is going to break you down and bring you back up. He's going to build you his way."

As the 1994 season approached, though, Aymond knew he needed results on the field, or all the intense discipline might start to chafe.

The Mustangs came through, winning five of their first six games on the field (the only loss in that stretch was later awarded to North Shore as a win by a Spring Westfield forfeit). Aymond said winning early was important. "It's critical, especially when I came in saying what we're going to get done and what the results were going to be, and immediately they saw results," he said. "It validated the hard work. From then on it brings you credibility, and credibility is everything."

The formula, with those 1994 victories as the catalyst, worked spectacularly. During the next twenty seasons, the Mustangs won 206 and lost only 42. North Shore began sending players to Division I college football programs in droves, and the school's name rang out throughout high school football.

Redding told me that when North Shore won the 5A Division I state title in 2003, it was as if every player who had ever played for the Mustangs won it together. At the same time, they all look back at the 1994 team as revered patriarchs. Even Cormier, who was a sophomore on the 1994 team, marvels at the transition the program made that season. "I most want to pay homage to the '94 team," Cormier said. "We were all young guys, and it started with Tiki Hardeman, who went to A&M, Robert Hall went to Miami. Those two guys kind of set it for us."

North Shore finished the 1994 regular season with an 8–2 mark and made the playoffs for the first time in school history. Who knows? That might have been enough credibility for Aymond to go on, but the Mustangs weren't finished. In the first round of the playoffs, they faced an old district nemesis, the Humble Wildcats. Humble entered the playoffs with a 9–0–1 record and the top ranking among Houston-area football teams.

It was the perfect setting for North Shore to take a huge leap forward. Hardeman was sidelined with a shoulder injury in the fourth quarter, so Cormier took command and threw a fourteen-yard touchdown pass to Scott Lindsey with sixteen seconds remaining, lifting North Shore to a 13–12 win.

Sportswriter Michael Murphy's follow-up story in the *Houston Chronicle* put the victory in perspective. "The irony? North Shore, which was making its first playoff appearance in the history of the school, had not been able to make the playoffs the past few years because the Mustangs were stuck behind all the good teams in District 21-5A," Murphy wrote. "District realignment put the Mustangs in 22-5A this season, and first-year North Shore coach David Aymond is making the best of it. Aymond remembers the 21-5A wars very well. So did the Humble fans, apparently."

Aymond, perhaps more given to eccentricities than most, went out of his way to claim an extra trophy from North Shore's first-ever playoff win. "I took a banner down from the Humble side," Aymond told the *Houston Chronicle*. "I went and got it personally. It said, 'Hey, Mustangs, welcome back to 21-5A.' It was addressing the fact that North Shore was out of 21-5A and was now coming back. Don't get me wrong; we have great respect for Humble. You just don't go through 21-5A undefeated. . . . That makes our victory even bigger."

Though the Mustangs fell the following week to Texas City, they had set the bar high. Two years later, with Cormier leading the team as a senior and Redding causing disruption on the defensive front as a sophomore, North Shore went undefeated in the regular season to set up another first-round playoff showdown with Humble. In 1996, both teams came in with 10–0 records. The clash had evolved from a David-and-Goliath matchup into a clash of the Titans. "It was like, 'We're the big dogs now,'" Cormier said. "We belong. When we were sophomores, it was more like, 'Can we hang with them?' We're a program now."

Humble gained a 21–20 lead just after halftime. But Cormier, who had an eighty-nine-yard punt return touchdown in the first half, took over later in the third quarter. He scored on touchdown runs of thirty-eight and thirty-four yards. Cormier finished with 142 rushing yards, and Mustangs running back Lavar Johnson pitched in 123 and a touchdown.

Humble scored in the fourth quarter on a twenty-yard throwback pass from wide receiver David Givens to quarterback Charlie Thames. But on a fourth-down play from inside the Mustangs ten, Givens, who went on to Notre Dame and won two Super Bowl rings with the Patriots, couldn't haul in the equalizing touchdown that Humble needed late in the fourth quarter. "This is what the playoffs are all about," Cormier told the *Houston Chronicle* after the game. "Two 10–0 teams playing before a packed house. The fans got a good show. I was just holding my breath [on the pass to Givens] because he's a great player."

North Shore ran its winning streak to thirteen before it ran into Converse Judson. Although the Rockets handed North Shore a 30–21 defeat, the Mustangs saw what the next level looked like. "For us to play them, to be on that stage, it was huge," Cormier said. "That was kind of the way Coach Aymond built our program was to be like a Converse Judson: a pure machine where everyone is dressed the same, everyone's doing the same stuff. It's a program."

North Shore reached that level in the early 2000s. The Mustangs didn't lose a regular-season contest from the final district game of 2000 to the season opener in 2009, stringing together a state-record seventy-eight straight victories. Including playoff games, North Shore went 94–7 in that stretch and won the 2003 state title with a 15–0 mark.

Aymond said that when he arrived at North Shore it was a basketball school. Football was an afterthought. When he retired after the 2013 season, North Shore stood among the elite.

On the inside, it's clearly a place where a coach's influence transformed the lives of countless kids. Though Redding didn't figure in the origin story of the Mustangs' success as much as I had expected he would, it's obvious that Aymond and North Shore football propelled Redding. "What I learned in high school has gotten me to this point, twelve years in the league," Redding said. "Coach used to always talk about play with the three Rs, and that's 'reckless,' 'relentless,' and 'ruthless.' He always used to preach that. Never give up as long as there's time on the clock. You keep going hard. If you don't give up on yourself, we're not going to give up on you. That's a huge ripple effect. He has been a big part of my success, just instilling those things in me when I was just a confused kid, disciplining me when I needed it and putting his arm around me when I needed that too. He understood as a coach—that's how his teams were so successful. He understood our rough upbringing, but he also understood how to channel that energy for us to be successful on the field."

# 22

# WORTHAM

## 1996

### *The Bulldogs Grow into Champions*

Long before Leonard Davis went to the Pro Bowl, before he was the second overall pick in the NFL draft, before he was all-American or all-Big 12, even before he was all-state, he was a young kid trying to earn his place with the older boys in the Sunday afternoon hoops game in tiny Wortham, Texas.

Not necessarily the bigger kids, mind you. Davis, who played offensive line in the NFL for a dozen seasons at six-six, 375 pounds, had his teachers looking up at him in elementary school. He stood five-nine in the fifth grade, so he's seldom known bigger kids.

Clearly, Davis was born big. But his is not the story of a gentle giant who had to be coaxed into playing sports. Davis was born with a ball in his hands and, with twenty-one siblings, plenty of competition. "The thing about growing up [in Wortham] is I started playing sports at an early age, playing Little League and basketball Little Dribblers," Davis said. "One of my older sisters, she played in high school, so she was one of my coaches. I had an uncle that played sports, and he was one of my coaches, and they taught me a lot about how to play basketball and play against people that are physically better than you, how to be a smarter player and use your size to your advantage.

"Then on Sundays growing up, after church everybody was playing basketball. We'd go up to the blacktop. You have people from all these different surrounding towns. The next thing you know, you've got forty or fifty people at the basketball court playing basketball. I learned a lot doing that."

Like any of us who grew up playing sports, Davis set his sights on wanting to be in the game, to see whether he could match his skills with those of everybody around him. But while he pushed himself, people around him were taking notice.

The big kid knew how to use his size and seemed comfortable with his amazing athleticism. He looked like a can't-miss. "Even in elementary and grade school, we knew that he would play pro football," Wortham teammate Justin Chapman said. "Early on in his life, it was a done deal. It was known that there was something different with him, that he was going to be a better athlete than everybody else. Mainly because of his size, but even at a young age he showed a lot of physical ability for his size, and that's really what kind of made the difference. Leonard was large and very skilled."

It didn't take long for the Wortham coaches to notice Davis. In fact, Davis was part of a class of young Bulldog standouts, and when he and his buddy Terrell Spence entered the sixth grade, the middle school coaches came calling. "We were like, 'Yeah, we'll do it,'" Davis said. "We talked to our parents and all of that. They sent a letter to the state, and it allowed us to play junior high football even though we were in sixth grade. There was a pretty good amount of us that played in the sixth grade."

Davis and Spence were quickly promoted to the eighth-grade team, where they kept up the practice of competing with older, more physically mature athletes. But it must have been difficult to tell which of the kids was a sixth grader. Davis, who later in his career blocked for Heisman winner Ricky Williams, toted the ball like Earl Campbell in middle school. "I remember a time or two he was carrying the ball, running people over," Chapman said. "He would walk into the end zone carrying five or six people."

Before he entered high school, Davis had established his reputation as a force. Once again, though, his story was anything but typical. Not only did he grow up in a small town, he grew up in a small town that lacked a winning tradition in football. So he's a larger-than-life athlete who also came up as an underdog.

Davis, who said he was a little taller than six-four and a little more than three hundred pounds as a freshman, went straight to the varsity when he reached high school. Several of his classmates joined him, and the young team proceeded taking its lumps. The Bulldogs went 0–10 in 1993 and didn't get much better the next season, going 2–8.

I spoke with Davis after he retired from pro football. Looking back from that vantage point, he could clearly see what had happened to the Bulldogs during those rough early years. "Even as freshmen, we had the mentality that we wanted to beat these guys," Davis said. "There comes a point when you're physically limited. One guy, as a freshman he was only 125, 130 pounds. It's just different. You physically can't do it. Even though you want to do it, you have the mind-set to do it, you're just physically incapable."

Just about the time Wortham folks started to think a winning football team wasn't in their future, new coach Tommy Roberson stepped in and found a group of Bulldogs who were primed to move forward. Roberson could see the pieces were there. He had heard of Davis years earlier from a fellow coach who was headed to Wortham, and when Roberson arrived in town, he saw the kid was the real deal. But Davis wasn't alone. "It was just a matter of moving some kids around to different positions," Roberson said. "Watching the game film from the year before, Terrell would get the ball out in open space and just do some great things with it. I thought he needed to touch the ball every play, so that's why I made him the quarterback. That worked out wonderful. We were able to get a kid by the name of Adam Barker to come out and go through the spring drills. He was uncanny as a veer back and had pretty good speed. He gave us that third threat."

Though the turnaround didn't happen immediately, Roberson could tell it was happening. Wortham lost four of its first five games in 1995, but neither the Bulldogs' resolve nor their coach's confidence was shaken. Roberson told the principal he still thought his team was on a collision course for a title. "'If things go like I think they'll go, we could be playing Bremond for the district championship,'" Roberson said, recalling the conversation. "She said, 'We haven't won but two games in two years. What makes you think so?' 'I know our kids and I really think we can be doing that.'"

Sure enough, Wortham opened district with a 32–0 win over Normangee, then thumped rival Frost 37–21 and crushed Dawson 46–0. When the Bulldogs upped their winning streak to four games with a 37–0 win over Oakwood, they set up a showdown with Bremond.

Suddenly all the potential that Davis and his classmates had shown from early in their athletic careers was combining with the experience gained from more than two seasons on varsity. But were they ready to overcome the area's small-school kingpin? Bremond made it to the state final seven times between 1981 and 2015, and a program like that doesn't just relinquish its place in the pecking order to an upstart. The Tigers walloped Wortham 60–22 to win the district title in 1995. But Wortham survived the beating and won the next week to make it into the playoffs with a 6–4 record.

Despite losing in the first round of the playoffs, Wortham harnessed momentum going forward, since most of their key cogs were coming back for 1996. Roberson knew he needed to figure out how to make life easier and more productive for Davis. Although the Bulldogs' opponents couldn't match him physically, they were finding ways to pester or avoid him.

Going into his senior season, Davis had grown to six-six, 340, and maintained the quickness and agility to run to the football. Wortham could have run behind Davis all day on offense if it wanted to, but it needed to better use his ability on defense. "The one area that I kept talking to college coaches about: everybody doubles and triples Leonard," Roberson recalled. "They're always grabbing his ankles, they're always biting his knees, they're always marking his shins. How can I give him a way to defeat that? They said back him up. Flex him off of the ball."

Instead of having a hand on the ground, Davis would be standing up and looking into the opposing backfield, a posture he liked. Not to mention that it must have made a few opposing quarterbacks shake in their cleats to look across the line at such a massive defender staring at them. "I was playing middle linebacker," Davis said. "If the quarterback dropped back, I just kind of read his eyes and mirrored the quarterback and kept my eyes on the running backs coming out of the backfield. I just played the football."

It led to perhaps Davis's favorite highlight of his entire career. "There was one game I actually scored a touchdown on an interception return," Davis said. "We got it on film and all that. It was against the Oakwood Panthers. I was supposed to be rushing, and then when I saw the running back come out of the backfield, the quarterback was scrambling. As soon as he threw it to him, I jumped over and picked it off, and eighty-one yards later I'm in the end zone."

The tweaks helped Wortham pick up the rhythm from the end of the previous season to start the 1996 campaign. The Bulldogs won three nondistrict games and then tore through their first three games of district play to set up another battle with Bremond. This time the Tigers entered the game ranked number nine in 1A, a slot ahead of tenth-ranked Wortham. The Bulldogs had already revamped their program by going from 0–10 to the state rankings, but they weren't finished.

Barker ran up the middle for a twenty-five-yard touchdown in the first quarter to put Wortham in front 7–3. Then Spence put his signature on the game with a brilliantly run option play. "Terrell Spence cut loose down the right sideline on an option before pitching to [James] Eggins at the last minute," *Waco Tribune-Herald* sportswriter John Werner wrote. "Nobody could catch Eggins as he ran for a 74-yard touchdown to give the Bulldogs a 13–3 edge with 3:50 left in the first half."

Bremond edged closer with a third-quarter touchdown drive. But given

Wortham's ability to control the pace of the game, the Tigers were running out of chances to take the lead when they punted early in the fourth quarter. "The thing I remember most about that game, I think there were eight minutes left in the fourth quarter," Roberson said. "We took the ball over on about the ten- or fifteen-yard line and kept the ball."

Roberson decided early in his tenure at Wortham that there was no other play call on third- or fourth-and-short than to run behind Davis. That strategy took center stage with the district championship on the line. "We were disciplined enough, and we believed enough, and we executed," Roberson said. "We must have gone for it on fourth-and-one—shoot, I don't know—four or five times [during the final drive versus Bremond]. We'd get in what we called our jumbo package, which had four linemen on one side and three on the other. I told Terrell, you just take it. We're going to run quarterback sneak on goose. We must have gotten four or five first downs in that drive that way."

The *Tribune-Herald* reported that Wortham drained the final 8:19 of the fourth quarter on its final drive. "To have a 13–9 lead and run the clock out, that might be the best drive I've ever had on any team ever," Roberson said. Wortham's victory over Bremond proved to be the highest hurdle on the way to a perfect 10–0 regular season.

Chapman saw the difference that winning made in his own house. "My dad hated football and didn't see any sense in it," Chapman said. "Especially with the losing seasons. I basically had to beg him to let me play. But like a lot of people, by our senior year he was at almost every game."

The Bulldogs believed they could ascend to the state championship. Tenaha ended that quest in the second round of the playoffs. But Wortham claimed a state title during Davis's senior season when it won the 1A basketball championship.

Not surprisingly, the kid who grew up earning his place in the Sunday-afternoon hoops game made a huge impact in the state tournament. He averaged a double-double in the semifinal and final, scoring as needed and dominating the rebounding category. But he was just part of a team that he said could have been mistaken for a 5A squad because of its size and swagger.

By that time, Davis was already signed and headed to Texas to play college football. The kid had grown up, and he was ready for the next challenge. "For me, it really wasn't a culture shock, because I always knew there was more competition out there," Davis said. "I just knew that when I get that opportunity, I'm going to show people that just because I went to a small school doesn't mean I shouldn't be out here on this field with you and everybody else."

# 23

# WACO

## 1996

### *University's LT Runs into Spotlight*

When LaDainian Tomlinson walked onto the field for pregame before the first game of his senior season at Waco University High School, he didn't know what to expect.

All he knew was he had put in the work to be ready. He had spent his junior season mostly blocking from the fullback position. When he learned he would take over at tailback as a senior, he went to work doing everything he could to be in shape for those tough carries in the fourth quarter. At seventeen, he was already outworking people. But he was still plenty nervous.

Keep in mind, this wasn't the player who led the NCAA in rushing for two straight seasons and won the Doak Walker Award as a TCU senior. He was still miles and miles away from being the best running back in the NFL for most of a decade. In fact, on September 5, 1996, a seventeen-year-old Tomlinson stared straight ahead at his first game as the go-to running back on his high school team. As the University Trojans prepared to meet the Austin LBJ Jaguars on a Thursday night at Nelson Field in Austin, Tomlinson experienced one of those "here we go" moments. "This game is fresh in my mind like it was yesterday," Tomlinson said. "The guys on their team, these were big guys. We couldn't just push them around. They had some guys that looked like DI-type guys [top-level college prospects]. Kind of looking back, walking on the field I was thinking to myself, 'You're going to find a lot out about yourself today. Either you have it or you don't.'"

I met Tomlinson at a Starbucks in Keller late in the spring of 2014. He wore a black tank top, white shorts, and a flat-brimmed TCU hat. The other coffee drinkers seemed to recognize him or at least sensed a larger-than-life presence, but to their credit no autographs or smartphone pics were sought. Thanks to Tomlinson's easygoing nature, it didn't take us long to settle into a conversation between two guys who grew up in the same town at the same time. I went to Waco Midway and graduated in 1996, a year ahead of Tomlinson at University. My best friend ran against Tomlinson, his good friend Lawrence Pullen, and their team in the 4 × 100-meter relay. If you had asked me in 1996 about University athletes, I would have immediately brought up Pullen, who played running back while Tomlinson blocked from his fullback position in 1995.

So despite almost two decades of other material to go over, Tomlinson and I began with Pullen. "He was always at my house," Tomlinson said. "We were really like brothers. He was older, and so I always kind of felt like I was following him around a little bit and trying to keep up with him. On my level, the kids my age, I was better than them. You knew that you could play, and you were one of the better athletes on your grade level, but [compared to] the older kids like Lawrence and some of the other guys that I used to play with, I was just an average kid."

That's why Tomlinson didn't know for sure how the game would unfold as he warmed up for LBJ.

I dug up the *Waco Tribune-Herald* game story in the microfilms at the Waco public library. It was written by Olin Buchanan, who a couple years later played a bit role as a reporter in the MTV football movie *Varsity Blues*. Buchanan worked for the *Austin American-Statesman* at the time, but since the Waco and Austin papers were both owned by the same parent company, Buchanan sent over the Thursday-night gamer to run in Waco as well.

LT and I looked at the story and sort of marveled at the opening paragraphs. They clearly delineate Tomlinson's transcendence: "It took University running back LaDainian Tomlinson 10 games to score four touchdowns last season," Buchanan wrote in his lead paragraph. "He needed one quarter to do it Thursday night."

It reads like Tomlinson's ascent happened in the blink of an eye. He rushed for 181 yards and scored six touchdowns in the season opener as University demolished the Jaguars 48–0. That set him on schedule to propel the Trojans to their best season in school history. University would go 12–2 as Tomlinson rushed for a city-record 2,554 yards and scored thirty-nine touchdowns.

But of course, it didn't happen in the blink of an eye. Tomlinson's success that season and beyond was the brilliant result of the work Tomlinson put in, but there was still a cause-and-effect relationship. "That's pretty much right if you just go by the work I put into it," Tomlinson said of his 2,500-yard season. "After basketball practice my junior season, I was going to run stadium stairs. Guys were looking at me like, 'This guy is nuts. What is he doing?' But I was preparing for my chance at tailback my senior year."

Tomlinson's four first-quarter touchdowns against LBJ included runs of thirty-seven yards and two yards around the right side, twenty-five yards up the middle, and around the left side for thirty-one yards. Fans live for that moment when their team's ballcarrier breaks into the open field and they can scream out, "He's gone!" Tomlinson just remembers biding his time, waiting for the hole to open. "For me, a lot of times things would look so bogged up you would have to be patient," he said. "A lot of these runs, I would be hiding behind those guys, and when I see that hole, I'm hitting it. A lot of those guys were like, 'Holy crap! Where'd he come from.' And they would miss me."

The reason Tomlinson played behind Pullen for a year, other than simple seniority, was because Pullen was faster, and Tomlinson admits that. I remember Pullen, who went on to play at Stephen F. Austin, as a basketball player that could defy gravity and dunk convincingly for a five-six guard.

Tomlinson, though, had football eyes. "He had great, great vision," said LeRoy Coleman, Tomlinson's high school head coach. "Lawrence was quick and had great speed, but LT could stop on a dime and make you miss. It was amazing to see the knack that he had, because he never got really hit. Nobody could get a solid lick on him because he had such great vision."

Football by its nature brings in a huge spectrum of personalities. There's usually no telling when the finer points of the game are going to click with a player. But like guards in basketball, running backs are almost required to be football junkies. If you don't have a head for the game that's up to speed with the other guys in the backfield, there's a good chance you're going to be watching them carry the football.

For Tomlinson, the desire to run with the ball began as a six-year-old. He watched Walter Payton play for the Bears, so when he went out for Pop Warner football, that's what he wanted to do. "When I first started playing, the coach put me at quarterback," Tomlinson said. "I was pissed about it because I wanted to be a running back. He said, 'No, you're going to always run the football.' But I didn't understand. I was thinking, 'What are you talking about? I'm going to give it to my friend.' 'He said, 'No, I want you to run it.' So the first play I go around the left side for a touchdown."

Tomlinson scoring touchdowns would become a trend for the next twenty-five years. He scored 100 touchdowns in fewer games than anyone in NFL history, making the 100th, 101st, and 102nd touchdowns of his career in 2006, in just his eighty-ninth game, at the age of twenty-seven. That same season, Tomlinson posted 2,323 rushing yards and thirty-one touchdowns.

But sitting in the Starbucks in Keller, I could sense how Tomlinson had felt before all those achievements came rolling in. "He was nervous because he really wanted to prove what he could do," Pullen said when I spoke with him on the phone later the same day. "People wondered about him, if he could do it when he got his chance. I knew his dedication and his work ethic, and I knew he was going to match that and beyond. I could see the maturation process developing. I felt like he could stand alone."

Tomlinson ended up scoring five rushing touchdowns in that first game of his senior year. The icing on the cake came in the second quarter when he went back in the game at linebacker. "One of my buddies, David Beverly, tells the story because they had taken me out of the game," Tomlinson said. "It was over, so I'm on the bench, and he has a cramp. He's supposed to be playing that spot. The very next play, I go in and I intercept the ball and run it back for a touchdown."

Tomlinson can't help but laugh hysterically when telling the story, especially the part about the anguish on Beverly's face. "He was like, 'That was supposed to be me. That was supposed to be me.' You cramped up, buddy. What do you want me to say?"

As he did so often in his career, Tomlinson found himself in the right place at the right time on that play. The trend continued when Tomlinson moved from high school to college.

He spurned the hometown Baylor football program, which was struggling to find a foothold in the newly formed Big 12. Instead, LT made a name for himself at TCU, leading the Horned Frogs' rise to national powerhouse. As a sophomore, Tomlinson helped TCU win its first bowl game in forty-one years. As a junior, he rushed for 1,850 yards and eighteen touchdowns. As a senior, he made those numbers look pedestrian as he posted a 2,158-yard, twenty-two-touchdown season.

Tomlinson smoothly transitioned to the NFL, where he rushed for more than 1,000 yards as a rookie with the San Diego Chargers. That was the first of eight consecutive seasons of more than 1,000 rushing yards. In 2003, he mixed in 100 receptions for 725 yards with 1,645 rushing yards. As of the end of the 2014 season, he is the only player to rush for more than 1,000 yards and catch more than 100 passes in a season in NFL history.

For me, it's surreal to think that a kid who was my age, who went to the same movie theaters and fast-food joints in the same town, became an all-American at TCU and then one of the biggest stars in the NFL. It's a phenomenal tribute to what can happen when a man prepares himself for an opportunity. Once he puts the work in, it's just a matter of waiting for the right moment and running straight ahead.

"This was a dream come true," Tomlinson told Buchanan after University's victory over LBJ. "My linemen did a good job. All I had to do was run through big holes."

# 24

# AUSTIN

## 1996

### *Westlake Breaks Through*

Jonny Rodgers's buddies could find any number of ways to introduce him when showing him off around Austin. For example, Rodgers was named the 2015 Austinite of the Year by the Austin Under 40 Awards for his charitable work with the Young Men's Business League. He's also a partner at his real estate firm. Before that, he graduated with honors from TCU, and before that he was the starting free safety on the Westlake Chaparrals 1996 state championship team.

But like all knuckleheaded buddies, Rodgers's friends choose to dwell on something he did when he was fifteen. "Just being around Austin, you know, I'll be sitting there talking with friends, and someone is like, 'Oh yeah, Drew Brees was Jonny's backup,'" Rodgers said. "Literally, I hear it every three or four days. It doesn't get old. It really doesn't."

As a freshman, Rodgers ran the offense on the Westlake freshman A team, and Brees quarterbacked the B team. Going into their sophomore year, Rodgers prepared to be the junior-varsity starting quarterback. Brees, who had come to the school as a freshman and had only limited experience playing tackle football, worked as Rodgers's backup.

Then perhaps the most fateful injury in the history of Texas high school football occurred in a JV scrimmage in mid-August. Rodgers blew out his ACL (anterior cruciate ligament), ending his sophomore season. Brees took over as the Chaparrals' JV starter and began tossing balls to his favorite receiver, Ryan Read, at a convincing rate. A year later, Brees had cemented himself as

Westlake's quarterback of the future, and Rodgers shifted to free safety and backup quarterback.

Westlake was loaded with senior starters and the junior Brees at quarterback going into the 1995 season. The Chaparrals took the momentum of four consecutive 10–0 regular seasons into the 1995 campaign and began ripping through another schedule. None of Westlake's first ten opponents came within twenty-four points of the Chaps. It looked as if Westlake might be headed back to the state championship game, where it had been twice already in the decade, losing in the state final in 1990 and 1994.

But another injury derailed Westlake. This time, Brees injured his ACL in the third round of the playoffs. Rodgers came on to lead the Chaps past Alice, but Westlake fell to eventual state champion San Antonio Roosevelt the next week.

I interviewed Brees at Saints training camp in the summer of 2014 when New Orleans was getting ready for the season in White Sulphur Springs, West Virginia. As we talked beside a practice field nestled in the Allegheny Mountains, the Super Bowl XLIV MVP still recalled the sense of urgency for Westlake to finally break through and win a state championship.

"We were used to winning," Brees said. "We were used to going deep in the playoffs. We made it to the quarterfinals and beyond every year that we were there. Certainly, it felt like just about every year we were always in contention for a state title, and yet it was always elusive, because we had been a few times but we had never won one."

In 1996, Westlake coach Ron Schroeder was ready to put the season on Brees's arm. Or at least, he eventually reached the point where he was comfortable with that scenario.

But during the cold days of the off-season following the 1995 season, Schroeder didn't know what he would do. The Chaparrals had lost plenty of starters and didn't have a whole lot of impact players or answers left in the building. Offensive tackle Seth McKinney, who went on to play at Texas A&M and then for eight seasons in the NFL, was surrounded in the Chaps locker room by a bunch of untested teammates. "I remember sitting in the off-season, starting when Drew was in the hospital having surgery and Seth McKinney was the only returning starter sitting in that room," Schroeder said. "McKinney had moved from Clear Lake. His father was hired by the Bush administration. They moved to Austin. I remember thinking when I was talking to the team after we should have won the state championship the year before, in '95. Seth is like the only guy sitting in the dressing room that was a big-time player. I remember thinking, 'Seth, are you glad you're here now?'"

But the pieces began to come together. Brees returned from surgery and was ready to go by the beginning of the 1996 season. Schroeder installed sophomore Bret Robin at halfback and moved senior Jamie Tyler from strong safety to fullback. The speedy Read came back from an ACL injury of his own to lead a solid group of wide receivers, and McKinney anchored the offensive line.

With Brees emerging as a star, suddenly throwing the ball around the field was too much fun to pass up. "We kind of made the decision to throw," Schroeder said. "Anyone will tell you that it's entertaining. I didn't want to throw if we're going to complete less than 50 percent. It wasn't a big risk. You go back to the days of Darrell Royal. Three things [can happen when you throw the football], two are bad. It was like that for a long time. Probably with Brees and Ryan Read and Jeremy Amos and some of these guys, it was probably the first time that more than likely when we threw a pass, it was going to be completed."

Brees passed for 3,528 yards and thirty-one touchdowns during his senior season at Westlake, earning Class 5A Offensive Player of the Year honors. He connected with Read 108 times for a then-state-record 1,993 yards and twenty touchdowns. Before the spread attack made it fashionable to see how many receivers a quarterback could find, Brees and Read essentially dared defenses to keep them from connecting. Amos caught thirty-seven passes for 571 yards, and running back Robin had the next-highest catch total with twenty-six.

As in 1995, the Chaparrals churned through a parade of regular-season blowouts. Westlake opened the season with a 28–14 win over San Antonio Holmes, which would be the last team to come within three touchdowns of the Chaps for the rest of the regular season.

McKinney said he could tell as early as Brees's junior season that the Westlake quarterback was headed for a special career. "In high school, I could have told you every game he was going to go out there and ball," McKinney said. "The way that he prepared himself, even in high school, and some of the things he could do in high school—I can recall days when we would set out trash cans, and he's dropping balls in trash cans from like fifty yards away. All you've got to do is look at our highlight film. Yeah, he's throwing a lot to Ryan Read, but he's throwing to other people as well, and they're not out there making circus catches. They're making great catches, but the ball is right to them."

Schroeder could sense that Brees elevated the Chaps to the level of a legitimate state-championship contender. But he could also see they needed a twist. From watching film of previous games, Schroeder saw that opposing defensive backs were starting to predict that the Westlake receivers would break off their routes at twelve yards. Schroeder responded by almost doubling the routes the receivers ran, making breaks at twenty yards. "When you're making a break at twenty, you've got to throw a laser for thirty-five yards, and I remember the first day we ran it at practice," Schroeder said. "It was kind of a break-and-go at twenty, and I mean he hit the guy right on the money. Just a laser. I'm just thinking, 'Man, Brees is going to be pretty good.' I think the very next game we played Churchill in the Alamodome, and we hit a couple of those passes where we ran those deep routes. They weren't bomb-type passes. They were on-the-line-type passes."

In the regional final, the round where the Chaps had fallen the previous season, Brees passed for 344 yards and three touchdowns, leading Westlake to a 49–23 victory over San Antonio Churchill. Robin and Tyler combined for four touchdown runs to balance Westlake's aerial assault.

Olin Buchanan covered Westlake throughout the playoffs for the *Austin American-Statesman*. He captured the importance of the change Schroeder made to the passing routes with a comment from the coach. "We put a couple of different wrinkles in on the post, and Drew just popped them in," Schroeder told Buchanan. "I definitely think Drew makes a difference."

Although Westlake didn't play many games in 1996 that were decided in the second half, much less in the fourth quarter, McKinney told me he's always balked at the suggestion that the Chaps played a soft schedule. He said Westlake took on the best teams that San Antonio and Houston had to offer just to get to the state championship game.

The Aldine team Westlake faced in the semifinals stood out in Brees's memory almost eighteen years after the game. "I remember looking at their roster, and you just went on paper, pound for pound, height, weight, all that stuff, it was an NFL roster," Brees said. "That's no joke. You look at this team, and you go, 'We're going to get destroyed.'"

That feeling prevailed during the week of practice leading to the Westlake-Aldine clash in the Astrodome. Rodgers said the Chaparrals players, particularly on the defensive side, were falling behind way before the game ever started. So much so that defensive coordinator Derek Long sat the team down for an attitude adjustment. "He basically gave us a pep talk that we were going to go out there and we were going to kick their butt," Rodgers said. "He was like, 'They're big. They're fast and they're strong. But we're disciplined, and we're going to beat 'em to the punch.' So when we started playing against Aldine and we were competing with them, we were like, 'Guys, we can do this.'"

Westlake's defense had been like a mint-condition, full-size, steel-belted radial spare tire, riding along under cover for most of the season. The Chaps didn't think much about it until they had to have it, which they did in the second half against Aldine.

Leading 28–21 and moving deep into Aldine territory late in the third quarter, Brees fumbled the snap at the Aldine six-yard line, and the Mustangs recovered.

But the Westlake defense kept Aldine from stealing away the momentum. On the second play of the Mustangs' ensuing drive, Chaparral linebacker Derek Hyzak drilled Aldine quarterback Bobby Gray, separating Gray from the football. "From my point of view, I can see the ball on the ground, and I'm running straight at it, and I see Devin Schade scoop it up and take it into the end zone," Rodgers said. "If you watch video of it, you can see me jump as high as I can and on top of Devin in the end zone. That play itself was . . . I get chills now even thinking about it."

Rodgers said the play validated the Westlake defense's effort of the entire season. They didn't mind being in the shadow of the Chaps' dynamic passing game, but it was a thrill to stand up and be counted in a key moment. "A lot of people just talked about the offense, to be honest with you," Rodgers said. "Drew and Ryan Read, Bret Robin and Jamie Tyler, and all those guys. We didn't have any big names on our defense. We were just kind of a hodgepodge group of guys that, when that happened, it was like, 'Yes! Yes! See guys, we're doing our part too!'"

Westlake defeated Aldine 42–21 and advanced to play Abilene Cooper in the 5A Division II state final at Texas Stadium. Cooper was led by the blazing fast and powerful running back Dominic Rhodes, who would claim a Super Bowl ring before Brees. Rhodes rushed for 113 yards and a touchdown to help Indianapolis defeat Chicago in Super Bowl XLI.

Rhodes got his yards in the state championship game as well, rushing for 230 and two touchdowns. "Dominic Rhodes was as good a running back as I had ever seen, if not better," Rodgers said. "We had played some good running backs, but Dominic Rhodes was special."

Cooper played Westlake to a first-half draw, 7–7. At halftime, Schroeder tightened up the Chaps' offensive game plan, and it helped them take over momentum in the third quarter.

Brees finished with 163 passing yards in the state final and tossed touchdowns to Amos and Matt Murphy in the fourth quarter. But it was Tyler pounding the football in the rushing game that made the difference. Tyler finished with 127 yards on twenty-four carries. Westlake won the third quarter 21–0 on the way to a 55–15 championship game victory.

Rodgers's playing career came to an end that day when he suffered another ACL injury at the end of the third quarter, just before the Chaparrals' coaches pulled the starters. He said it took him almost the entire fourth quarter to get through the bittersweetness of winning a state championship but suffering another blown-out knee. But the pain subsided in time for the postgame celebration. "It was the last play that I was ever going to play in high school football, and I blow my knee out," Rodgers said. "Drew is one of the first guys that came up to me and said, 'Hey, man, we're going to finish this out for you.' I knew my career was over, but all the work that we had done, the goals, all the stuff that all of us had been working for, it came true. We won it."

Brees carried with him the sense of that accomplishment as he moved on to Purdue and then the NFL. "I think that's how you fight through the tough times," Brees said. "Every team faces adversity at some point during the season. The teams that are able to push through that and come out better on the other side are the teams that have that tight-knit community within. If you really love each other and you really trust one another and you don't want to let each other down, you're going to pull through, and you're going to come out better on the other side, and it's going to serve you well the further you go along. I think the teams I've been on have always had that, maybe just because we had good guys. Character before talent, because people help you win, not players."

That's the story behind the story when Rodgers is introduced one more time as the guy who was ahead of Drew Brees at quarterback on the Westlake ninth-grade depth chart. Rodgers views the intervening knee injuries as divine providence. "That was God's way of saying, 'Jonny, we've got some special plans for this Drew Brees kid. We want you to go and take another route in life,'" Rodgers said. "I take that to heart because I have a strong faith in God. I'm doing wonderful in Austin, Texas, and Drew is Drew Brees."

# 25

# NEW BRAUNFELS

## 1997

### *Father and Son Build a Winner*

As images go, a coach could do much worse than Kliff Kingsbury's persona in the media. When Texas Tech hired Kingsbury late in 2012, he became the second-youngest coach in college football's bowl subdivision. Youth and a sharp jawline go a long way in branding a man as dynamic. But then someone noticed that Kingsbury looks more than a little bit like Hollywood heartthrob Ryan Gosling. After that, it seemed no one could see anything else. Like this one, every story began with Kingsbury's looks. That's not a bad problem, for sure. Trouble is, many of the storytellers find it hard to stray very far from that narrative.

But I forgot about all of that almost immediately after walking into Kingsbury's Texas Tech office. I didn't feel as though I were shooting bull with a frat boy or some bro in love with his public image. Instead, I was speaking with the son of a football coach. Kingsbury is a true football guy. He's a man who was bitten by the coaching bug while walking his own path. If the rest of the story appears to have gone in fast-forward, well, that perception might only be skin deep as well.

For one thing, the sons of football coaches learn that the job is heavy on grinding and light on glamour. Kingsbury's dad, Tim Kingsbury, was promoted from an assistant to the head coach at New Braunfels High School before the beginning of Kliff's sophomore year. Despite its appearance, the move didn't guarantee success or accolades for either Kingsbury.

In fact, Tim Kingsbury kept his son on the junior varsity that first season, even though the New Braunfels Unicorns' varsity wasn't very good. During Kliff's junior season, it became only more difficult for the Unicorns after New Braunfels was bumped up from 4A to 5A. Kliff came up to lead the varsity squad just as realignment put the Unicorns in a district that included 1995 5A Division I state champion Converse Judson and Division II state champion San Antonio Roosevelt. "We got moved into 5A, and probably the toughest 5A district in the state," Kingsbury said. "My dad became the head coach my sophomore year, when we were 4A, and then my junior year we went into that district and got blasted by all those teams."

I can imagine Kliff Kingsbury in 1996 being just another kid playing quarterback on an also-ran ball club. He wasn't on anyone's top 100 prospects list, even in the San Antonio area. College scholarship offers were not arriving in the mail.

But there was something brewing.

Tim Kingsbury knew that his senior class in 1997 could change things. The group had gone through middle school, freshman team, and junior varsity without losing a game. They had speed and skill, and Tim Kingsbury had the insight to use those things. "I went and listened to [Kentucky coach] Hal Mumme speak and determined we were going to spread people out," Tim Kingsbury said.

Mumme's offensive coordinator at the time was Mike Leach, who would play a gigantic role in Kingsbury's career. But at the time, Tim Kingsbury was just a football coach trying to get some help. And the Unicorns needed it. "If we tried to line up and pound it, we didn't have the bodies to do it," Kliff Kingsbury said. "We had 1,400 kids [enrolled in the high school], and they had 3,500. That was every team we were playing."

Hindsight being 20/20 and all, it's easy to see that Kingsbury in a spread system was a fateful match. It took hold pretty quickly for the Unicorns. New Braunfels ripped through its nondistrict schedule, scoring 122 points in three games and winning by an average of more than thirty-five points a game. By winning its District 26-5A opener, the Unicorns set up one of those larger-than-life games: the mighty Converse Judson Rockets appeared next on the schedule. Converse Judson, which had slammed New Braunfels 41–10 in 1996, was slated to come to Unicorn Stadium in 1997.

This is where the past becomes inflated a bit. Kliff Kingsbury told me the Rockets were nationally ranked when they came to town. Actually, Converse Judson had lost two straight before traveling to New Braunfels. But those details don't smudge the picture much. It was still the Converse Judson program that had won the state championship in Texas's largest school classification in 1995 and had reached the state final in 1996. The Rockets had compiled a 27–3 record during the previous two seasons, and two of the losses came against teams that won state championships.

The Rockets, by all measures, were still way out of New Braunfels's league. "It was Judson," Kliff Kingsbury said. "You weren't supposed to beat 'em. They came to New Braunfels and our little stadium, and the place was packed." What happened on the field that night in front of an estimated crowd of 8,000 created the impetus for the Kingsbury story.

The *San Antonio Express-News* ranked New Braunfels and Converse Judson as the sixth- and eighth-best teams in the area, so their meeting drew top-of-the-page coverage. The article described how Kingsbury led the Unicorns on a fourteen-play, eighty-three-yard touchdown drive the first time New Braunfels had the ball. To cap the drive, Kingsbury tossed to Eric Graves for a twenty-yard gain to the Judson four. Graves fumbled there, but offensive guard Randy Jones recovered it in the end zone for a touchdown.

Kingsbury and Graves made up for the hiccup by hooking up for a sixty-seven-yard touchdown midway through the second quarter, and the Unicorns surged ahead 14–0 going into halftime.

Tim Kingsbury told me Kliff took a forearm to the head sometime during the game. Years later, they discovered Kliff didn't remember many details from the Judson game. But some things couldn't help but stick. "I'll never forget the atmosphere, because it was standing room only all around the track," Kingsbury said. "I remember we ran a hitch-and-go to a receiver for a big play early, and the place kind of went crazy. It let everybody know. It kind of backed them off, and it kind of set the tone for the game."

Judson bounced back with a touchdown early in the third quarter. But Kingsbury responded with touchdown passes of thirty-six yards to Joel Tienda and sixteen yards to Graves to secure New Braunfels's 28–7 victory. "Everyone in the stadium rushed the field," Kliff Kingsbury said. "It was just that moment of, 'Hey, these guys can do this.' That's the one that I always remember."

Kingsbury completed sixteen of nineteen passes for 243 yards and three touchdowns. Following the game, Tim Kingsbury gave first credit to the defense, but he didn't wait too long before praising the spread offense's impact. "Our defense won us this game, but our offense was clicking," he told the *Express-News*. "We knew we couldn't rush on them, so we had to get our passing game going and it worked."

The win over Converse Judson launched New Braunfels on a district title run, and they finished 5-1 in 26-5A. San Antonio MacArthur handed the Unicorns their only regular-season loss, 17–14, but New Braunfels avenged it by defeating MacArthur 29–21 in the playoffs. The Unicorns won thirteen games in 1997 and advanced to the state semifinals, losing to Alief Hastings.

Tim Kingsbury said when he took over as head coach, the program had lost the confident edge that it had during the 1980s. The community was skeptical of the Unicorns' ability to compete in 5A. "We had to work hard at convincing them," he said. "We really didn't know how good we were, so that showed our kids we had a good ball club and could play with anybody."

As for Kliff, the win over Converse Judson played a vital role in his senior-season success, and that platform presented more opportunities for him to play college football. Or more accurately, it opened up *an* opportunity. "I ended up having one offer, to Texas Tech," Kingsbury said. "Right before signing day, they had a guy that didn't end up coming. Coach [Spike] Dykes came down and offered me."

Kingsbury's first start came at the end of his redshirt-freshman season. It would be Dykes's final game after leading the Red Raiders for fourteen seasons. Kingsbury passed for 259 yards and three touchdowns, and ran one yard for another one, as the Red Raiders defeated Oklahoma 38–28. Oklahoma's offensive coordinator that day was Mike Leach. He would be named Texas Tech's head coach after Dykes retired, and Leach tabbed Kingsbury as his starting quarterback. That set off one of the most prolific careers for a passer in college football history, and Kingsbury went on to pass for 12,423 yards and ninety-five touchdowns.

After banging around with five NFL teams in four seasons, and then spending time in NFL Europe and the Canadian Football League, Kingsbury was about to take a shot at a pro league start-up team in Houston. Before that venture began, the Houston Cougars' offensive coordinator, Dana Holgorsen, asked Kingsbury to come work with Cougar quarterback Case Keenum in an informal summer workout. Kingsbury clicked with Keenum, and the coaching fire was ignited.

Kingsbury admits he was lucky to switch when he did. Instead of plugging away in a fledgling off-brand football league that soon failed, he took a seat on the fast train to big-time college football coaching. He spent four seasons coaching at Houston, the last two as the co–offensive coordinator. When Cougars coach Kevin Sumlin left Houston for Texas A&M, he took Kingsbury with him as the Aggies' offensive coordinator.

Meanwhile, Leach's relationship with the Texas Tech administration fell apart. After an acrimonious breakup, Texas Tech hired Tommy Tuberville. When he split for Cincinnati, Texas Tech was in desperate need of a coach who wanted to be a Red Raider. The time was right for the thirty-three-year-old Kingsbury to mend the fence. "It's just been a whirlwind, but I couldn't be happier, beyond ecstatic, to be back. It feels like home," Kingsbury said after Texas Tech hired him late in 2012. "This is where I wanted to be, it's where I've wanted to be."

One thing Mike Leach picked up on from Spike Dykes was to find outliers who could drive Texas Tech's program. Dykes brought Kingsbury to Lubbock (the first time), and Leach followed suit by bringing in players like Wes Welker, Graham Harrell, and Michael Crabtree.

Kingsbury definitely has his eye out for players who, like himself, began to ascend as seniors. "If, by your junior year, you're not on anybody's radar, it's a done deal," Kingsbury said. "I have some empathy for that situation. I want to make sure we scour the senior tape and not just the junior tape."

That's not the Hollywood lookalike speaking, it's the underdog.

# 26

# KATY

## 1997

### *Tigers Pound Their Way to a Title*

In 1994, the final four teams playing in the 5A Division I playoffs were Converse Judson, Katy, Plano, and Odessa Permian. That would be like the college hoops Final Four coming down to Duke, North Carolina, Kentucky, and Kansas.

It's a who's who, especially when viewed from the second decade of the 2000s. But at the time, it was also like the old *Sesame Street* game in which children were asked, "Can you tell me which thing is not like the others / By the time I finish my song?"

At the time, Converse Judson had won back-to-back state championships in the previous two seasons. Plano would go on to win its seventh state title and its third in nine years. Odessa Permian claimed the most prominent place of them all, both because the Panthers had won four state championships since 1980 and, even more famously, had been the subject of the Texas high school football tome *Friday Night Lights*.

That left Katy.

Although the Tigers were no slouches, they didn't really belong in such rarefied company in 1994. Katy began changing that perception by knocking off Judson in the semifinals, ending the Rockets' ten-game unbeaten streak in the playoffs. But Plano stomped Katy in the state final 28–7, meaning the Tigers were still looking for their second state title and their first since winning the 1A championship in 1959.

Katy head coach Mike Johnston, who at the time was in his second decade as the Tigers' coach, saw clearly why his team fell short, and he knew it wasn't a total loss. "We just fell flat on our face," he said. "We lost control of the whole situation; the community was so excited and everything. I'm glad. You've got to go through that. It'd been so long, especially at that level. It proved we can be there."

Moving the program to that level took a huge chunk of Johnston's twenty-four-season tenure at Katy. He arrived at the school in 1980 as Bill Branum's offensive coordinator. Two years later, Johnston took over as head coach and made a key addition to the coaching staff when he brought on Gary Joseph as a defensive coach. Two years after that, Joseph was promoted to defensive coordinator, and the key pieces of the next three decades were in place.

Joseph took over as Katy's head coach when Johnston retired following the 2003 season. Between the two of them, they had guided the Tigers to a dozen state-championship-game appearances. That statistic is even more amazing because it took them more than a decade to reach the first one. Johnston and Joseph built the Tigers from a program that hadn't been in the playoffs since 1964, and it took some time. "We were everybody's homecoming the first two years I was here," Johnston said.

I met with Joseph late in the school year in 2015 at his Katy office. A reserved man who is much more comfortable running football practice than speaking with reporters, Joseph quickly put me in touch with Johnston. But his succinct description of the building process told me more than the sum of his words. "The biggest thing was the kids learned how to win," Joseph said. "It's easy to talk about winning, but you have to learn how to win, too. First time in '86 we went undefeated in the regular season. It was a big jump. We went from 4–6 in '85 to 10–0 in '86. That was a big, big jump. Mike will tell you that the '85 team lost four games by twelve points or something, real close. I think more than anything else, they were learning how to win."

Katy's building process took place in one of the most talent-concentrated cities in the country, so the Tigers were forged in the fire of intense district and playoff battles before they reached elite status in the later rounds of the playoffs. Houston-area schools like Madison, Lamar, Yates, and Fort Bend Willowridge kept Katy from finding its playoff footing in the late 1980s and early 1990s.

But in 1994, the Tigers broke through. After dropping the season opener versus Klein, Katy churned out nine straight victories to finish the regular season. Another three wins in the playoffs put the Tigers in that prestigious final four with Converse Judson, Plano, and Odessa Permian.

Fans at big-school playoff games in late November will notice a mob of players on each sideline. Most football teams will use about three dozen players in the course of a game, but in those postseason contests, a thriving program might have eighty to more than a hundred kids in uniform on the sideline. A closer examination will reveal that many of the smaller athletes are wearing an alternate version of the jersey and helmet. Those are the freshmen and sophomores brought up for the experience, and to serve as living, breathing, tackling, and blocking dummies.

For Katy, those young players on the sideline were the leaders of the group that would elevate the program to the final frontier. Eric Heitmann, who went on to earn all-Pac 10 and all-American honors at Stanford and play nine seasons for the 49ers, watched the 1994 state championship run as a Katy freshman. After a full career at the highest level of football, Heitmann still looked back at that year as a significant rite of passage. "That was awesome for us," Heitmann said. "When you grow up in Katy, Texas, and all the sudden you're able to stand on the sideline for a varsity football game, that's one of these crazy dream-come-true kind of experiences."

Heitmann played pro football at six-three, 312. By his senior year at Katy, he had grown into an important piece on the Tigers' most fearsome unit. When the 1997 season began, Johnston knew he had an offensive line on which he could build a real contender. Heitmann was joined by center Kevin Sijansky, who went on to Mississippi State and whom Johnston said was the strongest player he ever coached. Tight end Michael de la Torre played at Texas A&M, and guards Emilio Montejano and Peter Wilkening played at Howard Payne and Texas A&M–Commerce, respectively. Tackle Walter Wigfall played high school football at 310 pounds and captured the attitude of the Tigers' offensive line in a brilliant quote from a *Houston Chronicle* story. "We pound on people," Wigfall told sportswriter David Barron. "We pound on people because we're bigger and stronger. We pound people and beat them down. We pound them. Pound, pound, pound."

Johnston said it's the best offensive line he's ever seen in high school football. According to Sijansky, that aptitude grew out of the depth of the program in multiple ways. They learned from the players in front of them, but those older players were too good to let a varsity spot get stolen. So by the 1997 season, the offensive line had been playing together from the sub-varsity squads on up. "I played with the same offensive linemen, the same five guys, pretty much all the way throughout," Sijansky said. "When we got together as seniors that '97 year, we had been playing together as an organized offensive line for at least three years. We had developed a very good knack for playing with each other.

Without even thinking about it, I knew what my guards would do, I knew what the tackles would do. We all worked as one unit."

Katy's strength up front dovetailed with a keen self-awareness of just how good the team could be in 1997. Heitmann and Sijansky were joined as captains by linebacker Rusty Bucy and safety Joaquin Garcia. All four players were entrenched in the program, and had been seen as quality leaders even before their senior season began. So much so that Johnston felt comfortable putting a heavy burden on them.

"I met with all of them in here and I told them then, 'Do you realize if we don't get back to the championship game this year, that there won't be anybody on this campus that knows what it's like to be in the state championship?'" Johnston remembered when I met with him in his old coach's office. "I said, 'All four of you guys were on the sideline as freshmen. If you guys graduate this next year and we don't get back there, there ain't going to be a soul on this campus, a student, that's going to know what it's like.'"

Not only did the captains embrace that challenge, they were actually way ahead of the coach. "We wanted to be the best team to ever come through Katy," Garcia said. "Katy had never won a state championship since any of us had been alive. We wanted to be better than the '94 team. I don't think it was a competition against the state as much as it was a competition against ourselves, a competition against the school, a competition against that '94 team, and so that was the biggest expectation. We were part of the leadership team, so it was our responsibility."

This group of Katy Tigers differed from many of the powerhouses recounted in these pages. The Tigers didn't demolish most of the teams on their schedule, partly because of the high level of competition Katy faced even before the playoffs, and partly because the Tigers didn't have the type of quick-strike offense that can demoralize an opponent quickly. Johnston told me he and his assistant coaches began preaching physical football early on in building the program. They knew they wouldn't be able to outrun opponents very often, but they could slow down the opposition by using their pads and helmets. The Tigers ascended on the strength of that physical, lunch-pail persona.

But one point is eerily similar among players on championship-caliber teams: they remember a particular loss more vividly than many of the victories. Langham Creek handed the Tigers a 20–9 defeat in the second game of the year, and it stung. "We knew we were good, and people told us we were good," Sijansky said. "But that loss—we all kind of took a step back and said, 'We got to go out there every day and every practice, and we've got to work, because nothing's going to be given to us. Unless we have that mind-set, we're going to get beat more than once.' That set our goals and our whole system on track."

Katy went undefeated for the rest of the regular season, claiming a 17–10 win over rival Katy Taylor in the Tigers' closest district game. As is often the case, the first two rounds of the playoffs presented huge challenges: Katy clung to a 17–14 overtime victory in the first round after Alief Elsik missed a field goal attempt.

In the second round, Katy faced Houston Lamar, which had eliminated the Tigers from the postseason in 1996 with a 31–3 thumping. But the Tigers won the rematch 35–12, and it served as a catalyst. "We were the underdogs because they had beaten us so bad the year before," Garcia said. "We knew we had our hands full. The team went out there and got after 'em and beat 'em pretty good. I remember thinking, 'If we can do this against that team . . .' Winning that Lamar game was a huge game."

The barrage of heavyweight opponents kept coming. After Lamar, Katy clashed with Aldine Eisenhower. Though Eisenhower has played in only one state championship game as of this writing, losing to Midland Lee in 1999, the Eagles seemed to be a gatekeeper to greatness in the 1990s. Converse Judson defeated Eisenhower four times to get to the state championship game in the decade, and in 1997 it was Katy's turn to clear that hurdle.

The Tigers met Eisenhower in the state quarterfinals. "That was almost like our state championship right there," Heitmann said. "It was probably the toughest team we played all year." The players described the Katy-Eisenhower game to me as a slugfest where the two teams exchanged epic drives. Sijansky said it felt like the kind of low-scoring affair in which the last team with the ball would win it.

Katy forced Eisenhower to punt for the first time with 9:13 left in the fourth quarter, allowing the Tigers to set up a drive from their forty-five-yard line. From there, Katy marched fifty-five yards in twelve plays. The *Houston Chronicle* reported that the Tigers ran behind Bronston Carroll on the drive, just as they had for much of the afternoon at Rice Stadium. Carroll finished the game with thirty-seven carries for 164 yards. But quarterback Matt Gore finished the go-ahead drive with a two-yard run on an option keeper, giving Katy a 20–13 lead with 3:04 left.

Eisenhower had time to respond. That set up Bucy's most crucial play of the season. The Eagles marched inside the Katy thirty, but on second-and-six from the Tigers' twenty-four, Bucy stripped the ball from Eisenhower quarterback

Jeremy Denson. Robbie McDaniel grabbed the loose ball for Katy, allowing the Tigers to run out the clock and preserve the win.

The way Katy went ahead and then held on to that quarterfinal win epitomized the character of the team—power football on offense complemented by a play-making defense. It was appropriate then that Bucy, who went on to play at Texas Tech, came up with the clincher. "Rusty was everywhere," Heitmann said. "He was the most instinctive defensive player that I remember ever playing against. We were very fortunate to have him on our team. Beyond that, he was an amazing leader. As much talk as you hear about the offensive line and the running game, Rusty owned that defense."

Katy eased past a semifinal game in which it was the favorite, claiming a 35–16 victory over San Antonio Taft, and into a state-title tilt in which the Tigers were decidedly not the favorite.

After facing vaunted Plano in the state final in 1994, Katy once again drew a titan in the state final, which pitted it against Longview at the Astrodome. The Lobos were nationally ranked, and supposedly outclassed the Tigers. "They were basically saying we didn't have much of a chance against Longview," Johnston remembered. "They were undefeated, and they had shut out two or three teams in the playoffs. It got our kids fired up now, especially those linemen. They took it upon themselves."

Despite all the games that had come and gone, Heitmann recalled how he felt going into the state championship game. "No one had us picked to win," he said. "By that point in the season, we had been through so much, and we knew how good we were. It was frustrating to see that no one else in the entire state thought we had a chance. It was like, 'Katy will lose this game. Absolutely.'"

Katy went toe-to-toe with the favored Lobos, resulting in a stalemate for much of the first half. Then in the closing minutes of the second quarter, the Tigers began to assert control. Gore capped a fifteen-play, seventy-seven-yard touchdown drive with a one-yard touchdown plunge, giving Katy a 7–3 lead with 2:43 left in the half. After Longview failed to do anything during its final drive of the first half, Katy threw a haymaker. Gore hit wide receiver Mason White for a thirty-seven-yard touchdown with five seconds left before intermission, giving the Tigers a 14–3 lead.

Carroll tacked on a nine-yard touchdown run, and kicker Ryan Nugent booted a thirty-four-yard field goal in the second half. Just like that, Katy toppled heavy favorite Longview 24–3, winning their first state title since 1959.

It was the product of fifteen years of work for Johnston and his assistants, and he walked away with a feeling of supreme satisfaction. "When we left the

Dome that day, it was 24–3, and there wasn't no doubt who had the best team in the state," Johnston said.

Johnston received a little more validation of the team's strength when he met up with Longview coach Robert Bero the following spring. "Robert told me that his kids, they would come off the field and make the comment 'We can't get off the blocks, their blockers are so strong,'" Johnston said. "That was the strength of our team, was the offensive line. They were really dominant. We were just a real solid football team."

Since then, Katy's red Tiger logo on its helmet has become a common sight in mid-December state championship games. A year after winning the 5A Division I championship, the Tigers appeared headed back to the final to face Midland Lee, but an eligibility issue disqualified Katy after the penultimate week of the season. Undeterred, Katy returned to the state final eleven times between 1997 and 2015, winning six more championships.

For Johnston's final act, Katy won the 2003 championship 16–15 over Southlake Carroll. The Tigers were the only team to slay the Dragons during a five-year stretch (2002–2006) when Carroll won four state titles. Joseph took over as the head coach the following season, and as of this writing has returned to the final seven times and won in 2007, 2008, 2012, and 2015.

It's easy to imagine how Heitmann's thrill of standing on the sideline as a freshman in 1994 has grown exponentially for generations of Tigers since then. It's the foundation on which Joseph continues to build the program. "You put a decal on your helmet," Joseph said. "That's a big deal. Even when those kids get moved up for the playoffs, the travel squad, they get decals on their helmets, so now they've arrived."

The second morning I spent at the Katy field house, current players were rewatching the game film from the 2012 championship. It's impossible to enter that building without recognizing Katy's success, but the Tigers seemed to want that taste of a championship to be as palpable as possible. "The first thing—[when] you walked in the field house—you saw was the trophy case," Joseph said. "You've got kids that want to be a part of the program. We have about 140 freshmen come out every year. By the time they're seniors, there's 60-something. Of those 60, all those kids aren't getting to play. It comes down to they want to be a part of something that people are successful at. That, for us, is important, having little kids that grow up and they want to be part of the program, to be Tigers. Here it's still important."

When putting together the prospective pieces of this book, I didn't have a specific idea for Katy, though I thought Cincinnati Bengal quarterback Andy

Dalton might be the subject of a chapter. I knew, though, that Katy had to be included. If there were only ten stories from ten Texas towns, Katy has put itself in that kind of company.

That's why when looking back at that 1994 final four—Converse Judson versus Katy, Plano versus Odessa Permian—the Tigers fit perfectly.

# 27

# MART

## 1999

### *"Cosby Show" Panthers Thrive in Prime Time*

It was a soggy afternoon at Pennington Field in Bedford when the Mart Panthers prepared to meet the Boyd Yellow Jackets for the 1999 Class 2A state championship. It was one of those state championship games that whetted the appetite of lovers of small-town football clashes. In that atmosphere, Mart offensive lineman Jerod King went right up to Coach Terry Cron and pretty much guaranteed a win.

Coach, we got this.

Quincy Cosby realized during the opening kickoff that the Panthers were already in control against vaunted Boyd. His twin brother, Quan, had dreamt about the Mart-Boyd state championship and had a pretty good feeling about how it was going to go. "I dreamed of having exactly the game I had against Boyd," Quan said. "I was like, 'Dude, this is going to be one of my best games ever.'"

The key phrase being "one of." To write about one Quan Cosby game, or even one Mart game, is to ask for trouble.

The Mart Panthers had a lot of those types of games in the late 1990s and early 2000s. Heck, Mart might be the most underrated dynasty in all of Texas, since it's hard to pinpoint a time when Mart wasn't a little powerhouse. The Panthers have won five state titles and have played in the final on four other occasions as of this writing. Cosby estimated that eight or nine of his family members have won state championships as members of the Mart football program. Cosby said that he attended a family reunion just days before I spoke with him at a rooftop coffee bar in Waco. He arrived late and, therefore, missed an hours-long raging debate about whose Mart team was the best.

I had the thrill of covering Mart all the way to the state championship in 2006 and could easily write a chapter on that team. The truth is, whatever Mart team I pick to write about, I'll be starting an argument. So I might as well write about the Mart team I wish I'd had the chance to cover.

Mart's "Cosby Show" compiled a record of 30–1 during the 1999 and 2000 seasons. At the end of the 2000 campaign, high school football fans saw the 2A state championship game we were craving—Mart versus Celina. The Bobcats won it, adding that feather to the cap of their dynasty.

And that leaves the 1999 championship game as the pinnacle of the Cosby Show Panthers. Of course, not every key player on the 1999 Panthers was named Cosby. Cron said Jerod King was perhaps the best blocker he ever coached. A couple of my sportswriter buddies who covered Mart during that era said linebacker–running back John Garrett dominated high school football more than any player they had ever witnessed.

As a whole, the Cosby Show brought the flash and the catchiness that high school football fans recall from the late-night highlight shows. Quan could feel the crescendo coming on before the Boyd game. He envisioned and then executed the kind of unforgettable day that elevated him to earn first-team all-state honors on offense, defense, and special teams. He began by throwing a twenty-two-yard touchdown pass to Adaris Kinsey to give the Panthers the initial lead. By the time he was finished, Quan had added two touchdown runs and an eighty-seven-yard kickoff return that started the second half.

He accounted for 332 of Mart's 453 all-purpose yards as the Panthers defeated Boyd 40–7. Quan's performance prompted Cron to refer to the quarterback–defensive back–kick returner as "my magic man" in the *Waco Tribune-Herald* game story.

Boyd, by the way, was no pushover. The Yellow Jackets entered the game with the same perfect 14–0 record as Mart. Boyd had developed the kind of precision spread offense rarely seen at the 2A level in those days. Yellowjacket quarterback Kaleb Tierce had passed for 2,009 yards and thirty touchdowns going into the state final. His favorite target, six-six wide receiver Brandon Autry, had hauled in a whopping seventy-one receptions for 1,097 yards.

But players can sense pace early in a contest. Quincy Cosby felt it from the very beginning. "This is interesting, that moment I knew that was the opening kickoff," he said. "You could see it in everybody's faces. It was amazing. From the opening kickoff, it felt like we were the Incredible Hulk going against the world."

It was the full-on Cosby Show against Boyd as Quincy scored on a four-yard run and kept Boyd pinned deep in its own end with crafty punting. Then there was Garrett, the decoy on Quan Cosby's eighty-seven-yard kickoff return to start the second half. Let that settle in: Boyd was concerned enough about Garrett that the Yellow Jackets were duped when Quan took the ball.

My friend David G. Campbell, who covered the game that day for the *Waco Tribune-Herald*, said Garrett had the ability to tackle anyone in his vicinity. And Garrett, playing in his final game at Mart, scored the Panthers' go-ahead touchdown on a one-yard dive. He went on to earn freshman all-American honors at Baylor and started for three seasons for the Bears.

To have two players as extraordinary as Quan Cosby and Garrett on a 2A team goes a long way toward explaining the Panthers' prowess. Even fifteen years later, Cron can't separate the two. "Quan was the fastest kid I ever coached," said Cron, who, it should be noted, also won state championships at Bartlett in 1992 and Commerce in 2001. "John Garrett—between the tackle box, there was nobody that could root him out. In the all-star game, they had him going down on kickoffs and breaking up the wedge, and he almost took out three players in the all-star game. They both were the best at their positions of any kid I've ever coached."

Two or three amazing football players can certainly elevate a team in any classification, but especially when you get smaller than 3A. Those players, who work out together every day, take on a group personality. In speaking with the Cosbys and Cron, it seems the Panthers hungered for hard work and hard hits. "It was like we were bloodthirsty hounds," Quincy said. "That's what we loved to do, and everybody wanted the next big hit. It wasn't just me or Quan—it was everybody. That's how it was at our practices. We had intense practices."

For that reason, Cron knew he had a state champion on his hands. In the months leading up to the 1999 campaign, he told his wife, Leslie, that he would shudder to see the team that could defeat the Panthers.

Mart lost to Brookshire Royal in the state semifinal in 1998. From that point forward, the Panthers made "unfinished business" their battle cry. "With their work ethic and their commitment, especially after losing in the semifinals, the year before to Brookshire Royal, I knew we were going to be tough," Cron said. "You couple that with the way they worked in the off-season. I felt good about it. Going through the spring and the off-season, rain, shine, cold, wet, we went out and did our stuff."

I met with Quan Cosby in the summer of 2014. While there was plenty to unpack about being a Mart Panther, the dramatic moments were harder to define, because there weren't many. Mart scored 789 points in 1999 and won on average by a margin of forty-one.

Quan told me one story that I had to confirm with the other members of the team, since it seemed like folklore. Since no one else rose to their level, the Panthers made a habit of playing harder against themselves than anyone else could. "Coach Cron had to stop it because we were knocking each other out," Quan said. "The only way he stopped us is he took the pads off. If we were in pads, we were going to hit. He had to take our pads off to keep us from competing on that level."

Cron backed up the legend told by the Cosby twins. "We were going to have to lighten up through the course of the season because we definitely needed to stay healthy," Cron said. "They had one way of going, and it was full speed."

Of all the Panthers from that era, Quan Cosby stayed in the sports limelight for the longest. He played four years of minor league baseball for the Anaheim Angels organization and then returned to play college football at Texas. His Longhorn career propelled him to four years in the NFL.

Cosby credits his Mart career with teaching him how to compete, and the state championship win with convincing him he could play at a high level. When a player knows the game can click the way it did at Pennington Field, a new world of confidence opens up for him. "I talk to schools about how football is not a perfect game," Quan said. "But that was as close a thing to it, as far as execution, that I've ever seen. It was insane."

Quan said he learned how to prepare during high school. That helped him perform in the clutch as a pro baseball player. It also had a direct impact on the peak of his Longhorn career. Texas quarterback Colt McCoy hit Cosby for a twenty-six-yard touchdown with sixteen seconds remaining to lift the Horns to a 24–21 victory over Ohio State in the 2009 Fiesta Bowl.

Those are the cold, hard facts. To hear them described in first-person detail and see how Quan's Panther days came back to him in that moment is awe-inspiring. "[The Boyd game] was the reason I was prepared for my senior year when I caught the touchdown versus Ohio State," Quan said. Then he described how the Buckeyes opted to cover him with only a safety over the top: "I watched that defense, and they only did it twice the whole game. The other time, Colt threw it to a freshman. We had a nice little conversation on the sidelines. The next time it came up, with twenty-three seconds left, I was like, 'Are y'all kidding me? Y'all are really going to run this again? All you got is a safety to tackle me?' I looked at Colt, he looked at me, we got a signal, and boom—because of the way we prepared."

Quan recalled his habit throughout his career of taking his playbook home for extra study, looking at it before bed, and, at times, falling asleep on it. It's no wonder, then, that he developed the habit of frequently dreaming of the way big moments would unfold. "I think that's where it all started for me," Cosby said. "I had big games before then, but that was on a different level. From that point on, it catapulted me into actually thinking this DI thing might actually be serious or, even more, maybe one day I can play in the NFL. My last game of my junior year changed my mind-set of where I could possibly go in football."

# 28

# EVERMAN

## 2001-2002

### *Bulldogs Unleash Dominant Streak*

The Everman Bulldogs of the early 2000s expected to win.

They didn't hope to win or will themselves to win. The players I spoke with didn't point to a moment of inspiration or a time when everything came together. They just never knew anything else. "That group of kids, they were pretty self-assured that things were going to go their way," Everman coach Dale Keeling said. "Sometimes to the point where it was like, 'You guys got no clue.'"

Keeling had certainly been around enough good teams to recognize the Bulldogs' confidence and their ability to back it up. Keeling was in middle school when his father, Jimmie Keeling, led the 1968 Lubbock Estacado Matadors to the state championship in the school's first year of playing varsity football (see chapter 6). Keeling, who followed in his father's footsteps as a high school football head coach, arrived in Everman, just south of Interstate 20 on the edge of Fort Worth, in the late 1990s and started building a winner.

I worked in Fort Worth from August 2000 to September 2003 as a freelance writer for the *Star-Telegram*. I looked forward to covering Everman on Friday nights during their heyday. The Bulldogs were top-notch in just about every sport, and Keeling was so accommodating that it made life easy for a cub reporter like me. Ask any sportswriter, and he'll admit it's a whole lot more fun covering a winner than an also-ran.

To that end, it didn't get any better than Everman. The Bulldogs won thirty and lost zero in 2001 and 2002. They added a state championship in basketball in 2003 for good measure. As a matter of fact, Everman won its two games in the state hoops tournament that year by twenty-eight points apiece.

The Bulldogs' 72–44 victory over Tatum in the state basketball final was the final playoff victory for Jonathan Harrell and his teammates after a long run of playing together and winning. "We ran through everybody," Harrell said. "Eighth grade, we went undefeated in everything—basketball, football, and track. We were used to winning. We weren't used to losing."

I spoke with Harrell on the phone in the spring of 2015, and we relived some of those games together. Harrell stood out more than any of the Bulldogs in those days as a playmaking wide receiver on the football team and a smooth swingman on the basketball court.

But when it came time to track down some of those Everman players and talk about those years, it was another former Bulldog who caught my attention. Nick Clark played tight end and defensive line for Everman and went on to play defensive lineman at Texas State. When I spoke with him in the spring of 2015, it wasn't football that was wearing him out. We sat down at an Austin coffee shop the week after South by Southwest, a week after Clark had been run ragged by gigs as an in-demand bassist. Clark is a Renaissance man of the highest order. After a successful football career, he earned bachelor's and master's degrees in mathematics. But at the time of our conversation, he was making a living by making music.

He was the kind of man who looked back at winning high school football games in the way most of us retrospectively view learning our multiplication tables. "Winning was just kind of in our DNA," Clark said. "We didn't know anything about losing. Losing wasn't even in our vocabulary."

Harrell said one of the Bulldogs' middle school coaches told Keeling that the class of 2003 was going to win the coach a state championship. By the beginning of the 2001 season, it was apparent that Everman had its program headed in that direction.

Everman lost a close call in the second round of the playoffs against Wichita Falls in 1999. Then reclassification shifted the Bulldogs from 4A to 3A before the next football season. The new digs suited Everman: it advanced to the 3A Division I semifinals before losing to Abilene Wylie. That was the setup for Harrell, Clark, quarterback Michael Benton, and company going into their junior season in 2001.

The Bulldogs had momentum, talent, and ample confidence, which proved to be well founded from early in the season. Everman got its footing with a season-opening 17–12 victory over an established 4A team from Fort Worth Eastern Hills. The Bulldogs then thrashed back-to-back 4A foes, winning 60–0 over Fort Worth Southwest and 45–14 against Wichita Falls Rider. After a 13–7 overtime win versus 4A Waxahachie, Everman had run through its nondistrict schedule with a 5–0 record that included four wins over bigger schools and a 74–0 walloping of 3A Robinson.

Everman's district slate didn't offer many more chances for the Bulldogs to prove their merit, but it didn't matter much, since they were already ranked number two in the state.

But as has been established in these pages so far, the Texas high school football playoffs are seeded by geography rather than poll hierarchy. Much of the time, maybe most of the time, a championship-bound football team will meet its toughest opponent sometime before the final battle. In Everman's case, it was on a collision course with Forney, the 3A Division II state runner-up the previous season and the top-ranked 3A team in 2001.

Number one and number two, Forney and Everman, each won their play-off openers, setting up the clash at Pennington Field in the second round of the playoffs. I worked every angle I could think of the week before that game, trying to convince my assigning editor, Eric Zarate, that I needed to cover the Everman-Forney game. Instead, the duty went to staff writer Carlos Mendez. Since the pervasiveness of social media was still several years in the future, I didn't have to suffer through the details of what I was missing at Pennington Field until the stories began to emerge early the next week.

For those who aren't able to regularly attend Texas high school football games on Friday nights, let me describe the usual atmosphere as honestly and accurately as possible. In just about every town, folks more or less fill the stadium on the home side, and sometimes a good team will bring a respectable number of fans to populate the visiting stands across the way. The stadiums usually reflect the size of the town, so city schools sometimes share big stadiums, and this can lead to some puny-looking crowds. But as the playoffs progress and the cream rises to the top, big schools draw big crowds in big city stadiums.

Still, rarely do games sell out and pack every seat. Pennington Field, which sits just off of Texas Highway 121 a few miles southwest of the DFW Airport, is a landmark of the Dallas–Fort Worth Metroplex. This game was easy to find, and fans flocked to it, filling the bleachers and spilling out into standing-room-only areas in the end zone and even on the sidelines. "I think Pennington seats 12,000," Keeling said. "Well, they sold 15,000 tickets, and there were people on the sideline. There were people in the end zone. It was just crazy. I had to call timeout in the first quarter to get the security people. I said, 'We can't play anymore until the sidelines are clear.' I looked back, and there's a line of seven women standing on our bench where our kids couldn't even sit down."

As sports fans, we say that great crowds for big games create an electric atmosphere. When it jumps up from there, "crazy" is the only word that fits. "Man, look, when I tell you I've never seen nothing like that before in a high school game—sold the stadium out, they started turning people away after 15,000," Harrell said. "There was so many people there, I seen my friends on the sideline with us. There were people lined up on the back of the end zone on both sides of the field. It was crazy. The atmosphere was the best thing you could ever wish for in high school."

Far from shying away from the moment, the Bulldogs lapped it up. Everman had been starved for a challenge since handling a barrage of 4A opponents in the season's opening stages. Now the challenge was at hand. "It was, 'Ah, cool! We really get to play against some people that it's going to be a big game, a big atmosphere, and everybody is going to be there,'" Clark said.

Everman thrived under the bright lights versus the top-ranked team in 3A. Running back Theo Miller scored on an eight-yard touchdown run, and quarterback Michael Benton kept on a fourth-down option play to score from two yards out, giving the Bulldogs a 14–3 lead at halftime.

Forney was driven by standout running back DaBryan Blanton, who went on to win two Big 12 titles in the 100-meter dash while running for Oklahoma. Blanton had Everman's full attention, but the Bulldogs had the speed to contain him. When Blanton broke loose in the second quarter, Everman cornerback Tremaine Wright crossed the field to run down the Jackrabbit, holding Blanton to a forty-two-yard run that stopped at the Bulldogs' forty-five. Forney managed a field goal on the drive for their only score of the first half. But instead of creating momentum for Forney, the play set the tone for Everman. "He went and, like, hawked him down the field," Clark said about Wright's tackle. "It's DaBryan Blanton. When he gets in the open field, it's out the gate. When Tremaine went and caught him, we were like, 'Ah man, we got this.'"

Everman owned the first half, but Forney pushed back in the third quarter. Blanton, who finished with 158 rushing yards on thirty carries, scored on a thirty-six-yard run to help Forney close the gap to 21–17.

Trailing by four points, the Jackrabbits took the ball a little more than a minute into the fourth quarter and began chiseling away the yards for a potential go-ahead score. Forney patiently picked up first downs until, twenty plays after the drive started, the Jackrabbits had a fourth-and-one at the Everman twenty-yard line with 1:01 left on the clock. Simply put, the huge 3A clash came down to a single play. Everman's moment of truth had arrived. "If they get this first down, we're not going to get the ball back, and they're probably going to score," Keeling said.

Everman deployed Harrell as a playmaker at defensive end during Forney's final drive. Harrell was such a mainstay on offense, and had the perfect body type to play wide receiver, that Mendez referred to Harrell as a defensive back in the second paragraph of his *Star-Telegram* game story.

But there's no doubt Harrell was in the game as a defensive end. "I was in the whole series because it was a crucial point of the game," Harrell said. "They were methodically moving the ball down the field. They kept running at me. They were getting some yards. They were driving on us. That was one of our biggest tests."

In the full-contact chess match of that moment, Harrell knew where he needed to move. "I was just like, 'Man, if they run at me, I'm just going to try to get inside of this tackle and just try to blow the box up,'" Harrell said. "That's all I can do, because they're blocking down on me and double-teaming me. All I can do is try to blow this play up. I wasn't even trying to make the tackle. I was trying to blow the play up."

Sure enough, Forney went up the middle at Harrell, but with fullback Bryson Brown carrying the ball instead of Blanton. "It just so happened that they gave the ball to the fullback on fourth-and-one, and I got inside of that tackle right off the line," Harrell said. "I'm like, 'Wow! I'm in perfect position.' I was already low, so I hit him in his thigh, and that's all it took right there. When I hit him in the thigh, he kind of bounced back a little bit, and the rest of the squad came and jumped on him."

Clark said he remembered Brandon Darden leading the charge as the Bulldogs swallowed up Brown for a two-yard loss. Mendez's story reported that Jonathan's brother Blaine Harrell and Andre' Simon finished off the tackle that preserved the win for Everman. "You couldn't hear anything," Keeling said. "Everybody was standing up. It was one of the most exciting things I've ever been a part of."

The Bulldogs had taken the best shot from the best opponent the 3A ranks had to offer. Getting past Forney launched Everman into the rest of the playoffs.

The Bulldogs smashed their next two opponents, winning 42–0 over Texarkana Pleasant Grove and 36–6 over Perryton. Even the state final at Kyle Field didn't match the fever pitch of the Forney game: Everman defeated Sinton 25–14 for the school's first state title in football.

In 2002, Everman went on a victory lap that mirrored its 2001 run. The second time around, I convinced my editor to let me cover the Everman-Forney rematch at Texas Stadium, which Everman won 21–14. The Bulldogs claimed their second-straight state title by defeating Burnet, led by Stephen McGee and Jordan Shipley, 35–14 at the Alamodome.

Of course, confidence, talent, and accomplishment do not make a person or group immune to vulnerability, even tragedy. The second straight state championship game left a lump in the Everman players' throats. Teammate Corey Fulbright suffered a paralyzing spinal injury in the game.

In a testament to the bond of competition in Texas high school football, the Burnet community joined with Everman in helping Fulbright cope with his injury. So much so that the next season, when Burnet returned to the state championship game to face Gainesville, the Everman team showed up to cheer for the Burnet Bulldogs.

When I spoke with Keeling and the Everman players in 2015, it was clear that Fulbright remained an important part of the Bullodgs' tradition. In the Everman field house, among the photos of former Bulldogs playing college football is a tribute to the one who will remain in a wheelchair for life. Harrell referred to the 2002 season as having Fulbright at the center of it.

Everman stayed relevant among the best programs in their classification, later battling with neighbor Aledo for area supremacy. By the end of the 2015 season, however, the Bulldogs hadn't added another football state title to their trophy case.

Harrell, who played college football at New Mexico, was back in Fort Worth when I spoke with him in the spring of 2015. He said his Bulldog teams and the legends of those days still resonate. "To this day, people still talk about it," Harrell said. "People who I don't even know, they'll find out who I am, what my name is, and they're like, 'You went to Everman. Y'all were like the best team I've ever seen in my life.'"

As I sat in an Austin coffee shop with Clark, I became swept up in conversation with the type of intelligent person who sees complex problems as being easy. Clark said he and his high school teammates expected to win, an attitude he has obviously applied to mathematics I can't begin to understand and to music I only wish I could make. "The common thread that I learned from all of that is, it's cliche, but you can pretty much do anything," Clark said. "There's nothing holding you back as long as you're willing to put in the work to do that, especially if you have the inherent talent for something. It's kind of your purpose in life. Putting the work in is the hard part, and then the stars will just align because you're acting within what you're talented in."

# 29

# ENNIS

## 2001

*Harrells' Lions Come Roaring Back*

Graham Harrell went to the sideline, anxious about what would happen next. The Ennis sophomore quarterback had just scrambled to find Jarvis Woodson for a touchdown, Woodson's first of the season, fourteen games in. But the Lions still trailed Highland Park by a touchdown with half the fourth quarter gone, meaning the Lions' twenty-four-game winning streak was still in trouble.

A couple of minutes earlier, the Scots had taken a 38–24 lead with 8:12 remaining. Harrell, who, according to the *Dallas Morning News*, had woken up with a fever that morning and thrown up before the game, was wobbly for three quarters. It was a dire situation. But in leading the touchdown drive, Harrell indicated that he had found his rhythm. And as defenses from Austin to Minneapolis would find in the coming years, it meant trouble when Harrell found his rhythm.

At that moment, though, Harrell felt a rumble in his gut that didn't have anything to do with whatever had caused him to vomit that morning. A huge Texas Stadium crowd watched the Ennis kickoff team and the Highland Park return squad take the field. Harrell knew the Lions' offense could erase the Scots' edge, only he wasn't in control now. He had to watch with everyone else to see whether the Ennis defense could halt a Highland Park offense that had already piled up more than 400 yards on that Saturday afternoon. "You're going to the sideline feeling pretty helpless," Harrell said. "Man, if we get the ball back, we've got a chance to win this thing. That's the game of football; you've got to play good offense, you've got to play good defense. Now you've got to go get a stop, especially against an offense that has done as well as they had all day."

Throughout his high school and college career, Harrell ran offenses that were feared for their ability to score fast and reel off big chunks of points in a hurry. He had grown up with that mind-set even before he became the Lions' starting quarterback as a sophomore.

Sam Harrell turned to the spread offense, jumping into it wholeheartedly before the turn of the millennium. When Sam and Graham Harrell were simultaneously inducted in the Texas High School Football Hall of Fame in Waco in 2013, the elder Harrell explained his thoughts about the spread to *Waco Tribune-Herald* sports editor Brice Cherry. "We'd had a couple of good years, making the playoffs, but we were always getting beat," Harrell told Cherry. "But whenever we jumped into our up-tempo gun package, nearly every time something good would happen. Finally we said, 'Shoot, we might as well do this all 48 minutes.' . . . It was the perfect fit."

The change vaulted Ennis to the top as the Lions went 14–2 in 2000 and won the Class 4A Division II state championship. Ennis dropped a couple of nondistrict games during that first championship season, but once district play began, the Lions started tearing through opponents. Ennis scored thirty-nine points a game during an eleven-game winning streak to finish 2000. The Lions edged Wichita Falls 23–20 in the state semifinal and defeated West Orange–Stark 38–24 for the title.

As a freshman, Graham Harrell watched that team and eagerly waited for his turn. "He went to the spread full-time to try to get our athletes in space," Graham Harrell said about his dad's decision about the progressive offense. "So that offense had a ton to do with me being able to step in and play because it fit my skill set well."

Handing the reins of an offense to a sophomore in high school, a kid barely old enough to have a driver's license, is a worrisome move. Sam Harrell certainly felt the stress of putting his son in that situation, so the coach went to work overpreparing Graham.

Going into the first game of the 2001 campaign, the Harrells exhaustedly covered all the situations and wrinkles a defense might throw at the Lions' offense. Before sending Graham onto the field for one particular play, Sam Harrell went over the probable coverage the defense would use against Ennis's four vertical routes. "Sure enough, they did exactly the opposite of what I told him," Sam Harrell said. "They rolled to Cover 2 instead of being in Cover 3, and he did exactly what he was supposed to do. He didn't throw it where I told him it was going to be, because that's where he shouldn't have thrown it, and he threw it right where he should've. [Receivers coach Brian Rogers] was standing right next to me. He heard me tell him all that, and he said, 'I think we're going to be all right.'"

Graham Harrell led Ennis to a 21–9 victory over Rowlett in that season opener. Then, whereas the Lions had faltered with losses to Mesquite Poteet and Marshall in 2000, the Graham Harrell–led offense produced a 31–14 win over Poteet and a 45–31 victory against Marshall, going undefeated in nondistrict games. "From then on, he did things over and over as a sophomore that really kind of amazed us," Sam Harrell said.

It helped a lot that Graham Harrell had veteran talent around him. In particular, wide receivers Vincent Marshall and Broderic Jones gave the Lions a pair of ultrareliable playmakers. "When you're in the locker room and you know the team that you have, there are just times when you have that feeling that this is a special team," Graham Harrell said. "After my freshman year, looking at the team we had coming back and knowing I had the opportunity to step in and play, I thought, 'Man, this team has the opportunity to be really good.'"

By the time Ennis had entered the waning minutes against Highland Park, it obviously was a great team. The Lions had won their first thirteen games of the season, and only one of those—the regular-season finale against Waxahachie—had been decided by fewer than ten points. Those thirteen, added to the eleven wins that finished the 2000 season, meant that Ennis had won twenty-four straight. But that streak was in serious danger.

That's when the Lions defense stepped in with a vital contribution. Instead of bending but not breaking, Ennis used the momentum that the offense had created and attacked the Scots. "Our defense fed off of it," Sam Harrell said. "They held them to three-and-out just bang, bang, bang. And our offense was biting at the bit to get back out there."

Now Highland Park was in trouble. Although a two-touchdown lead seems like an enviable position, against a spread offense in the fourth quarter it can be anything but comfortable. The Scots went from the illusion of being in command with a little more than eight minutes left to getting drenched by a tidal wave of momentum with four grueling minutes still left on the clock.

And as usually happens in that situation, it got worse in a hurry. Ennis lined up at its own twenty-seven needing a touchdown to tie the game. Graham Harrell described to me how Vincent Marshall, one of the fastest athletes in the state that year, was better at running a fade route from an inside receiver position than he was on the outside, so the Lions made that formation change to fit the receiver's blazing speed. With Marshall lined up on the inside on that critical play, Harrell took the snap and almost immediately saw a defensive glitch.

"They like blew a coverage," Graham Harrell said. "Their safety didn't play Vincent, and their corner came up on the hitch, and I'm thinking, 'No way!' This is probably our best player on the team. He's not a guy that you just want to ignore, and for some reason on that play they ignored him. It really caught me off guard. Whenever the ball is snapped, it's almost like I'm getting tricked. No way this guy's that open. As soon as he caught it, I started running and celebrating. I knew it was a touchdown, because you're not going to catch him."

Marshall's seventy-three-yard touchdown catch from Harrell tied the game at 38. Though its two-touchdown lead had evaporated quickly, Highland Park could still have the last word.

But sometimes it's hard to get that massive, intangible boulder of momentum to roll the other way. On their ensuing possession, the Scots committed a holding penalty on the first play, which pushed them back to their own eleven. On the next play, Highland Park quarterback Alexander Webb eluded pressure and tried to make something happen at the last second. "He fires it back across his body into the field and throws an interception," Graham Harrell said. "It's the only mistake he made all day, really."

Anthony Jenkins picked off the pass for the Lions. The game story in the *Dallas Morning News* reported that Jenkins fumbled on the return, but free safety Alberto Martinez recovered at the Highland Park eleven.

Ennis wasted a couple of downs, but then Harrell went back to Woodson for a ten-yard gain to the Scots' one. Woodson, a sophomore, made six catches, including at least two vital ones, in the regional final against Highland Park. "That drive and that game kind of set up the rest of his career," Harrell said. Woodson, the sophomore who caught the first touchdown pass of his career in the fourth quarter against Highland Park, went on to catch 192 passes for 3,007 yards and fifty touchdowns in his Ennis career.

With a first-and-goal at the one, Harrell didn't waste any time, diving across for the go-ahead touchdown on first down. Highland Park still had 2:12 remaining and three timeouts, according to the *Dallas Morning News*. But the Ennis defense, which had been gashed for the first three and a half quarters, stood strong at the end and closed the door on the Scots' attempt to rally. The comeback gave the Lions' players on both sides of the ball a feeling of invincibility.

Southlake Carroll tested that momentum on the next Saturday, back at Texas Stadium. The Dragons grabbed a 10–7 lead at halftime as the Lions again struggled to find their rhythm.

Not to worry, though. "You're in a spot where most of the time you're not going to win," Harrell said about the fourth quarter of the Highland Park game. "When you come back and win in that situation, you really feel like, no matter what happens, for some reason we're going to win. It doesn't matter what happens from here on, we're just meant to be."

Harrell opened the second half against Southlake Carroll with a sixty-five-yard touchdown pass to Jones. That touched off another firestorm, and the Lions won the second half 42–7. "Golly, that second half was just boom, boom, boom," Sam Harrell said. "Broderic Jones—we threw a wide-receiver screen to him, a tunnel screen, and he busted it for about sixty-five yards and a touchdown, and then it just seemed like the floodgates opened."

Ennis advanced to the state championship game and skipped the drama in the final, dismissing Bay City 21–0 at the Astrodome.

In the next season, the Texas Stadium magic deserted the Lions as Denton Ryan pulled off an upset of Ennis that made the Ennis–Highland Park game seem humdrum. The Scots, ironically, ended Harrell's career by eliminating Ennis from the playoffs in 2003.

But Harrell's high school football legacy was set. He finished his Ennis career with an astonishing 12,532 passing yards and 167 touchdowns. He graduated as the leading career passer in Texas high school football history. As the spread crept across the landscape, Harrell's eye-popping stats were eventually surpassed. As of this writing, he is fourth in career passing yards and second in touchdowns in the Texas high school record book.

And as mentioned earlier, Sam and Graham Harrell entered the Texas High School Football Hall of Fame together in 2013.

Graham Harrell's legacy didn't end after high school. In fact, the fourth-quarter comeback against Highland Park now seems like a prelude to his best moments at Texas Tech. In the 2006 Insight Bowl, Harrell, a sophomore starter, and the Red Raiders were awful for more than thirty-five minutes of game time, falling behind Minnesota 38–7. But then Harrell ignited. He threw two touchdown passes and ran for another as Texas Tech rallied. Harrell finished with 445 passing yards as the Red Raiders defeated Minnesota 44–41 in overtime.

As a senior in 2008, Harrell orchestrated one of the most memorable game-winning drives in Texas Tech history in a game against top-ranked Texas.

Harrell led the sixth-ranked Red Raiders from their own thirty-eight with 1:29 left to a game-winning touchdown with a tick remaining on the clock. Harrell's twenty-eight-yard touchdown pass to Michael Crabtree for the win might never be surpassed in Red Raider lore. "I think situations like that, fourth-quarter comebacks, became something I expected to do," Harrell said. "I think a lot of that can be traced back to Highland Park. These aren't moments to veer away. These are moments to thrive in, that can set you up for the greatest moments of your career. I think those kind of set the tone for things to come."

# 30

## PALESTINE

### 2002

### *The Call That Changed Adrian Peterson's Path*

It was the first Friday of September 2002 when the best running back in Palestine, Texas, became the best running back in the nation. But for that night to happen, a man sitting in prison, unable to see his son play, had to care enough to make a phone call.

The way Adrian Peterson tells the story, he was floundering the summer before his junior season. Flourishing in track by the end of his sophomore year, he figured that sport might be the way forward for him. Peterson had enjoyed success in football as soon as he stepped on the field as a seven-year-old, but by the beginning of his junior season, he had been bumped around and banged up enough to have some doubt. Peterson played on the varsity squad as a freshman at Palestine Westwood before an injury knocked him out for the season after just a few weeks. He then transferred to Palestine High School and played junior varsity as a sophomore. Going into his junior season, football was low enough on the priority list that he was sleeping in at his mother's house after two-a-days began.

"I kind of got off track and really didn't have my head on right," Peterson said. "I'll never forget talking to my dad, because going to the summer of my junior year, I wasn't going to two-a-days or anything like that. My dad was incarcerated at the time, and I remember him calling early in the morning because he knew what time it was and that I should have been at practice."

When I interviewed Peterson during the Vikings' training camp in Mankato, Minnesota, I wasn't sure whether we would broach the subject of his father.

Of course, I knew the story: how the imprisoned Nelson Peterson wasn't able to see his son play in person until Adrian was a junior at Oklahoma. But Peterson's connection with his father came through as we sat on the back of a golf cart, about thirty yards from droves of adoring Vikings fans.

A few days later, I spoke with Nelson Peterson on the telephone. Peterson went to prison, convicted of money laundering for a cocaine ring, when Adrian was twelve years old. Nelson told me how vital it was for him to stay connected with his son, to do everything he could to raise him despite the separation. On an August morning in 2002, Nelson Peterson was expecting to hear that his son was on the practice field with his teammates.

"His mother's husband answered the phone, and I said, 'Frank, did Adrian go to practice today?'" Nelson Peterson said. "He said, 'Nah, Adrian didn't go to practice. That boy's not doing nothing. He's in the bed in there.'" That struck fear in the father's heart. "I said, 'Get him to the phone,'" Nelson remembered. "He got Adrian up and took him the phone, or Adrian came to the phone, and I said, 'Adrian what are you doing, son?' I said, 'Make this the last time that I call this house and your butt is in bed and you're not at practice.'"

In the years before Nelson Peterson went to prison, he coached his son, so he knew the kind of talent that was growing up before his eyes. That morning, he reached out to his son in the only way available to him: parenting via telephone, encouraging and exhorting his son. "One thing he said to me that I'll never forget was 'Son, you've been doing it for a long time, and I know that you are the best running back in the nation,'" Adrian Peterson said. "'I know you're the best running back in Texas. But you've got to go out there and put in the work and show everybody that you are.' That kind of hit home for me."

Adrian Peterson and his father had a long conversation that day. It ended with the son going into school and making sure he was part of the team. First-year coach Jeff Harrell said he had established a relationship with Peterson, who had qualified for the state track meet as a sophomore in the 100-meter dash, so he was eager to have Peterson ready to go for football. "We were excited about him and thought he could be good," Harrell said. "We didn't know he was going to be as good as he was."

Peterson wasted little time in making an impact. Palestine opened Peterson's junior season by easily defeating Cleveland High School as Peterson continually beat the Indians to the corner for long runs. That season opener, on a late-August night, didn't cause too many ripples. The next week, Palestine faced a tougher test, and a personal challenge for Peterson and his Wildcat teammates.

In 2001, Cornel Thompson had taken over as Palestine's head football coach, but he and several other members of the Wildcats' coaching staff departed the next season for Huntsville, where Thompson became the defensive coordinator. The Palestine players had their say about the matter when the Wildcats played Huntsville on the second Friday night of the season. Peterson took the game personally, wanting to send a message to the departed coach.

The message he sent resonated much farther. Peterson rushed for 338 yards and four touchdowns. He scored on plays of seventy, forty-six, sixty-one, and eighty-eight yards, running past the Hornets and right over them when necessary.

Steve Eudey, Peterson's youth football coach, who played a key role in guiding Peterson when Nelson went to prison, watched from the stands, sitting beside Palestine superintendent Gary Mayo and principal Richard Scoggin. All three felt spurned by the previous coaching staff, yet hopeful of Peterson's and the 2002 team's potential. "The third play of the game, Adrian runs up the middle, runs over the middle linebacker, steps on him on the way to about a seventy-five-yard touchdown," Eudey said. "We whipped them pretty well, and there wasn't anybody happier in that stadium than Gary Mayo and Richard Scoggin and me."

The headline splashed across the sports page of the *Huntsville Item* the morning after Palestine romped over Huntsville 40–12 read "Defense Rests." But there was more to this story than questionable defensive play. Huntsville sports editor Tom Waddill, who covered the game, didn't miss the key story line. Waddill quoted Huntsville head coach Mark Foreman on the subject of Peterson. "He's the real deal," Foreman said. "He's hard to tackle. I didn't know if he'd be able to continue to do that the whole ball game. Apparently he was. We just couldn't tackle him."

Waddill stayed on the angle of the Palestine players, and Peterson specifically, feeling shunned by their previous coaching staff. "They're missing out" was Peterson's most poignant comment in the *Huntsville Item* game story.

When I asked Peterson about unforgettable moments, almost twelve years after that night in Huntsville, he went directly to that game. "The coaches we had previously left Palestine and were like, 'You'll never win there,' and this, that, and the other," Peterson said. "They end up going to Huntsville, and we end up playing them. On the second carry of the game, I broke it."

Earlier, I wrote that Peterson went from being the best running back in Palestine to the best running back in the nation that night. It wasn't an exaggeration for effect. Within days, scouts who had previously seen Peterson perform only at camps were ready to bump him to the top of their lists. "After that game, we began to get a lot more phone calls inquiring," Eudey said.

Less than two weeks after the Huntsville game, Harrell said Texas A&M came forward with the first scholarship offer. That started the avalanche of Peterson's recruitment. Sometime the next summer, Eudey was having breakfast with a writer from *Sports Illustrated* in College Station, where he had taken Adrian for a photo shoot. The writer revealed just how high Peterson had soared in the eyes of scouts. "He said, 'Steve, do you have any idea what's fixing to happen?'" Eudey said, recalling the conversation. "'You know that tomorrow Rivals [Rivals.com, a sports website] is coming out with Adrian as the number one recruit? I said, 'You mean in the state?' I kind of figured he was going to be pretty high. He said, "No, Steve, he's going to be the number one kid in the nation.'"

It was as if the Huntsville game had verified for everyone that Peterson was on track to football stardom.

Peterson finished his junior season with 2,051 rushing yards, twenty-two touchdowns, and 8.3 yards per carry. He upped those numbers to 2,960 yards, thirty-two touchdowns, and 11.7 yards per carry as a senior, despite playing in just eleven games. Peterson dominated the competition to such an extent that his name was bandied about as a talent that could jump from high school to the NFL.

Instead, the six-two, 210-pound running back with track-star speed became a true freshman starter at running back for Oklahoma. Peterson rushed for more than 100 yards in each of his first nine games. He racked up 1,925 yards as a freshman, setting a freshman record with eleven games of more than 100 yards, earned first-team Associated Press all-American honors, and finished second to USC quarterback Matt Leinart in Heisman voting.

Despite foot and collarbone injuries during his sophomore and junior seasons at Oklahoma, Peterson rushed for 4,245 yards, less than 100 yards short of Billy Sims's Sooner career record. That kind of success in the face of adversity has become a theme during Peterson's career. When he suffered a torn ACL and a torn MCL (medial collateral ligament), ending his 2011 season, he came back to start the season opener in 2012 and rushed for 2,097 yards that season, earning the NFL Most Valuable Player Award.

Nelson Peterson attended the Oklahoma–Iowa State game in 2006, his first time to see Adrian play in person since coaching his son in youth football. The media celebrated the supposed reunion. But the truth is, Nelson has remained present throughout his son's life.

When I shook Peterson's hand at the Vikings' camp, I was amazed by the strength in the grip. I remember thinking that I would be shocked if I ever saw him fumble again. That handshake was a trained quality. "I remember him coming to see me one day, and I taught him his handshake that is known around the country now, his firm handshake," Nelson Peterson said. "I told him, you have to be able to look a man in the eye, give him a firm handshake, and introduce yourself: 'I'm Adrian Peterson.' We did that during a prison visit."

Adrian Peterson said that of all the influences around him while he was growing up, his father had the most sway. "I had guidance, but it was like, 'If you want to do it, then do it,'" Peterson said, referring to voices other than his father's. "My dad really pushed me into it. I think about it all the time because I know guys that I played with that had great talent, that could've played college ball, that could have gone off and played professional basketball, that made the decision to stay at home, and now they're still at home in Palestine."

When I spoke with Nelson Peterson, I almost off-handedly asked him how often he makes it to Viking games. He said he hadn't missed one since the Vikings drafted Peterson with the seventh overall pick in 2007. It was clear that he still felt his role was to push Adrian as far as his son could go. "I never wanted Adrian to think that he was so good at an early age that he would settle and stop working," Nelson Peterson said. "I told him, 'You're a pretty good player. But you're only good in Palestine. It's not good enough just to be the best player in Palestine.'"

A few weeks after I spoke with Peterson at the Vikings' camp, and after I had conducted all the interviews for this chapter, Peterson made headlines that began the most tumultuous year of his career. Peterson was indicted for "reckless or negligent injury to a child" in mid-September for disciplining his son with a switch. In November, he pleaded "no contest" to a misdemeanor reckless assault charge.

As Peterson sat out the final fifteen games of the 2014 season, I had dozens of conversations about the controversy. I found the differences of opinion to be dizzying. They ranged from unflinching support for the way Peterson had spanked his son (mostly by people who also had been spanked with switches as children) to unmitigated disapproval of that type of corporal punishment.

Peterson maintained in his statements to the media throughout the ordeal that he loved his son and desperately wanted to be part of the child's life. Having sat outside the Vikings' practice field and listened to Peterson talk about his relationship with his father, I'm convinced that bond has been vitally important in his life. "When I sit back and think about it, I'm able to reflect and go,

'You know what? If he wouldn't have called, would I have not went in?'" Peterson said. "Would I not have been encouraged to get back involved and prove that—You know what? My dad, even though he was incarcerated, he still remembered and knew what I was able to do and what I've done. It just remotivated me."

# GEORGETOWN

## 2002

*Mason Crosby Kicks His Way to the Top*

Like many of us fortunate sons, Mason Crosby's football career began with playing catch with his dad.

Jim Crosby took his kids to Georgetown High School's Eagle Stadium for afternoons of tossing the ball around the big yard. Just Mason and his older sister, Ashley, younger brother Rees, and Jim made up games of football. A couple of years later, the same field would serve as the setting for the movie *Varsity Blues*, which portrayed another kind of made-up football, a flashy, intense, anything-goes version of high school football. Mason, an eighth grader at the time, sat in the stands as an extra for many of the home-field scenes, cheering for the fictional West Canaan Coyotes. But on the afternoons with Mason's dad, brother, and sister, the Crosbys planted the real seeds for a less dramatic but more substantial football career.

It began as just father and kids acting out the roles of quarterback and receivers. For kicks, Jim let Mason try a field goal. "We started kicking because he played a lot of soccer," Jim Crosby said. "We decided, 'Let's do some kicking.' The first time I noticed he had a strong ability for it was when he was ten. I put the ball down, and he kicked a thirty-yard field goal at ten years old. This was just me holding it at the twenty-yard line, and he booted it through, but it was a really nice-looking kick. So after that, we decided every time we went out, we would kick loads of footballs. It was my job to hold it, and we'd race and get the ball and come back and hold it again. We did that literally thousands of times."

Jim Crosby said his son kicked that first thirty-yarder soccer style. The work that followed came from the sheer enjoyment of playing a game, but the payoff was massive.

When I met Mason Crosby in July 2014, I had the thrill of shaking his hand inside the Green Bay Packers' locker room at Lambeau Field as he was preparing to start his eighth season with the team. Crosby's current contract with Green Bay was set to pay him $2.65 million during the 2014 season, and he'd earned it. He had led the NFL in scoring with 141 points as a rookie in 2007 and had scored at least 112 points in each year of his seven-year career when I interviewed him. At that point, Crosby had finished in the top ten in the NFL in scoring five times. That's a thriving pro football career.

So, much like Earl and Tiger Woods with golf clubs and balls, Jim Crosby held footballs for his son for hours and hours during Mason's childhood in the hope of cashing in later in life, right? Not really.

In fact, when Mason Crosby started playing junior high football, he didn't even press the coaches to let him kick. Earl Woods would have marched his son into the coach's office and demanded a kicking audition. Jim Crosby simply asked his son whether he was getting to kick. "I'll take you back to middle school," Mason Crosby said. "I remember coming into seventh grade, and it was just kind of like, 'Yeah, Coach, what do you need me to do?' I remember my dad telling me, 'Tell them you can kick.'"

Crosby was a football player who could kick from the very beginning of his playing days. Sure, he played soccer, but by the time he started as a junior at defensive back and kicker for the Georgetown Eagles, he was anything but a transplant from the soccer team. Crosby was already a football player in junior high, and he became the kicker only after an injury opened a window of opportunity. "They threw out a big guy, a D-lineman or something, and they would just try to power it down there on kickoffs," Crosby remembered. "We didn't actually kick extra points or any field goals. Fast-forward a couple games in, and my dad is still, 'Tell them you can kick.' A guy gets hurt in a game, and it was middle school football, so they hadn't really prepared for who is going to be the backup. The coach is going, 'Who can kick?' So this is my moment. I went out there and kicked a good kickoff. They realized those are good kickoffs, maybe we can try some extra points."

That's Mason Crosby's humble version of the story. His mom, Karen Crosby, remembered a much more promising debut. "His very first kickoff—I mean, in the seventh grade—went in the end zone," Karen Crosby said. "You are now the kicker. And he was the kicker always after that."

When Georgetown head coach Larry Moore met Crosby, he could see and hear the freshman's kicking talent. "When Mason kicked the ball, it sounded different," Moore said. "It was different. He hit it with such speed and power—it was beyond a good kicker. It was explosive. I still remember watching film of our own game, and they filmed some pregame stuff for some reason or another. There were scouts down in the end zone about where the high-jump pit would be. They kept looking back over their shoulders, and we never could figure out what they were looking at. We finally found out they were looking at Mason kicking field goals during pregame. He was kicking the thing clear across the track, back up to the field house. It was just phenomenal."

Moore kept Crosby on the freshman and sophomore teams because he had a decent kicker on the varsity. More importantly, the Eagles needed Crosby to gain experience at defensive back while playing on sub-varsity squads.

But Crosby's talent kicking the football still had plenty of time to shine through. In 2011, Crosby set a Green Bay record for longest field goal with a fifty-eight-yarder against Minnesota. He owned the top five spots in that category in the Packers' record book going into 2014. But none of those kicks surpassed his longest effort as a Georgetown Eagle.

On October 18, 2002, Georgetown played at Cedar Park on a calm night. I asked Jim and Karen Crosby whether it was the kind of night when the wind was howling and a kicked ball might fly forever. They said it wasn't, and Jim pointed out how excessive wind, even at a kicker's back, might make a long kick more difficult.

Cedar Park kicker Chris Price threw down the gauntlet by nailing a fifty-one-yard field goal. Crosby, who had played soccer with Price, would have the chance to top his erstwhile teammate.

Still, the call to try the field goal came as a bit of a surprise. It wasn't until Crosby saw the holder that he realized the coach had called his number for a fifty-nine-yard attempt. "I actually punted also, and I was under the impression that we were going to punt," Crosby said. "I was kind of down away from Coach when he called us out for the field goal, so I'm going out there with the mind-set that we were going to punt. I see my holder and see the big guys, and I think, 'All right,' and kind of reframe my mind. I hit the perfect ball and put it right through."

According to a note in the *Austin American-Statesman* the following week, Crosby's field goal tied him for the fifth longest in Texas high school history. Later on the same night, Jim and Karen Crosby fretted that Moore might want to go after the top spot and send out Mason for a sixty-two-yard attempt.

"Georgetown got stopped, and he had the potential of kicking a sixty-two-yarder at the time," Jim Crosby said. "Coach did the right thing and punted it away. There was probably four or five minutes left. If he had missed it, they would have gotten the ball at the other side of the fifty-yard line."

While the parents in the stands began to contemplate seeing their kicker hit a sixty-plus-yard kick, the Crosbys had mixed emotions. "Would everybody hush," Karen Crosby thought. "That's a long way." Football sense won out, allowing everyone to assume Crosby had the sixty-yarder in him. "If the coach had elected to do that, everybody felt pretty confident he could make it from there, me included," Jim Crosby said. "If it was straight, he could make it."

Such is the case with legends, and Crosby, as much as any player from the state of Texas, has legendary ability and the folklore to go with it. During Crosby's career, his leg caused headaches for the football team's support staff. Crosby would consistently boot footballs through the uprights and into the trees in an adjacent park, sending the ball boys on constant errands to retrieve them. Eventually, the booster club jumped in and raised money to erect a net to catch the field goal attempts. (It should be noted that Georgetown, as the site of the UIL state soccer tournament, saw its share of talented strikers.)

So the net went up, only it couldn't hold Crosby. "When I looked at it, I knew immediately that there's no way it's going to control any of his kicks," Moore said. "I told him, 'Just kind of punch this into the netting for the booster club. We really appreciate what they've done.' He said, 'Sure, sure.' He got back to the forty-yard line, and I said, 'Go ahead and kick one.' He kicked it over the dang net from there too."

Crosby's favorite kicking story came coupled with his prowess as a defensive back. After intercepting a pass and taking it to the house, Crosby fired off what he thought was an innocuous celebration, but it turned out to be the kind that makes life more difficult for the kicker. "I think I spiked the ball," Crosby said. "It was somewhat unintentional. I meant to spike the ball, but I think there was a guy on the ground, and I spiked it, and it was basically on him. They made me kick the extra point a little bit longer. Honestly, I was pretty winded. I was tired from the play, but I focused in and fortunately made the kick. That was kind of cool, scoring all the points on one play."

Crosby's kicking attracted the attention of both Texas coach Mack Brown and Colorado coach Gary Barnett, who saw Crosby personally shut down a Buffalo recruiting camp by putting on an impromptu kicking exhibition. That same day, Barnett offered Crosby a full-ride scholarship, trumping Texas's offer of preferred-walk-on status. So Crosby went on to kick ultralong field goals in the Rocky Mountains.

Then the Packers drafted Crosby in the sixth round of the 2007 NFL draft. In 2011, he kicked a twenty-three-yard field goal for the final points scored in the Packers' 31–25 victory over the Pittsburgh Steelers in Super Bowl XLV.

Of course, all that turned the Crosby family into the most passionate bunch of Packer fans in Central Texas. I met with Jim and Karen at a deli in Georgetown just before Green Bay's preseason game against the Oakland Raiders in 2014. They were decked out in their green and gold, ready to watch the game on TV.

In the parents' enjoyment of telling the high school stories, I could see the evolution from a dad holding a ball on the twenty-yard line for his ten-year-old to mom and dad in the stands. Professional-football parents aren't that different from their high school versions. "We love the Packers, we love being Packers fans, our family loves it," Karen Crosby said. "But we're Mason's mom and dad first. When we're at games and people say stuff, it's like, 'We're Mom and Dad. This is our child out there.' Those other boys out there are our son's friends and teammates. It feels the same even at the Packers level as it did in high school."

With all due respect to *Varsity Blues*, the true story from Georgetown—the one in which the elementary school kid goes from kicking field goals at Eagle Stadium to doing the same thing at Lambeau Field—is straighter and truer every time.

# 32

# SOUTHLAKE

## 2002

### The Carroll Dragons' Ascent

Southlake Carroll's ascension to the absolute top of the Class 5A elite was just about dead in the water before it ever really began.

Carroll, of course, proved to be the gold standard for high school football in Texas in the 2000s. The Dragons lost just one game from 2002 to 2006, going 79–1 and claiming four state championships in that span, also known as the Todd Dodge era. Carroll's only loss in five seasons came against fellow 5A power Katy, which grasped a 16–15 win over the Dragons in the state title game in 2003. During the decade of the 2000s, Southlake Carroll was synonymous with "the team to beat."

But the first of those title seasons fell into serious jeopardy in the state semifinals. Playing at a packed Waco ISD Stadium in December 2002, the defending state champion Lufkin Panthers began to assert control. After leading 20–14 at halftime, Lufkin upped its advantage to 30–14 midway through the third quarter when juggernaut sophomore running back Jorvorskie Lane scored on a thirty-two-yard run. It looked bad for the Dragons.

Carroll reached the desperation point with three minutes left in the third quarter when Dodge elected to go for it on a fourth-and-one from the Dragons' own thirty-eight.

Instead of converting, Lufkin swarmed Carroll quarterback Chase Wasson for a four-yard loss. When I spoke with Wasson more than twelve years later, he recalled the sinking in his gut after being stopped on that fourth-down play. "I still remember this to this day. I went to the sideline obviously pretty dejected,"

Wasson said. "I sat on the bench, obviously head down. Like most high school students, [the Carroll fans] weren't probably as fired up about us not getting the first down for many reasons, so we were getting our own crowd ripping us."

The Panthers took the ball away on downs, and with Lane in their backfield, they were well equipped to run out the clock on the Dragons' season. "The thoughts in my head were, 'Wow! What a great season we've had,'" Dodge said. "What am I going to say to these kids when the game's over? Those thoughts start coming into your mind. The very next play, they get the ball back. They run a boot throwback post to try to stick the knife in us, and we pick it."

Lufkin's Terrance Parks threw the pass, and Christian Merritt intercepted it to give Carroll new life late in the third quarter. That's all it took for the fire-breathing Dragons to ignite.

Dodge knew his team needed a spark, so despite facing a rabid Lufkin defense and coming off a fourth-down failure, the Carroll coach decided it was time to go big or go home. "We got the ball back, and Coach Dodge dialed up. We called it 60 Box High," Wasson said. "A lot of people don't remember this, but that game the wind was one of those swirling winds, and that stadium, when the wind starts swirling, it's ridiculous. I'm thinking in my head, 'I don't know if I've got a forty-yard post in my arm with this wind.' But we got the coverage we wanted. Andrew [Hansen] broke over the top, and it really sparked us for that next run."

Wasson hit Hansen for a thirty-five-yard touchdown to cut the Panthers' lead to ten points, so the Dragons lined up for a two-point try. On the play, Wasson, the 2002 5A Offensive Player of the Year, planned to hit future NFL tight end Scott Chandler on a quick slant. But the Panthers aggressively took away that option, so Wasson improvised and found Chase Daniel, a future 5A Offensive Player of the Year and NFL quarterback, who played receiver for Carroll as a sophomore that season. "I'm sure they said they pressed [Chandler] pretty good, but more or less they mauled him at the line, so that took away what we wanted to do," Wasson said. "I scrambled around trying to find a few guys. I saw Chase Daniel in the middle of the end zone. I kind of jumped and threw it and heard the crowd roaring and knew he caught it, and that kind of gave us some more momentum."

For Carroll, momentum meant moving at maximum speed at all times. Dodge was the head coach at Austin Westlake when I chatted with him on a golf cart at Roy Kizer Golf Course in the spring of 2015. He explained to me how a logistical change before the 2002 season had made a huge impact on the Carroll program.

The Dragons established themselves among the Texas elite as a 3A school in the late 1980s and early 1990s, winning state championships in 1988, 1992, and 1993 under Coach Bob Ledbetter. As the Dallas–Forth Worth metroplex began to rapidly expand at the end of the millennium, Carroll quickly outgrew its small-town roots. The Dragons, who moved up to 4A in 1994, experienced only middling success for the rest of the decade. Dodge took over in 2000. In two seasons under Dodge in 4A, the Dragons notched a 19–10 record before getting bumped up in classification to 5A.

Dodge could sense that the ascension from 3A to 5A in less than a decade had made the Southlake community uneasy, but instead of panicking, he found a wrinkle. "We'd always been a little enamored with the no-huddle stuff," Dodge said. "I never was a guy that wanted to just do things off video. So we took a trip to Murfreesboro, Tennessee, to Middle Tennessee [State University]. Larry Fedora was the offensive coordinator there at the time. When we made the trip, he'd already gone to Florida, but he said, 'Go on. There's an old fellow there named Coach Robinson, that's our quarterback coach, and he will give you everything you need.' We went and spent four days. I told the guys, 'I don't want a concept, a screen. I don't want a run concept. All we want to do is talk about your no-huddle communication, how you do it.'"

Carroll wide receiver Tre Sellari told me the Dragons took to the new system immediately. He said that for the receivers, it was both relaxing and empowering to be able to run a deep route then jog to the line of scrimmage without having to get to the huddle, then line up and do it again.

Dodge said Carroll didn't change anything except how plays were called as the team shifted to no-huddle. "We're running the same offense we had," he said. "Just now we're doing it with hand signals and tempo, and we lit into the 2002 season."

Carroll unleashed its offense on an unsuspecting district in 5A. The Dragons posted a 63–7 win over Flower Mound Marcus, a 56–10 thrashing of Flower Mound, and a 52–14 victory against Lewisville to set the tone in district play. This was not the 3A power of a decade earlier, nor was it the better-than-average 4A program of recent days. These Dragons, who were ripping through their 5A district, were clearly a different breed.

Then came the playoffs. Carroll had won its share of games in blowouts throughout its dynasty run, including a 41–17 win over powerhouse Abilene Cooper in the third round of the playoffs in 2002. But for the two weeks after the Cooper win, the Dragons worked via the comeback. When the rally began against Lufkin, it was built partially on the experience of a week earlier.

Carroll played another DFW mainstay, Arlington High School, in the fourth round of the playoffs. As Dodge and Arlington coach Mickey Finley scrambled to find a site for their matchup, they finally agreed to flip home-and-home. Carroll won the chance to play in Dragon Stadium, and the Dragons and Colts fans were so ready for the postseason clash that they showed up en masse very early on that Friday evening. "That's the best home-crowd environment that's probably ever been to a Southlake game, because it was the fourth round of the playoffs," Wasson said. "There weren't any other teams around the Metroplex playing, so I remember [that] as high school seniors, we pulled up at the stadium probably three, four hours before game time, and you couldn't even get a seat at that point. It was an electric atmosphere. It was electric at probably five o'clock, and we didn't kick off until seven-thirty."

Once Arlington finally kicked off, it asserted itself. Colt quarterback Joe Jon Finley threw three touchdown passes to lead his team to a 27–21 halftime lead. Though Arlington led by only six points, Dodge and the players had the sense that they were on the verge of a very bad home loss. Wasson told me the Colts physically dominated the game, especially in the first and second quarters.

But Dodge gave the Dragons two choices: be embarrassed at home or come back. Carroll chose the second route. "We realized that playing at home is something, especially at Southlake, that there's a lot of pride at stake," Wasson said. "When we took the field that second half, it was pretty special, because everything that we were maybe a hair off in the first half, everything clicked. The one thing I would say was special about that year was that offense, defense, special teams, scout team guys—everyone bought into the overall mission."

Wasson began the scoring in the second half with a twenty-nine-yard touchdown pass to Hansen, igniting a third-quarter rally. The Dragons scored seventeen unanswered points in the third, taking control of the contest. The Carroll defense allowed only six points in the second half on the way to a 52–33 win.

When a no-huddle spread offense finds its rhythm, it's often very bad news for the opponent. That was the case for Arlington when the Dragons got it going, and Lufkin faced the same monster in the state semifinals after Wasson once again hit Hansen for a touchdown and then found Daniel for the two-point conversion.

Still ahead by eight points, Lufkin took the ball near the end of the third quarter and attempted to power its way down the field while running off as much clock as possible. The Panthers successfully drained more than six minutes from the time remaining, but it wasn't nearly enough. Carroll eventually forced a punt and regained possession at its forty-two with 6:17 left.

Wasson engineered a twelve-play drive that included one of the more memorable plays in Dragon history. Lufkin forced Carroll into a fourth-and-six situation, a play that might have decided the outcome of the game if the Panthers made one more stop.

Wasson said the Carroll coaches sent in several options for the play call, but he knew he wanted to go to Chandler. "We ended up with another isolation route with Scotty," Wasson remembered. "They mauled him on that side, took him out of the equation. My second option was Andrew Hansen, and he was tangled up with his guy. And then out of the corner of my eye I saw Tre Sellari kind of flash and wrapping around this middle backer, that basically he looked wide open. I just lofted it over the middle, didn't even see the other outside backer. Hindsight 20/20, probably should have never made the throw."

Sellari, who went on to play college baseball at Hardin-Simmons, had to react on the fly to keep the Dragons' season alive. "He threw it, and all I remember is this linebacker cut right in front of me," Sellari said. "He did what every defensive guy does: 'Here comes the ball. I might as well try to intercept it.' Nobody's thinking, 'Hey, it's fourth down. Just knock it down.' He tries to make a play. It hit him in the chest or the arms, he tried to catch it, it popped up, and I swear it felt like the ball was just floating in the air. All I remember doing was diving, and the next thing I knew I was holding the ball up in the air, and the ref was saying completed catch, first down. It was really one of those things almost like a car crash. It slows down just enough where you can tell what's going on, and before you know it, it was over."

After Sellari's catch, Chandler untangled himself from the Panthers' defense long enough to catch a nine-yard, fade-route touchdown from Wasson. Hansen caught the two-point conversion pass to tie the game at 30 with 2:33 left.

Pressed for time, Lufkin tried for a quick answer. Instead, Carroll cornerback Aron Morgan came up with a play that he's been arguing with his teammates about ever since.

All his buddies say that Morgan "probably couldn't catch a cold" and that the ball must have just stuck to his gloves. But Morgan intercepted a Parks pass near the fifty-yard line and began sprinting toward the Panthers' goal line. "I just read his eyes, and I just jumped the route, and off I went, going down the sideline," Morgan said. "A couple of things I want to make a point about. One: No one blocked for me on my team. I should have had a cavalry because it was on the back side, and I ran by two or three of my own guys who were not blocking for me. Two: The cramp. No one believes me. Halfway through the return, I felt a cramp coming. I say this because I ended up running track in college, so I'm pretty prideful on speed. The thing that still pisses me off still today is the receiver on the other side of the field is the one that tackled me. He clearly was booking."

Even so, the interception return gave Carroll the ball at the Lufkin two. That set up kicker Garrett Hartley for an eighteen-yard game-winning field goal, which the future NFL kicker put through the uprights. Left with only forty-four seconds, Lufkin couldn't answer, allowing the Dragons to celebrate a thrilling 33–30 win.

As I sat on a golf cart with Dodge in 2015, listening to him describe the drama that unfolded against Lufkin at Waco ISD Stadium was almost as exciting as being there. "There are certain ones that you absolutely feel like it was yesterday," Dodge said. "In the game against Arlington High, I can remember the situation more than I can remember all the plays. I can remember specifically the plays and who made the plays in the Lufkin game."

Carroll advanced to play Smithson Valley in the state championship game. One of the teams was guaranteed to make history as the first to step up to 5A and win a state championship in its first season at that level.

It was Carroll. And then it was Carroll at or near the top of the 5A heap for the next decade. As mentioned, Wasson was named the 5A Offensive Player of the Year, a tradition that would be carried on by his successors Daniel, Greg McElroy, and Riley Dodge.

The Dragons added the school's eighth state championship when Kenny Hill passed for two touchdowns and ran for two more in a title-game victory over Fort Bend Hightower in 2011.

The thing about origin stories is that there's only one way to interpret them. There's no alternate universe in which the Arlington Colts turn back Carroll's second-half rally or Lufkin turns to Lane to salt away a state-semifinal victory. We have the reality in which Sellari made the fourth-down catch, Morgan came up with the catch of his life, and Hartley kicked the game-winning field goal.

So those Dragons claim a unique place in Texas high school football history. "It changed the entire mentality of what it meant to be a Carroll Dragon," Wasson said. "I still take pride in that today: the swagger and just the edge that when the opponent looks over and they know they're facing Southlake, mentally they're fourteen points behind. That's kind of the mentality we all played with. Southlake is a really cool place in that they honor the past. It gives an opportunity for these up-and-comers to look at the wall and see what was before them and kind of what the expectation is. I think that's what transcends into always making that place special."

# 33

# TUSCOLA

## 2003

### *McCoys Lead Jim Ned to the Brink*

Brad McCoy likes to remember the first pass his son Colt ever threw in a real, live-action, full-pads football game.

Not a proponent of youth-league tackle football—and at any rate, not living in a big city where it was readily available—McCoy was the head coach at Tuscola Jim Ned, and he was watching the seventh-grade team play the first time he saw his son under center.

Colt McCoy, already in training to be a field general, glanced over to check the coverage on Cam Holson, who, at six-two with good speed, was the Dez Bryant of West Texas seventh-grade football. McCoy liked what he saw from the Albany defense and was already envisioning Holson open on a fly route. "I'll never forget. Colt threw the ball—I don't know, he probably threw it forty yards in the air and hit Cam in stride for about an eighty-yard touchdown," Brad McCoy said. "I was watching those kids from Albany, those seventh graders. They all just kind of stopped. They're watching the flight of the ball like 'What is that?' We kind of looked at each other after the first play of their seventh-grade year, after they threw a touchdown, and were like, 'Okay, this may be a lot of fun before it's over.'"

I watched Colt McCoy throwing touchdown passes and pumping his fist in excitement during a relatively mundane Washington Redskin practice in June 2015. Though more than fifteen years had passed since McCoy hit Holson on a deep route versus Albany Junior High, the quarterback's enthusiasm for the game hadn't waned. A little while later, sitting on a couch outside the Redskins' locker room, I asked him about that first touchdown pass in the seventh grade. "I remember a lot of touchdowns to Cam Holson," McCoy said with a friendly smile.

McCoy started for his dad for three seasons, winning thirty-four games and losing just two as the starting quarterback of the Tuscola Jim Ned Indians. A few years later, when McCoy became the winningest quarterback in University of Texas history and led the Longhorns into the BCS National Championship Game, it was hard to fathom that he came from a tiny town in West Texas. It was almost too much like mythology.

But to McCoy, it was perfectly logical. "You can't replicate it. You really can't—it's impossible," McCoy said. "I would never trade anything for the way that I grew up, going to a small school, being from a small town. Those bonds that I had in high school with my teammates and coaches, I don't think that I'll ever have something as strong as that in sports."

McCoy started at quarterback and safety as a sophomore for the Indians and helped them win their first seven games of the 2002 season. But in the eighth game, McCoy came up to tackle standout Bangs running back Jacoby Jones, and the collision cost Jim Ned. A concussion knocked McCoy out of action for the rest of that game and the next one. The Indians lost to Bangs and fell again with McCoy out of action the next week versus the Winters Blizzards, freezing Jim Ned out of the playoffs.

We'll never know how much that one tackle altered football in Texas. Brad McCoy told me his oldest son was a fantastic defensive player. R. C. Slocum saw a young Colt McCoy at a Texas A&M summer camp and said the kid might be the best safety for his age in the country. But Jim Ned needed a quarterback too badly to let McCoy go looking for people to hit.

Brad McCoy said Colt's sophomore season was the last time he played defense. It worked out, though, since the Indians had strong junior and senior classes, which made for plenty of depth on the roster going into 2003. And they were motivated. "We kind of had a sour taste in our mouths and were looking forward to our junior year," McCoy said. "From the beginning, we were just really looking forward to the season, because we felt like it ended the wrong way for us."

The Indians missed McCoy's presence on defense, but still won a shootout with Wall 48–40 to start 2003. Jim Ned found its rhythm after that, rolling through the next three games with three-touchdown victories and then the three after that by more than fifty points each. That set up a rematch against Bangs, with McCoy and Jones taking center stage.

Both McCoy and Jones will likely make it into the Texas High School Football Hall of Fame. Jones finished his career at Bangs with 7,889 yards and 101 touchdowns. After getting the better of the matchup between Jim Ned and Bangs in 2002, Jones tried to steal the show again in 2003. Jones ran for 308 yards and the *Brownwood Bulletin*'s game story emphasized that the Dragons had the edge in most statistical categories.

But McCoy was too efficient, completing fourteen of twenty-one passes for 201 yards and three touchdowns. Indian running back Terry Smith pitched in with 160 rushing yards and scored three times, including a sixty-yard romp that gave Jim Ned the initial lead.

The Indians walked away with a 58–38 victory over Bangs and the certainty that they would make the playoffs this time around. For good measure, though, Jim Ned pounded Winters the next week 75–0 and then finished a 10–0 regular season by easing past San Saba.

Jim Ned didn't have to wait long to test its playoff mettle. The Indians went into the playoffs ranked number seven in the Associated Press 2A poll. After skating through the first round of the playoffs, the Indians met sixth-ranked Jacksboro.

There's something about expecting to win a state championship and setting the bar that high that turns good teams into tenacious ones. Although Jacksboro wasn't a usual contender for a state title in the early 2000s, Brad McCoy told me the 2003 team had a collection of seven or eight players whose fathers had played on Jacksboro's state championship teams from 1962 and 1971. Like Jim Ned, the Tigers entered the game with a perfect 11–0 record, determined that their season would not end on that Saturday afternoon at Brownwood's Gordon Wood Stadium.

Jacksboro opened the game exactly according to script, running off fifteen plays and more than six minutes of game time. That kept McCoy and the prolific Indian offense on the sideline.

But in the second quarter, that old go-to weapon came into play. Just as he did in the seventh grade, McCoy looked Holson's way and liked the coverage he saw. Holson liked the vibe too. "I was sprinting from the other side of the field and I looked at Colt," Holson told *Abilene Reporter-News* reporter Joshua Parrott. "We've been best friends and grown up together, it was like he knew I was there. I guess that's what comes from playing five years together." McCoy hit Holson for a sixty-yard touchdown pass that tied the game with 3:17 left before halftime.

After that, the clash became a war of attrition. The *Reporter-News*'s game story credited Smith with sixty-nine rushing yards, a somewhat pedestrian total. But that afternoon, they were difference-making yards. He ran for touchdowns of two and twenty-five yards, the only two scores of the second half for either team. Jim Ned wide receiver Chase Cook caught five passes, but his real contribution came on defense, where he intercepted two passes to stymie the Tigers' offense.

The Indians had been lighting up the scoreboard all season, but they were able to switch gears to beat Jacksboro. "We weren't used to beating people 21–7," Colt McCoy said. "But to be able to have the poise and the confidence and beat a team and kind of grind it out, that was big for us. We did have a lot of confidence after that game."

Brad McCoy told me that beating Jacksboro was a big hurdle to clear, and it gave Jim Ned the momentum to ascend to the state championship game. The next week, the Indians thumped Maypearl 35–10. Smith had been subtly great against Jacksboro, but he was blatantly brilliant versus Maypearl, rushing for 302 yards and all five touchdowns.

Jim Ned advanced to play Shallowater in the state semifinals, and the winning continued before that game even started. The two teams agreed to flip a coin for the right to choose a neutral site. Brad McCoy won the toss, so the Mustangs traveled to Abilene to play Jim Ned at Shotwell Stadium.

Maybe it was the close-to-home venue or the ride they were on, but the Indians clicked against Shallowater. Jim Ned's offensive weapons complemented each other as well as they had all season, or maybe even better. McCoy passed for 297 yards and threw touchdown passes to Smith, Holson, and Justin O'Dell. He also ran for eighty-four yards and touchdowns of thirty-five and two yards. Smith gained 142 rushing yards, and Holson hauled in four passes for 155 yards. Jim Ned led 36–7 at the end of the third quarter and left Shotwell with a 43–21 victory. "It was just one of those nights where the ball went our way, and it was kind of a landslide for them," Brad McCoy said. "By that time of the year, our defense had really risen up. It was one of those nights where it just all came together."

For many state championship combatants, reaching the final is a gradual process. They knock on the door for a couple of years before breaking through. Jim Ned went from a late-season slide that left them out of the playoffs in 2002 to the championship game in 2003. The pieces came together quickly and convincingly.

But at least one factor went against the Indians leading up to the state final. Brad McCoy said he's jealous of the format that took effect a few years later in which all the state championship games, 1A through 6A, are played in the same location. The Indians hoped to play San Augustine at Texas Stadium in a semi-climate-controlled environment, but it was already booked. So Jim Ned faced the Wolves at Lion Memorial Stadium in Ennis on a cold mid-December night. Brad McCoy remembered that the game-time temperature was eighteen degrees.

The Indians struck first when McCoy threw a seven-yard touchdown pass to John Starnes early in the second quarter. But Jim Ned's chances to crank up its usually prolific offense took a hit when McCoy inadvertently smacked a helmet with his throwing hand. He said his thumb was jammed. Brad McCoy told me it was broken. Colt battled through the injury, but the pain and the cold made gripping the football extremely difficult.

With the Indians limited on offense, San Augustine charged. The Wolves tied the score before halftime on quarterback Brandon Sharp's sixty-yard touchdown pass to Dominique Edison. San Augustine running back Tydrick Davis scored three touchdowns in the second half, and the Wolves' defense shut out Jim Ned in the final two quarters to claim a 28–7 victory.

When it was over, Brad McCoy shook hands and offered his congratulations, then turned to find his son. "Colt was just distraught at the end of the game, on the field on his knees and in tears," Brad McCoy said. "I got to him, and of course it was emotional for all of us. When I finally got to him, I couldn't settle him down. I said, 'Hey, let's go. We'll get over it. It's a game, blah, blah, blah.' He looked at me with teary eyes and said, 'I don't know how. I've never been here before. I don't know how to do this.'"

Brad McCoy thought about his son's words and realized that his seventh-, eighth-, and ninth-grade teams had gone undefeated. The Indians' two defeats at the end of the 2002 season came after Colt was sidelined with a concussion. His first loss came on the biggest stage possible for a 2A high school football player. "It was hard," Colt McCoy said. "We all took it hard. It took us about three weeks to get ready to play basketball, we were so hacked off that we lost the game."

That's what makes Colt McCoy one of the athletes worthy of holding up as an ideal. For him, it was a group hurt, and it required a group effort for the Indians to pick themselves up and pursue another championship. Somehow, he ascended to stardom in college and success in the NFL while maintaining the soft-spoken guilelessness more common in small-town high school players than among well-paid professionals.

As we sat on the couch outside the Redskins' locker room, McCoy wanted to talk more about his experience as a five-sport athlete in high school than anything else. He played basketball, golf, and tennis and ran track, and said all of them played a role in his development. When the Indians finally recovered from losing the football state final, they bounced back and claimed a district title in basketball.

Jim Ned followed up their state final run in 2003 by winning the first twelve games of 2004, though they fell to Canadian in the quarterfinals. But the Indians still played for a championship that school year. Holson and McCoy led a talented basketball team to the state tournament.

Holson scored twenty-five points and grabbed thirteen rebounds, and McCoy had twelve points and a pair of assists in Jim Ned's state-semifinal win. The Kountze Lions beat the Indians in the final, even though Holson poured in thirty-three points and McCoy added eighteen.

McCoy went on to win forty-five games as the starting quarterback at Texas. The Longhorns claimed a Big 12 championship and victories in the Fiesta, Holiday, and Alamo bowl games during that run. As a pro, McCoy showed he could command an NFL offense when he led the Redskins to a 20–17 overtime victory at Dallas in the 2014 season, one of Washington's few bright spots in that campaign.

There are many guys who would take that success and forget about their high school days. But not many guys are Colt McCoy. "That [2003 Jim Ned] team had a bond that I wouldn't change for anything," McCoy said. "We were so close. We trusted each other. We had fun. It was just small-town football that if you didn't play it, you don't know about it. That camaraderie that we all had was pretty amazing."

# 34

# CRAWFORD

## 2004

### *Pirates Put the President on Hold*

The red phone is a reasonable place to begin the story of the 2004 Crawford Pirates.

It's astounding, the combination of intricate pieces that fell into place to cause that red phone to be sitting in the middle of the locker room at Birdville Stadium when the Pirates arrived for the Class 2A state championship game against Troup. For example, the president of the United States, who hailed from Texas, carried enough state pride to want to establish his Texas ranch as his favorite office away from the White House. George W. Bush's ranch happened to be near the 2A town of Crawford. For their part, the Pirates happened to have a strong football team led by a stellar collection of seniors who were closely enough connected with football to have served as ball boys for the Pirates ten years earlier, when Crawford fell in the state championship game. And that football savvy came into play as the Pirates overcame a gauntlet of obstacles to reach the state championship game again, this time at Birdville Stadium that evening.

In fact, Crawford entered the final game of the season with a perfect record, 15–0. They derailed mighty Celina's fifty-four-game winning streak as a Class 2A program along the way. During the week leading up to the championship game, the Secret Service asked Crawford coach Robert Murphy to give President Bush a chance to speak with the team. Murphy told the president he could deliver his message during the Friday pep rally. "You don't tell the president no," Murphy said. "It kind of caught me off guard. I said, 'Can I get back to you on this?' I go and visit with the principal, and we think about it. I don't have my mind on that. I've got my mind on how to stop Troup and score touchdowns. We decide the more people we could get involved in this experience, the better it would be. We decided he was going to speak to the pep rally."

But unseating dynasties and advising the president of the team's availability—and the red telephone—followed the most dramatic moment for Crawford.

Four weeks earlier in the second round of the playoffs, the Pirates found themselves trailing Cisco by two touchdowns with less than nine minutes remaining at Tarleton State's Memorial Stadium in Stephenville. Murphy was wondering whether basketball coach Clark Moore would want to begin hoops practice the next day or wait until Monday.

He wasn't the only one. Running back–linebacker Derek Dumas had to give himself a stern pep talk for having the exact same inner monologue. "In the second quarter, I remember wondering if we were going to have basketball practice on Monday," Dumas said. "I quickly snapped out of that. I scolded myself for thinking that."

Dumas described the Crawford-Cisco game as a boxing match in which Cisco landed the first punch and continued to hit hard throughout while the Pirates attempted to fight their way back. That's how the Lobos gained a 17–3 edge as the clock ticked down in the fourth quarter.

Besides leading on the scoreboard, Cisco kept Crawford from gaining a momentum foothold by staying a step ahead of the Pirates. The game's flow came as a bit of a surprise to the Crawford players, who remembered slightly underestimating Cisco. "One of the things that may have given you a false sense of confidence was that they had lost to Hamilton earlier in the year," said Lee Murphy, the quarterback and coach's son. "We had beaten Hamilton the year before pretty good."

By the fourth quarter, the Pirates were ready to admit having made a mistake in their calculations. Crawford's chances were running out, partly because the Lobos had an answer for everything the Pirates attempted. "If we blinked, they knew what we were going to do," Murphy said. "We were so predictable. If it's third down and we're on this hash mark, we're going over here."

So Coach Murphy walked over to offensive coordinator Delbert Kelm and made the suggestion that turned the tide. "We're on the left hash mark, right in front of our bench, 'Let's throw 38 Convoy back into the boundary,'" Murphy said. "Sure enough, they had everybody on the wide side of the field. When Dumas caught the ball, it was basically, 'Just don't trip and fall.'"

Lee Murphy saw the same thing once he eluded a bit of pressure and let go of the ball. "It set up about as perfectly as you could," he said. "The linemen went downfield and got the blocks that they needed to, and it was kind of off to the races from there. That worked, and thank goodness it did."

But Dumas remembers an entirely different scenario. As the running back making the catch, he said that waiting for the play to set up felt like running in quicksand. "It did not look good at all," Dumas said. "Then I remembered it's kind of set up like that. It's not supposed to look good. All the sudden, you see a couple of our linemen get out there and kind of cross my face and chop down a couple of the guys, and it's just the perfect tunnel. It's exactly how the play is supposed to work, but it didn't look good at the beginning. That play is made in the first three or four steps."

Dumas took the screen pass fifty-eight yards for the touchdown that began to turn the tide. Murphy called for a fake on the extra point, wanting to take advantage of the momentum, but running back B. J. Christian had a run-pass option on a halfback pass and threw incomplete. The Pirates still trailed 17–9 with less than half of the fourth quarter remaining.

Cisco, having run the ball right at Crawford with success all night, continued to make life difficult for the Crawford defense. The Lobos marched into Crawford territory past the forty-yard line before they finally faced a fourth-and-six from the Pirates' thirty-six.

I should mention here that I was covering the ball game for the *Waco Tribune-Herald*. My dad, who lives just down the road from Stephenville in Granbury, spotted for me that night. In the press box, a *Dallas Morning News* stringer sat to my left. My dad sat to my right, and to his right sat Grady West, the father of Cisco coach Brent West. Of all the stories in this book, this is the only one for which I saw the key game in person, and it's the most memorable game I've ever covered. What happened next is a huge reason why.

Dumas said that earlier in his career he probably would have been more focused on his specific assignment on the pivotal play. Cisco went for it on fourth down, and Lobo quarterback Jason Ballinger dropped back to pass and then scrambled to his right. Dumas, having seen the running back in the backfield, knew it was his job to cover that man. But he waited, and when the back broke out of his blocking position to run an impromptu pass pattern, Dumas jumped the route. "We learned a long time ago: don't coach caution into your kids," Murphy said. "Sometimes you just have to play the play. That's what Dumas did. See it and go get it."

The running back stumbled and Ballinger's pass floated. "The ball is up in the air, and it's honestly the best break on the ball I've been able to get at any level," Dumas said. He intercepted the pass at the line of scrimmage, and none of the Lobos were in position to catch him. "The first couple of steps, I was leaning so far forward that I almost got ahead of myself," Dumas said. "My body almost got a little faster than my feet."

Dumas scored on a sixty-four-yard interception return, and the Lobos incurred a penalty for unsportsmanlike conduct, helping Crawford add the two-point conversion, which tied the score at 17.

In the press box, the *Dallas Morning News* stringer roundly criticized the Cisco coach's decision to go for it on fourth-and-six from the Pirates' thirty-six. As Dumas raced toward the Lobos' end zone, and in the seconds that followed, the writer foolishly went on and on, berating the Cisco coach within arm's reach of the man's father.

Eventually, Grady West had had enough. He rose from his chair and awkwardly shuffled toward the reporter. I can still see the scarlet grimace on the man's face. It was clear that West was using every ounce of restraint he could access to keep from pummeling the bespectacled writer. The old coach's anger spewed out of his mouth as he pronounced his intention to inflict punishment. The moment was so surreal that I can't recall the coach's exact words. My dad said he remembers West moving toward the writer and repeating the phrase "I'm going to hurt you!"

I stared in amazement, but not disbelief. In my view, West was within his rights to punch the reporter at least once. But West's better judgment won out. He sat back down and seconds later opted to leave the press box. In the wake of it all, the reporter made some remark about the insanity of the moment. I replied that it was the man's son down there, so he wasn't going to have a sense of humor about it.

On the field, the momentum clearly shifted to Crawford. But as Dumas said, Cisco continued to punch away. The Lobos connected on a sweep pass, and linebacker Sam Moody had to make a touchdown-saving tackle. Cisco's last-second field goal attempt missed, sending the game to overtime.

Both teams scored touchdowns in the first overtime period, and the game went into double overtime tied 24–24.

Cisco had been a difficult stop for the Crawford defense all night, methodically chewing up yards. But in the second overtime, Crawford defensive end Andrew Judy sacked Ballinger on a third-and-eight play from the Pirates' thirteen. Cisco's field goal attempt missed, meaning Crawford needed only a field goal to win.

The Pirates conservatively moved into position, setting up kicker Shawn Fulwider for the twenty-four-yard game winner. Crawford advanced 27–24. In the postgame interview beneath the goalposts, Coach Murphy had a sense of what his team had just accomplished. "You've got to win a game like this to go all the way," he said.

In the weeks that followed, Murphy repeated on several occasions that he believed his team won the state championship that night in Stephenville. Almost ten years later, we relived the moment while sitting in the Coffee Shop Cafe in McGregor. Murphy said he's slightly augmented that sentiment. He believes that to win a state title, you have to win a game you probably shouldn't have won, or defeat a team you probably shouldn't have been able to beat.

The Pirates went on to defeat a series of tradition-rich programs—Cooper, Canadian, Celina, and Troup—to win the state championship, but they were never pressed to desperation as they were against Cisco.

"I don't think a large majority of the people following us other than maybe you perhaps realized that that was the state championship," Lee Murphy said. "Cisco was the second-best team in the state in 2A that year." I reported on the Pirates' entire run to the state championship, covering all six playoff games. I remember two moments more than any other—Dumas's interception return and another instance in Sweetwater's Mustang Bowl when Murphy rambled on about a disagreement we had regarding our all-area team. Finally, I told him, "Coach, I have to write a story and drive home." Murphy is the most interesting coach I've ever covered, high school or college, because of his combination of old-school practices and his desire to analyze the game. They say baseball is a "talking sport," but I would rather chat about football with Murphy than talk baseball with just about anyone.

People more important than I apparently felt the same way. The president wanted to congratulate Murphy on the team's state championship after Crawford dismissed Troup 28–14. But the Crawford community celebrated the victory for so long on the Birdville Stadium turf that Murphy missed the call. "When we finally got off the field, the guy that was in charge of the dressing room, he came up to me," Murphy said. "He said, 'That phone was ringing over there, and I went over and answered it, and they said it was the White House. They wanted to talk to the head coach.'"

President Bush finally made contact with Murphy and the Pirates when he returned to his Crawford ranch that Christmas. The players and coaches presented the president and First Lady with Pirate jerseys with numbers 43 and 1. "The first thing he said to me was, 'I tried to call you after the game, and you wouldn't get off the field and answer the phone,'" Murphy remembers. "We put him on hold, I guess."

# 35

## ABILENE

### 2004

*Wylie Wins First Crown on Final Play*

The ritual had almost nothing to do with football.

It didn't help the Abilene Wylie Bulldogs get in better condition for the looming state championship game. It didn't make the Bulldogs more familiar with their opponent, the Cuero Gobblers. It didn't sharpen their instincts on the plays they had been running all season, nor did it add a new wrinkle.

But it stuck, and it made a difference. Wylie quarterback Case Keenum looked back at the 2004 season more than a decade later and remembered one afternoon of practice more vividly than anything else. Bulldog coach Hugh Sandifer gathered his troops and took a moment to reinforce team unity. One by one, each of the Wylie players was singled out. His teammates chanted his name in rapid succession, followed by three rapid claps.

Chase Browning, Chase Browning, Chase Browning. Clap, clap, clap.

Michael Kiger, Michael Kiger, Michael Kiger. Clap, clap, clap.

Case Keenum, Case Keenum, Case Keenum. Clap, clap, clap.

Jared Robertson, Jared Robertson, Jared Robertson. Clap, clap, clap.

Tyler Driskill, Tyler Driskill, Tyler Driskill. Clap, clap, clap.

"We don't do that a lot, but we do it kind of to show you the power of your team," Wylie coach Hugh Sandifer said. "One of the big things, one of the sayings we have is 'You're never out there alone on the field.' It kind of reiterates that everybody on the team has a role, and everybody on the team has the same responsibilities, the same importance. When you hear sixty guys chanting your name back to you, it kind of gets you pumped up."

By that time, Wylie had been battle-tested by a stellar 3A schedule and had made it through four rounds of the playoffs. The Bulldogs had one more huge test in front of them, the top-ranked Gobblers, and Sandifer perhaps sensed that his team would need every last player to contribute in order to win a state championship.

In 2004, Wylie yet again had the pieces to be a serious contender for the 3A state title. The Bulldogs were already in the conversation. They lost to Gatesville in the state final in 2000. In 2002, Wylie lost in the second round of the playoffs to Everman, the defending and eventual state champion. Then in 2003, the Bulldogs returned the favor by defeating Everman in the third round, but fell the following week against Gainesville.

All that served to tell Wylie that it was in line for a championship. In addition to that mentality, the Bulldogs had a top-notch running back in Kiger, a ruthless defensive lineman in Robertson, a big target in six-five receiver Josh Archer, and Keenum at quarterback.

As long as there is football, there will be quarterbacks coming out of Texas and making names for themselves on the college and NFL stage. But the early 2000s seem to have been the golden age of the Texas QB prospect as spread offenses popped up and thrived all over the state. The list that includes Kevin Kolb from Stephenville, Matt Stafford from Highland Park, Robert Griffin from Copperas Cove, Colt McCoy from Tuscola Jim Ned, Chase Wasson, Chase Daniel, Greg McElroy and Riley Dodge from Southlake Carroll, Graham Harrell from Ennis, and Andy Dalton from Katy also includes Keenum.

In fact, Keenum ascended after high school like few others. At Houston, he passed for more than 5,600 yards in 2009 and 2011, so far the only player to do that twice in college football. He threw a career-record 155 touchdown passes. Of course, that helped him get branded as a system quarterback, and NFL teams passed on him in the draft in 2012. But he signed with the Houston Texans, played on the practice squad for a year, and then started eight games for the Texans in 2013.

When I spoke with Keenum in the spring of 2015, he was on the move. After starting two games at the end of the Texans' season in 2014, Keenum was headed to St. Louis to begin his fourth season in the NFL. A couple of our plans to talk fell through, partly because of his busy schedule and partly because he wanted to get reacquainted with his high school football scrapbook before the interview. When he finally called me, he gave a humble but sincere description of the 2004 Bulldogs without putting himself at the center of their success. "Going back and looking at stuff, we were kind of that boring team that our defense was so freaking good that we just stopped everybody," Keenum said. "We had a couple of guys on offense that could play."

That perspective certainly has merit, especially since Wylie wasn't in the forefront of the spread-offense charge. The Bulldogs won nine games and advanced to the state semifinals in 2003 despite scoring more than thirty-five points only once. Wylie's quarterfinal win over Snyder that season best reflected the Bulldogs' modus operandi: they knocked off the rival Tigers 18–6.

The meat-and-potatoes style contrasted with the more common mode of the time, particularly when Sandifer and the Bulldogs took on a couple of the state's most prolific offenses in their 2004 nondistrict schedule. Wylie couldn't control the tempo the way it wanted at that point, and it resulted in a couple of losses. Aledo edged the Bulldogs 42–28 in the third week of the season. Three weeks after that, Decatur slammed Wylie 44–7.

Though the Bulldogs took their lumps in those two games, Sandifer could tell his team still had plenty of fight in it. In the postgame huddle at Decatur, instead of ripping the troops, Sandifer set the bar high. "It was their homecoming," Sandifer said. "They're going nuts. Our guys were pretty down. I could see it, really down. So I challenged our guys that night at the Decatur field. I pointed over to Decatur. I said, 'That team will be playing in week thirteen. Now our challenge is to make sure we're their opponent.'"

In the moments following a thirty-seven-point loss, that no doubt seemed like a fantasy. "Those guys looked at me like, 'These guys just beat us unmercifully,'" Sandifer said. "We knew we were better than the way we played, but we also knew that Decatur was really, really good. That's our opponent in week thirteen. Our job's to get there."

To do that, Wylie had to survive another gauntlet in district play. Wylie, Sweetwater, and Snyder all looked at the district championship trophy as if winning it were their birthright. Sweetwater had won the 4A state championship in 1985, the pinnacle for a program that has fielded contenders in football since the days when Sammy Baugh was slinging the ball around the field for the Mustangs in the 1930s. A few miles down Highway 84, Snyder had yet to reach the state's highest postseason achievements, but the Tigers still had a legacy. Grant Teaff came from there, as did Sonny Cumbie. Snyder ultimately claimed bragging rights among the District 4-3A triumvirate in 2004, sort of.

Wylie, Sweetwater, and Snyder finished in a deadlocked three-way tie that season. Wylie narrowly defeated Sweetwater 13–7, but Snyder knocked off the Bulldogs 27–23. Sweetwater claimed a 35–25 victory over Snyder, so all three programs went 1–1 against the other two. But Snyder had the final say, defeating Sweetwater 21–20 in the 3A Division II Region I final. The Tigers fell the next week to Gilmer, the eventual state champion, but since they had defeated both Wylie and Sweetwater, they unofficially broke the district tie.

Wylie avoided the whole Sweetwater-Snyder melee in the playoffs, since the Bulldogs went into the 3A big-school bracket. As Sandifer predicted, that put them on a collision course with Decatur. After Wylie won its second-round playoff game against Canyon, and Decatur edged Gainesville, they were set to meet again.

The rematch took place at Memorial Stadium in Stephenville. Decatur entered with a 12–0 record and a number two state ranking. Eagle quarterback Chandler Dane had thrown forty-seven touchdown passes already that season, and Decatur was scoring more than fifty points a game, according to *Abilene Reporter-News* sportswriter Troy Shockley's advance story about the game.

But Wylie had been on a mission to flip the script from their nondistrict meeting ever since that painful night in October, and the Bulldogs' offense took the fight to Decatur in the first half. Kiger scored the game's first points on a thirteen-yard run, and Keenum lunged across the goal line for a one-yard touchdown that put Wylie ahead 14–0 late in the second quarter.

The Bulldogs' defense held Decatur to a field goal on the final play of the first half and held back an Eagle surge in the second half. Dane threw a twenty-one-yard touchdown pass to Jonathan Jones with four minutes left in the third quarter, cutting Wylie's lead to 14–13. But on Decatur's final offensive series, the Bulldogs made the plays they needed. The Wylie defensive line sacked Dane, and defensive backs Brady Bounds and Josh Poorman each batted away Dane passes. Poorman's deflection, which came on fourth down, allowed Wylie to take the ball and run out the clock. The Bulldogs had avenged a 44–7 loss with a 14–13 victory. "I can't say enough about the defense," Keenum told the *Reporter-News*. "This was really a defensive game, and those guys came through again."

By surviving the week-thirteen clash with the Eagles, Wylie advanced to the state semifinals, where they dispensed with Royse City 28–0. Sandifer told me that his team was a far stretch from the state's top ten, but for the second time in three weeks, the Bulldogs earned the right to face a team at the top of those rankings. Wylie met number one Cuero in the state final.

Thus, the emphasis on team unity and the importance of every player at the special roll call during championship week. Beyond that, Sandifer had to convince his players that they could carry away the championship trophy. "I remember telling the guys when we played Cuero, 'We've just got to beat 'em one time, so let's make sure we have our best shot at it that Friday night,'" Sandifer said.

Wylie faced off with the Gobblers at Floyd Casey Stadium in Waco. The Bulldogs forced the tempo they wanted, taking a 7–6 lead to halftime, but Cuero took the lead late in the third quarter with a touchdown and a two-point conversion.

Keenum, a junior in 2004, was still a few years from being deployed as the uber-prolific arm at the helm of the Houston Cougars' offense. He completed seven passes in fifteen attempts for ninety-eight yards against Cuero. But with the Bulldogs trailing 14–7 in the fourth quarter, Keenum threw a dart. He hit Archer for a twenty-five-yard touchdown pass, zipping the ball past a Cuero defensive back who went for the interception and into the big receiver's arms.

The focus then turned to the Wylie defense, which was thrown into a dire situation deep in its own territory. The Gobblers forced a turnover on a botched punt to take over at the Wylie fourteen-yard line, but the Bulldogs' defense rose to the challenge.

Robertson sacked Cuero quarterback Matt Schumacher, and the Bulldogs front snuffed out two more running plays. The Gobblers surrendered five more yards on a delay-of-game penalty, forcing them into fourth-and-nineteen from the Wylie twenty-three. Schumacher's fourth-down pass fell incomplete, giving Keenum and company a chance to break the tie with time running out in the fourth quarter.

The Bulldogs quickly moved into Cuero territory at the 48, but then stalled a bit. The Gobblers forced Wylie into a third-and-eleven with less than a minute remaining. That set the stage for the biggest play in Keenum's high school career. Sandifer said that earlier in the game, Keenum reacted to a Cuero blitz by hitting Archer for a big gain. The Gobblers gave the same look again on the critical third-down play. "This time, Case was able to take off and ran and got to the sideline to make the first down," Sandifer said. "I think everybody on both teams thought he was getting ready to go out of bounds, or get hit and go out of bounds, and then he turns it back up and got us down inside the ten-yard line."

Keenum escaped the grasp of Cuero defensive end J. T. Rudd, freeing the Wylie quarterback to make the deciding scramble. Keenum told me he ended up being close friends and roommates with Rudd at Houston. When the subject of bragging rights came up in their residence, all Keenum had to do was set his state championship ring on the table.

Wylie ran the ball once on first-and-goal from the Cuero nine-yard line and then called timeout with 4.6 seconds left. At that point, Keenum had to be held back from taking the game into his own hands, or onto his own foot, as the situation dictated. "I wanted to go kick it," Keenum said. "I had actually kicked some at the beginning of the year and made one and shanked, like, three."

Keenum had yielded the kicking duties to Driskill, a backup offensive tackle and a toe-punch kicker, earlier in the year. Driskill had proved himself to San-difer throughout the season, so Driskill got the call. Sitting in his office when I spoke to him more than ten years later, Sandifer chuckled at the idea of mak-ing that decision in the dramatic moments of that game, despite the fact that Keenum had got them there and had made a forty-seven-yard field goal early in the season. Sandifer said that, to him, the straight-on approach of Driskill was the safe and smart play, and he never doubted that the kicker would make it. Sandifer was more adamant about not giving Cuero any chance to respond.

It all came together. "As soon as I kicked it, I saw the ball going through the goal posts," Driskill told the *Reporter-News*. "I knew it was good." Driskill's twenty-five-yard game winner went through with no time left on the clock and sent the Wylie sideline and their fans into euphoric celebration. "It was pretty much pandemonium," Sandifer said. "It took us a while before we ever shook hands. That's one of the highest highs, to win a state championship on the last play of the game. But it's also, on the flip side of that, it's one of the lowest lows. I understood that because we'd been there. In 2000, we lost within the last couple minutes of the state championship game after having the lead. We were trying to be very respectful. It was people running everywhere, people coming out of the bleachers, jumping over the wall there at Baylor."

The *Reporter-News* described Kiger's reaction of looking out at the field, dumbfounded and overcome by what had just happened. The senior running back had been Wylie's go-to offensive weapon for most of the season. Keenum rushed for 128 yards to lead the Bulldogs in the championship game, but Kiger pitched in 72 yards. The local paper chose to see the state-title victory through Kiger's eyes. "It had to process there for a bit," Kiger told the *Reporter-News*. "But pretty quick, it hit me so hard. We just won state."

Some of the fans running around the Floyd Casey Stadium field were shirt-less seventh graders who would become the next Wylie football players to reach the state championship game. Sandifer pointed that out when we talked about the lasting effects of the championship. Keenum, of course, took his knack for making the right play at the right time to stardom in college and an NFL career. But when Sandifer looks back at the 2004 championship, he thinks most fondly about what it did for all the people who came before that team, some of whom were on the field as well.

"Our coaches had been together for a long time," Sandifer said. "I was think-ing how neat that was that we got to experience that. But the thing that kind of got me emotional pretty quick after that was all the guys that had played before that, like the 2000 team that didn't get to experience that. That was for them. [The 2004 team] was an extension of those guys. To this day, that's what we talk about. You're not the first one that's ever worn this jersey. That hit me."

Wylie Bulldogs, Wylie Bulldogs, Wylie Bulldogs. Clap, clap, clap.

# 36

# HIGHLAND PARK

## 2005

### *Scots Prevail in Epic Battle*

Some of the stories in this collection happened in far-flung stadiums in moments that might have flown under the radar had it not been for the transcendent personalities that brought them to light.

But the story of the 2005 matchup between Highland Park and Stephenville does not fit in the "untold" category. In fact, it almost had to be *the* game of the 2005 season in Texas. In any year of high school football, you might get a game like this one: two storied programs led by bona fide star quarterbacks playing so late in the playoffs, so close to the state championship game, that it was no stretch to assume it was the de facto 4A title match.

Stephenville rolled in with quarterback Jevan Snead (committed to the University of Texas) and the war cry "Win 5" boldly emblazoned on the front of their jerseys. The Yellow Jackets won four state championships in seven seasons under Art Briles, but they were starving for a fifth, and their first one after Briles had departed for the college ranks. In the way stood the nation's top-rated quarterback prospect, Matthew Stafford, and the Highland Park Scots. If you were an alumnus of either school, you cleared your schedule to be at the game. If you were a fan of high school football, you considered the possibility of dedicating a Saturday to driving up to Fouts Field in Denton to see it.

When I was preparing, in a Chicago hotel room, to interview Stafford at the Detroit Lions' camp before the beginning of the 2014 season, I had already landed on the Stephenville state semifinal as the moment that Stafford would likely want to recall. That's when I found a ten-minute highlight video of the game in question. As I let it play and let the volume of the crowd and the sound of the Stephenville fans' ball-bearing-filled propane tanks fill the hotel room, I was enveloped by the feel of playoff football. The video wasn't narrated or subtitled, but that wasn't required. It was clear that a special game was playing out on my computer screen.

As expected, it was the game that Stafford spoke about, losing himself in the details to escape from one of those dog days of summer football practice. "It was just such a tight game and such a big win, and the way the state championship happened, you can't help but think that was the one we had to win to get it done, and we did," Stafford said.

Stafford showed that day in 2005 why he's the type of quarterback whom, when he drops back to pass, the opposing fans hold their collective breath. He broke the Stephenville fans' hearts that afternoon in Denton when he threw a seven-yard touchdown pass to Holt Martin with thirty-seven seconds left to lift the Scots to a 41–38 victory.

Yeah, it was that type of game.

After speaking with Highland Park coach Randy Allen and several members of that 2005 Highland Park team, I've come to understand Stafford's place among the Scots. Sure, he was a highly touted quarterback. Wide receiver John Dickenson told me the guys were in the fourth grade the first time they saw him throw the ball the length of the field (it was a forty-yard track, but still), so they had known for a long time that he would be a star. But Stafford was one of a group of driven players, and just part of the picture that day.

In fact, the man with the real insight into the drama of that particular football game was John Dickenson's twin brother, Charley. In the state championship game, Charley Dickenson returned a punt forty-nine yards for the final touchdown of the Scots' undefeated season as they dusted Marshall 59–0 for the state title. John and Charley Dickenson were Highland Park's two starting inside receivers, which, in a spread offense, means they were legit playmaking studs as a matter of necessity. But as I interviewed Stafford and Highland Park coach Randy Allen, they mentioned a fumble late in the fourth quarter when the Scots were trying to score the winning touchdown. They casually avoided mentioning the name of the player who fumbled. I wondered whom they were protecting.

Then John Dickenson, recapping the same sequence, let the cat out of the bag with the phrase "my brother fumbled." He suggested maybe I shouldn't include that detail. But to leave it out would be to leave out the greatness of Charley's perspective. "I'd like to never talk about that play again," Charley said, laughing a little when I told him I figured out who fumbled. "But I'll gladly shed some light on what happened."

Despite the fact that Highland Park raced to a 27–10 first-half lead, Stephenville charged back in the second half and took a 38–34 lead when running back Dallas Neal darted ninety-four yards for a touchdown with 8:07 left.

Highland Park then took over, looking for a score to take back the lead. Stafford saw an opportunity to pick up a first down on a route known as a "crawfish." Charley Dickenson caught the ball and fought for a few extra, Wes Welker–esque yards. "I had gotten away with, like, a swim move when you're carrying the ball," Dickenson said. "You kind of stop, and once you approach the defender, you kind of swing the ball over their head. And I had gotten away with it all year. This time, the ball hit the top of the linebacker's helmet. The feeling was as if I had just gotten gut-punched."

The Highland Park offense slumped off the field. Stephenville took over with 4:12 left and the chance to run out the clock. In the defensive huddle, the Scots knew there was no time to outsmart the Yellow Jackets. "I remember sitting on the sidelines after the fumble happened, and there was nothing left to do or say," Highland Park free safety John Callahan said. "Our coaches were just like, 'Guys, we've got to get a stop.' I remember running out and thinking I have to do something."

So Callahan, who would go on to start for Princeton for three years and then go to China to launch a career in international business, stepped in and saved the day for Highland Park.

Stephenville, unsure of its ability to run for first downs against the Scots, opted to try to get one through the air. On second-and-eight from his own twenty-three, Snead looked for wide receiver Brent McElfresh. "I remember thinking I need to get inside leverage on him in case he does run a slant," Callahan said. "I have to help outside too, but that's a harder throw. The ball is snapped, and it's kind of a blur, but I was lucky enough to see the kind of play and hop in front and get the interception. He kind of had one hand on it, and I pulled it away from him."

A few feet away, outside linebacker Fred Rowsey witnessed just how clever a play his teammate and buddy made. "I saw [Snead] throw the ball, and I kind of broke to the inside to try to get involved in the play if [the receiver] made the catch. And I saw John step right in front of the receiver and intercept it," Rowsey said. "They both had their hands on the ball. It was a battle as they went down to the ground, but John came up with it, which was awesome."

In the plays between his fumble and Callahan's interception, Charley Dickenson began visualizing a punt return for a touchdown. "My first reaction was a feeling that I've never felt before, and the second feeling was 'How can I correct this? How can I make up for this?'" Dickenson said.

Of course, he's glad he never got the chance. "Luckily, fortunately, John Callahan made an unbelievable play when they chose to pass the ball," Charley Dickenson said. "He came up with the ball, and it's almost like it never happened. I had a huge burden lifted off my shoulders."

In the seconds following Callahan making the right read and the play, the Scots' outlook went from blurry doubt to total confidence. Stafford took the offense back on the field to start at the Stephenville thirty-two, all the players knowing they could move in for the kill.

Almost ten years later, while sitting in a corner of the Lions' facility in Allen Park, Michigan, Stafford recalled the exact attitude he and his teammates felt. "We had all the confidence in the world because we had moved it on them all day," Stafford said. "It was just getting it down there and punching it in. When we got out there on offense, it was go time."

Highland Park coach Randy Allen actually had a bit of concern that his offense would score too quickly and give Stephenville too much time to answer. "Our goal was to score with as little time left on the clock as possible," Allen said. "If we scored on a big play, so be it. But it was more of a drive. We ran the ball quite a bit on that drive, and we got down to about the seven-yard line going in to score."

At that point, Holt Martin entered the game. Martin was perhaps Stafford's favorite target, according to Charley Dickenson. Martin had been an outside receiver who could be counted on to make clutch, drive-extending catches. But after suffering a midseason injury, he had yet to catch a pass in the playoffs.

That drought ended with 37.7 seconds left in the fourth quarter when Stafford hit Martin on a slant for the winning touchdown "It happened to be the junior's turn to play, but he knew it was Holt's last chance to redeem himself," John Dickenson said. "So he let Holt go in, and then Holt came in and caught the game-winning touchdown. It was pretty cool for it to end like that."

The Highland Park defense stifled Stephenville's desperate attempt to score in the final thirty seconds. When Snead's final pass fell to the turf with 0:00 showing, the Scots' entire bench emptied onto the field. The student body was close behind. "A lot of people thought that was the state championship game," Allen said. "Both crowds were tremendous. It was a packed stadium, and everybody was into the game. After the game was finally decided, our student body stormed the field. It was just a great atmosphere to play a high school football game."

According to the conventional wisdom, a team that wins so dramatically might struggle to get back up emotionally for the following game. With that in mind, Allen pulled the captains together after the Stephenville game, before he set off to scout the other semifinal matchup, between Marshall and Pflugerville Connally. He asked them their opinion about where the site of the championship should be, and in that way he pulled their minds toward the remaining task.

Not to worry, though. The Scots were both focused and standing firm on their metaphorical surfboard, riding a massive wave of momentum. Despite having a dynamic running back named Jackie Robinson, Marshall couldn't keep up with the Scots.

Highland Park running back Jake Feldt scored five touchdowns in the first half, one on a thirty-three-yard pass from John Dickenson. Stafford didn't throw a touchdown pass in the championship game, a statistical anomaly in a game that Highland Park won 59–0, though he did move the Scots along with 202 passing yards. Highland Park led 42–0 at halftime, and it was all over but the crying.

Highland Park, a school that had amassed more than 700 wins in its history by the late 2000s, won its fourth state championship in 2005, but the first in forty-eight years. The Scots made it back to the championship game against Lake Travis in 2007, but as of this writing they're still looking for their fifth state title.

Still, Stafford believed the 2005 team reset the standard. "It was a ripple effect for our high school," he said. "We'd punched through that last door, and it was like, 'Hey, you know, most people don't see us as a super-talented team, but we're good enough to make it.'"

Allen knows that's true. I spoke with him a week before the start of the 2014 season, and he had fresh evidence that the 2005 team's accomplishment resonated strongly with his players. "They have a realistic goal of winning the state championship, and I asked them what their memories were of our program," Allen said. "They go back to, 'When I was in the fourth grade, I saw the 2005 state championship game.' That's kind of ingrained in our kids."

# 37

# COPPERAS COVE

## 2007

### RG3, Bulldawgs Come Alive

Robert Griffin could've avoided a lot of pain in his athletic career.

He could've chosen a pursuit in which he faced nothing more treacherous than an endless succession of forty-two-inch hurdles. As a junior at Copperas Cove High School, running in the state track meet in 2007, Griffin set the meet record for all classes by clocking 35.33 seconds in the 300-meter hurdles. A year later, after graduating from Copperas Cove in December and enrolling at Baylor, Griffin won the Big 12 championship in the 400-meter hurdles.

In an alternate universe where Griffin pursued track and field, RG3 might be synonymous with Olympic gold medals.

But Griffin is a football player, and that identity comes with contusions, scrapes, torn ligaments, crutches, rehab, and, most of the time, just good old playing through the pain.

One morning in November 2007, Griffin sat up in bed and realized that getting ready for the day was going to be a much bigger problem than he had anticipated. The night before, Griffin's Copperas Cove Bulldawgs had fallen in overtime to rival Waco High 27–21 in the final game of the regular season.

As a staff writer for the *Waco Tribune-Herald* at the time, I had frequently covered both the Dawgs and the Lions that season. But senior writer Brice Cherry pulled rank and grabbed the Waco High–Copperas Cove assignment that week. I was a little irked by that. For a year, we had been talking about the legendary physicality of the Lions-Dawgs showdown at the end of 2006. Waco High won that game too, claiming the district championship. Both teams went on to play in state championship games in separate divisions.

The rematch promised to be electrifying, and it delivered. I didn't blame Cherry for swiping it. Games like that are the reason seniority exists. With three seconds left in the fourth quarter and Waco High leading 21–14, Griffin sprinted up the middle on a quarterback draw from the Lions' ten-yard line. A Waco High defender angled in on him near the goal line, but Griffin turned his back to absorb the hit and protect the ball. He scored, and Michael Roell's extra point forced overtime. "Griffin makes chicken salad without chickens, and it's never over with a guy like that," Waco High coach Johnny Tusa told Cherry.

But Tusa's team prevailed when the Lions' defense shut down Copperas Cove in overtime. Running back Bronshae'Keon Dugas scored the walk-off touchdown on a twenty-five-yard scamper to give Waco High the district title for the second straight season.

Overnight, the soreness from the hard-hitting game set in for Griffin. "It was one of those days when you wake up and everything is hurting," Griffin said. "I woke up on Saturday, and I couldn't walk. I had done something to my groin, but I didn't remember what play it was on, because I walked off the field, and I was fine that night. I woke up, couldn't walk, didn't practice the whole week that week leading up to Waxahachie. Didn't know if I was going to be able to play, because I just couldn't do anything."

Losing to Waco High in consecutive years stung the Dawgs' pride, but it was no big deal, really. Copperas Cove coach Jack Welch said as much as soon as the game was over. "The key for us is we've lost nothing, except the district title," he told Cherry. "We're both moving on to the state championship playoffs and we've both got a chance."

Welch didn't know at the time, though, that his quarterback's availability would be in doubt for most of the week leading up to round one of the postseason. Not having Griffin would be a huge problem, since Welch and his brother Tracy Welch, the Dawgs' offensive coordinator, had essentially designed their offense around the quarterback's unique skill set.

Griffin had wanted to be the Dawgs' quarterback for as long as he could remember. As an elementary school student, he would write Tracy Welch notes on Fridays, wishing the coach good luck in that night's game. He would sign the notes "Your future Bulldawg quarterback." But when it came time for Griffin to suit up with the Copperas Cove varsity, he wasn't a shoo-in to lead the offense. The Welches took a long, studied look at Griffin and fellow up-and-comer Logan Brock to decide which would play quarterback.

When I spoke with Jack Welch at his office late in the 2014–2015 school year, he explained the decision process. "They both looked good," he said. "Logan is throwing the ball really well. He's a drop-back, set-in-the-pocket type of guy who operates the offense well. We saw the talent that Robert had. He had the great speed, the world-class speed. So our thought was—and Tracy did it—start developing him, because he was so talented. Let's start throwing in the short game, concentrate on the short game, get his technique on the short game. So we threw the hitches, the screens, all the things that [the University of Houston] does, and we started doing the read option."

Through that strategy, the Copperas Cove coaching staff uncovered yet another of Griffin's skills. "Very accurate on throwing the ball short, because he was throwing it on the run," Welch said. "When you go and look at him, what he's done well at Baylor and what he's done well at Washington, when he throws the ball on the run, he's throwing it up over his front leg. Because on the run, you have to. So our little short stuff, that's the way we'd do it."

That formula worked better than anyone could have predicted. For the Bull-dawgs, it resulted in two of the best seasons in school history. Griffin passed for 2,001 yards and rushed for 876 with a combined thirty-three touchdowns to lead Copperas Cove to the state championship game in 2006. Griffin, who is the most astute high school or college athlete I've yet interviewed, understood the process and why it worked during his junior season. Then he saw the need to tweak it in 2007.

When I sat down to talk with Griffin in the Redskins' facility during June OTAs [organized team activities, that is, preseason training sessions] in 2015, he went back through the strategy of those two seasons. "I actually threw the ball less my senior year than my junior," he said. "It wasn't because of me—it was what we had. [In 2006] we had Rashad Hawk at receiver, we had Jer-rard Millsap at running back, we had Brian Jones at receiver, we had Donnell Greer at receiver. We ran a more pro-style system my junior year, running the ball, play-action pass, throw it deep, three-step drops, all of that. And then our senior year, with Troy Vital at running back and myself, we ran the heck out of the zone read."

Despite the loss to Waco High in the final district game, the Bulldawgs went into the 4A Division I playoffs with their focus set on getting back to the state championship game. To get there, though, they would need to survive a first-round clash with Waxahachie. Copperas Cove had defeated the Indians 33–28 in the playoff opener the previous year, so they knew it was going to be a battle. "They were so powerful," Tracy Welch remembered. "They were so good. They played so hard. We really felt that if we had not beat Waxahachie, they would have gone to the state championship."

Copperas Cove really needed Griffin to be ready to go. He told me that after sitting out practice for a week, he finally felt strong enough to play when game day arrived. But even with Griffin on the field, it didn't look like a battle the Bulldawgs were going to win. Back at Waco ISD Stadium, where Waco High had defeated Copperas Cove in overtime eight days earlier, the Bulldawgs fell behind Waxahachie by two touchdowns early in the second quarter on a Saturday afternoon.

Vital scored on a three-yard run to cut the Indians' lead in half at the end of the second quarter. But Copperas Cove still went to the halftime locker room with their heads drooping. "Everyone's got negative thoughts running all through their heads," Griffin said of that halftime. "You're kind of like, 'Dang, we don't want our senior season to end like this.' We go into halftime, and it'd be great to say I had some great speech that fired everybody up and just super-indulged the moment, but I didn't. I didn't tell anybody anything. There was no great speech that we came out in the third quarter and started getting it going. We came back out and stunk it up some more."

Waxahachie running back Dominique Carson scored on a seven-yard run with less than ten minutes left in the fourth quarter to put the Indians ahead 28–14. The Bulldawgs, a state finalist the previous season, stared at a possible first-round exit from the playoffs.

Vital knew the rest of the team was looking to Griffin for a spark. "He kind of just looked at me, and he told me, 'Man, we kind of need you to just go out there and be Rob,'" Griffin remembered.

Meanwhile, Welch had been playing what he described as a game of Battleship, trying to figure out how to exploit the Indians' defense. "Some things aren't going to work," Welch said. "This didn't work; let's keep working. Let's find what's going to work. When we find it, it's going to click. The kids stayed focused, and a lot of that was Robert's leadership."

At just the right moment, the Bulldawgs called the right number. Tracy Welch dialed up a tight-end screen, and Griffin hit Brock. "I remember Logan rumbling, bumbling, stumbling down the field," Tracy Welch said. "He takes just a routine tight-end screen about thirty-five, forty yards."

The play cranked up a momentum-changing touchdown drive. Vital scored on another three-yard run with 5:18 left, meaning the Bulldawgs had little room for error on offense or defense the rest of the way.

The Copperas Cove defense forced a punt, and then Griffin and company responded with a swift and convincing touchdown march. Rolling out and on the run, just as the Welches wanted him to, Griffin launched a thirty-one-yard scoring pass to Josh Boyce. The extra point tied the game at 28 with 2:04 left in the fourth quarter. "That was probably one of the better moments of my career," Griffin said. "When we were coming back, everybody had that great vibe, even when we were down in the fourth."

Amazingly, Copperas Cove didn't even need to get the ball back to take the lead. After the kick-cover team pinned Waxahachie deep in its own territory, the Indians faced a third-and-fifteen from their own three. That's when Bulldawg linebackers Joseph Wright and Tanner Brock shot through the line of scrimmage to drop Carson for a safety.

Waxahachie, which had led by fourteen points just a few minutes earlier, suddenly trailed by two and had to kick to the red-hot Copperas Cove offense. Griffin added an insurance touchdown on a twenty-seven-yard run, and it turned out to be important. The Indians scored with four seconds left when quarterback Boomer Collins hit Sam Gagliano for a seven-yard touchdown. But Copperas Cove successfully ran out the last few ticks and clung to a 37–35 win.

John Werner, a Copperas Cove native, covered the game for the *Waco Tribune-Herald* and gathered an exceptional statement from the Bulldawgs' head coach. "Robert and Troy were amazing, and they just kept getting better as the game went on," Jack Welch told Werner. "Our kids kept playing until the final seconds. You teach it, you preach it, but the kids went out and did it."

Copperas Cove sailed through the next two rounds of the playoffs to set up a state semifinal against rising powerhouse Aledo. The Bulldawgs won another close one over the Bearcats 15–9. But this isn't a story of ultimate high school glory. Houston-area Lamar Consolidated claimed a 20–14 victory over Copperas Cove in the state final.

Instead, this is a story of how something that happened on a high school football field wound up having a dramatic, resounding echo. Griffin's entire career at Baylor was a comeback story. He and Art Briles took the Bears from the deepest, darkest corner of the Big 12 basement to relevance for the first time in the conference.

Then Griffin's career ascended like few others in the history of college football. In a five-game span, Griffin took Baylor from a feel-good story to the hottest thing going in the nation. He posted his signature *SportsCenter* highlight with a thirty-four-yard touchdown pass to Terrance Williams with eight seconds left to beat fifth-ranked Oklahoma. The next week, he torched Texas with 320 passing yards and two touchdowns and tacked on two rushing TDs in a 48–24 victory. Griffin had won the Heisman Trophy when he left Floyd Casey

Stadium that night, though he wouldn't officially collect the hardware until a couple of weeks later in New York.

When I asked Griffin about the correlation between the Waxahachie game and his Heisman run, his eyes lit up. "We were actually losing to Kansas in a similar fashion that we were losing to Waxahachie in high school," Griffin said. "I would say the Kansas game was more serious because we were down by seventeen in the fourth."

Indeed, the Jayhawks took a 24–3 lead over Baylor late in the third quarter. Then Griffin summoned more fourth-quarter magic. He began the surge with a forty-nine-yard scoring run and then heaved touchdown passes of thirty-six yards to Williams and sixty-seven to Tevin Reese to send the game into overtime. Griffin's fourteen-yard scoring toss to Reese in overtime helped the Bears outlast Kansas 31–30. "Crazy, crazy game," Griffin said. "But if we don't win that game against Kansas, not only are we not winning the Heisman, now we have four losses. We're also probably not going to that bowl game."

In Griffin's story, the Bulldawgs won that Waxahachie game, and the Bears won that Kansas game and all the ones that followed in 2011. The Washington Redskins took Griffin with the second overall pick of the 2012 draft, and as of the 2015 preseason, his NFL chapter is still being written.

# 38

# BRENHAM

## 2009

*Cubs Advance with Improbable Rally*

Angleton quarterback Quandre Diggs and running back Henry Josey tore through Brenham for two quarters.

Josey, a future star running back at Missouri, popped a fifty-six-yard run and another for a nineteen-yard touchdown, and threw a seventy-seven-yard pass on a halfback pass. Diggs, who went on to stardom at cornerback at Texas, broke a sixty-two-yard quarterback keeper for a touchdown and guided a Wild-cat offense that piled up 334 yards in the first two quarters of the 2009 4A regional semifinal game.

Diggs, Josey, and Angleton went to the halftime locker room with a 21–0 lead, seemingly in firm control of the contest. The Brenham coaches huddled in the locker room at Conroe's Woodforest Bank Stadium and just looked for a way to stop the bleeding. "We're like the little boy with his finger in the dike," Brenham coach Glen West said.

As I listened to West describe the game in his office in the spring of 2015, he candidly recounted details of the Brenham-Angleton game. A little more than five years had passed, allowing West to gain some perspective without losing any of the specifics. "We're just trying to plug up the holes, really not to even win the ball game at this point, to try to keep from being embarrassed," he said. "It's already 21–0, and it looks like it could be 42–0 easy. That was going through my mind. It's no longer just about winning; it's about a good showing. When it becomes a game you could be eliminated on, you start thinking about where does this set our program? If you can't win, you at least want to play on an honorable note where you feel good about yourself."

West and defensive coordinator Craig Agnew, both products of the Brownwood dynasty, debated the risks and rewards of changing their defensive strategy. West said he doesn't like to change in the middle of the game, because it means gambling on which direction the game turns. A change is as likely to cause further damage as it is to shift the momentum.

But as West and Agnew talked about how to slow down Angleton, one of the Cubs' defensive senior leaders weighed in on the matter. Middle linebacker Michael Walker argued for sticking with the game plan. "He walked up to us as we're talking at halftime, and he said, 'Don't change anything,'" West said. "I looked at him and said, 'Why?' He said, 'Coach, what we're doing will work.' He said, 'The reason they made one of the long runs, I slipped down. I was there; I just slipped down. It will work. It's a good plan. I promise you. They ran the play later, and we stopped it. This is a good defense. Stay with it.'"

Walker knew it took gumption to make his case for sticking with the same strategy, and sure enough, it ruffled the head coach. "I remember getting mad at him and saying, 'Well, it better work, because we're down 21–0,'" West said. "His comment to me was 'It will.'"

Walker also knew that if he didn't say something, his high school career could be over quickly. "Being in the middle of the defense, I knew my teammates' assignments as well," said Walker, who went on to play at Utah. "I could tell if it was the defense that's not working or if it was just a player that missed their assignment. At halftime, as they're making adjustments, I knew it wasn't the defense that they put us in—it was us as players that made mistakes. I think I made a mistake on one play. My fellow linebacker made a mistake on a couple of plays. I knew we were going to have to come back on a great team like Angleton, and I felt like we were good enough to do it."

Walker and the Brenham defense came up with a big stop to start the second half, pushing Angleton to a fourth-down fake-punt attempt and then stuffing it. That proved to be a foothold for the entire Cubs sideline. "It made our coaches mad, it made our team mad, and it gave us some confidence," West said.

But Brenham's twenty-one-point deficit seemed even direr because Angleton's defense had not allowed a touchdown in the playoffs through two and a half games. If the Cubs couldn't put a dent in that run, it didn't matter how well the defense played in the second half.

During the halftime powwow, though, West came across something he thought would work. With Angleton playing a tight man-to-man defense and pressing at the line of scrimmage, West wanted to get running back Troy Green in a pass route down the seam and force the Wildcats to cover him with a linebacker. West put the idea into practice midway through the third, and

Brenham quarterback Ty Schlottmann hit Green over the top in the middle of the field for a thirty-eight-yard touchdown. "That's what really got us going," Schlottmann said. "Just got a little momentum in the third quarter, and we kind of just fed off of that."

Brenham inched closer with Tanner Schmidt's thirty-four-yard field goal later in the third. But on the final play of the quarter, Angleton struck back when Diggs raced forty-two yards for his second touchdown of the game.

That set up a whirlwind fourth quarter and perhaps the most thrilling twelve minutes in Brenham football history.

The Cubs were driving early in the period when Schlottmann took a late hit on an incomplete pass from the Angleton twenty-nine. A personal foul against the Wildcats moved up Brenham to the fourteen, but Schlottmann, dazed, went to the sideline. In stepped backup quarterback Michael Buro, whom Schlottmann said could just as easily have been the Cubs' starter. "Coach Oehrlein, our offensive coordinator, says over the headset, 'Let's go deep. They'll never expect it,'" West recalled. "'He's got the arm to do it. Let's go deep.'"

On his first pass attempt of the playoffs, Buro hit wide receiver Derek Edwards for a fourteen-yard touchdown. "I definitely didn't know we were going to swing it deep there," Schlottmann said. "But he made a perfect pass, and it was pretty cool, because he didn't get a whole lot of chances. But when he did, especially in the playoff run, he for sure made the most of it. So that was pretty awesome."

The transition from Schlottmann's injury to Buro's opportunism worked so seamlessly that many watching from the stands at Rhodes Stadium figured it was all part of West's shrewdness. "In the state game that year against Aledo, the same thing happens," West said. "Quarterback gets hurt again, put the same kid in, and he throws another fifty-yard touchdown pass to Derek Edwards. We actually had people in this town that thought that was a trick—have the quarterback act like he was hurt."

The Buro-to-Edwards connection cut Angleton's lead to 28–17 with 10:15 left, and the Cubs had once again stolen the momentum. The amplification on the Brenham sideline increased when the Cubs defense forced a three-and-out.

After the Cubs took the ball back, another late hit on the Wildcats spurred another drive. This one was capped by Schlottmann going to Edwards for a twenty-three-yard touchdown. When Green ran for the two-point conversion, Angleton's margin was sliced to three points with 7:18 still on the clock.

With an unbelievable comeback victory within reach, West had one more trick up his sleeve, and he was in the right mood to use it. He candidly described the kinds of emotions that coaches won't often admit to feeling. Or at least it takes years after the fact to confess them. First of all, it is rare for a sportswriter to hear a coach admit that he was just trying to keep from getting blown out. On top of that, when Brenham started to roar back, West said he began to feel like someone playing with house money, though he steered clear of that specific gambling phrase.

"It kind of shows you how relaxed we were, because, you know, obviously a quarterback gets hurt, our second-team quarterback comes in, and we go deep with him the first play he's in there," West said. "When we were down 21–0, I would've taken a fourteen-point loss. We were looking at a disaster, a total disaster. And to this day, Diggs says he still hasn't gotten over that loss. They were in complete command and probably the best. I feel like they would've been the state champion. They were so talented."

The Cubs' feeling that they had nothing to lose came into play on the game's decisive drive. Angleton, which had shredded Brenham in the first half, couldn't build a drive with a three-point lead. Walker's assertion held true that the Cubs' defensive strategy was sound. "For the second straight time in the fourth quarter, Brenham's defense held firm, giving the Cubs the ball at their own 36," *Brenham Banner* sports editor Richard Bray wrote in his game story.

West told me Angleton's in-your-face man-to-man defense was the same kind of aggression that his team had played with that season. So he knew that running the ball, methodically moving toward a tying or winning score, was out. He had to keep going over the top of the Wildcats. Schlottmann found Green over the middle again for a forty-yard gain into Angleton territory.

But the Cubs soon faced a crucial fourth-and-one at the Wildcats' fifteen. A thirty-two-yard field goal would have tied the game and completed Brenham's climb out of a twenty-one-point hole. But here's where West made a call that embodied the team's attitude at that point. West wanted to roll the dice with a fake field goal, and no one I spoke with questioned the logic of the decision. "When he called that play, we all felt like it would work if we could get the ball off the ground from the holder's hand and throw it in time," Walker said. "We knew it would be wide open."

Oh, by the way, Schlottmann was the holder. So that helped.

When the ball was snapped, Schmidt flailed as if it had been snapped over everyone's heads. In the meantime, wide receiver Terrell Reese darted behind the line of scrimmage from one end of the line into the opposite flat, where Schlottmann found him. Reese took the reception to the two-yard line before Angleton stopped him.

Green finished the drive with a two-yard touchdown run, Schmidt kicked the extra point, and the Cubs had the lead 32–28. Brenham safety Jeremy Hall intercepted a Diggs pass to end Angleton's chance to retake the lead, and it was celebration time for the Cubs. "The clock hit zero, and you look up, and you're like, 'Holy cow!'" Schlottmann said. "We have more points than them now. Just from the halftime to the end of the fourth quarter, it was totally different. At halftime, you're kind of defeated. You're like, 'Dang, I don't want this to be the last game with these guys.' And at the end of the fourth quarter, you're like, 'I can't believe we just pulled that off and we get to spend another week together.' It was awesome. It was crazy."

Brenham surfed the wave of momentum from the Angleton win into a similar situation in the next week versus Dayton in the regional final. On that occasion, the Cubs merely overcame a 17–0 margin at halftime to win 30–24. After easing past Johnny Manziel's Kerrville Tivy team 31–21 in the state semifinal, Brenham ran into the Aledo buzz saw in the state final. Johnathan Gray and the Bearcats prevailed 35–21.

The Cubs lost three state finals between 2002 and 2013. Going into the 2015 season, they were still looking for that first state title. West won a state championship as a player in 1978 in Brownwood, where his father, Kenneth West, was a longtime member of Gordon Wood's brain trust. By knocking on the door of a state championship, Brenham raised expectations for the football team in a town where the baseball program had won six state titles by the summer of 1988.

Schlottmann, a part of both Cubs sports' legacies, gained valuable wisdom from the dramatic comeback when it looked as if Angleton was about to blow out Brenham and laugh its way into the next round. "When you play in games like that, when you're down twenty-one at half and have to kind of look to your left and right and trust in your teammates and coaches, it helps you when you get to the next level," said Schlottmann, who was a relief pitcher at Texas A&M when I spoke with him in 2015. "For sure, I've been in games like that in baseball, down by so many runs with so many innings left. You just have to stick with your game plan and trust in the guys around you. It definitely helped me grow into the athlete and person that I am."

# 39

# ALEDO

## 2008-2011

### *Johnathan Gray Runs into the Record Book*

From here, the ingredients seem to point clearly and directly to a spectacular outcome.

Take a perennially strong football program, one that had made the playoffs for twelve consecutive seasons under the same head coach. The Aledo Bearcats won the Class 3A Division I state championship in 1998 in coach Tim Buchanan's fifth year at the helm. Under Buchanan, the Bearcats made a smooth transition from 3A to 4A in 2002, growing in prominence as they grew in size. Buchanan led Aledo to the state semifinals in 4A in 2004, 2006, and 2007.

Add the top-rated running back in the nation, one who would be every bit the high school football sensation that Cedric Benson, Adrian Peterson, and even Kenneth Hall were before him. Johnathan Gray would earn a five-star designation from multiple recruiting publications and the top spot at running back as judged by Rivals.com.

And indeed, from here it seems as if a trophy case full of state championships was served to the Bearcats buffet style. But don't be deceived by how easily it all seems to have unfolded. Anyone who has ever suffered through a hard-fought contest on a Friday night or a Saturday afternoon knows that winning one game, much less enough to claim a state title, takes a ton of elbow grease.

For Gray, the work started in earnest as soon as he stepped onto the Aledo High School campus. Gray, the son of Texas Tech all-American running back James Gray, always wanted to top his father's accomplishments. He'd heard his dad talk about the legendarily hard work put in by the elder Gray's Fort Worth Trimble Tech teams.

So on the Wednesday night before Gray was set to play in his first high school sub-varsity game, he stayed late on the practice field to put in some extra work. "We were getting ready for the first game," Buchanan said. "I'll never forget this. I'm sitting in my office, and I see some of them running 100-yard sprints out on the field on Wednesday after practice. And I look out there, and I went, 'What is he doing?' He's got a sled out there with about two hundred pounds of weights on it. He's doing 110-yard sprints. I watch him, and I see him run back, and I realize it's Johnathan, and I realize, 'Crud, he's playing tomorrow! He plays on Thursdays.'

"I walked out there. I said, 'John, what are you doing?' He said, 'Coach, I got to get ready for the game tomorrow.' I said, 'Hey, I appreciate you wanting to work hard and all that, but you play tomorrow.' He said, 'Yes, sir, I know.' I said, 'Let's do this on Monday or Tuesday. Let's not do it the day before the game.' He goes, 'Coach, I'm going to do a couple more.' That's when I realized he was a different-type kid from just about any other great athlete I've ever coached."

This is a trend with running backs. Every great one I've spoken with has an internal motor and motivation that makes them want to outwork everyone else. I've said that running backs and guitar players are a dime a dozen because every good team or band has one or two, but that's not completely true. With the ballcarriers, the guys who keep getting stronger in the fourth quarter, the truly great ones, are rare.

Buchanan pointed out to me that although it appears the running back is getting stronger, he is actually growing fatigued at a slower rate than everyone around him.

Gray's motivation to work hard on the sub-varsity squads only grew after his freshman season didn't live up to his expectations.

When I met Gray at Texas during a bye week of the 2014 season, he described how the final game of his first season at Aledo fueled him for the next three years. Gray quickly moved through the sub-varsity squads and began toting the ball for the Aledo varsity. He rushed for 969 yards and fifteen touchdowns as a freshman on the Bearcats varsity (not including yards gained on sub-varsity teams), helping the Bearcats go undefeated in the regular season. But the success built up Gray and the Bearcats for a painful sting when Everman ended Aledo's run with a 24–7 defeat in the second round of the playoffs. "That hurt our seniors," Gray said. "I said to myself, 'I don't ever want to be crying my senior year or my sophomore year or my junior year in a playoff game after I lost.'"

And Gray kept that promise to himself, with a ton of help from his Bearcat teammates. Buchanan left little doubt that Gray had served as the bell cow, but he wasn't alone in his willingness to put in the hours. Quarterback Matt Bishop was right there too, demanding a high standard. "Very seldom did we ever have a bad practice," Buchanan said. "Both of those kids worked so hard in practice that it made everyone around him work."

Gray, in particular, needed the work. His freshman season, though successful by any standard for a freshman, revealed a couple of flaws in his game. Gray fumbled, for one, and Buchanan said he couldn't catch even a lateral if the ball was above his navel.

The solution, Buchanan figured, was to half fill a football with water and make Gray carry it. Well, actually, Buchanan intended to fill the ball entirely with water, a trick his dad used on him when he was a player. The problem, though, was that it was difficult and time-consuming to fill a football with water. Buchanan gave up halfway through, which proved to be a revelatory accident. "You felt like you had to carry it high and tight," Buchanan said of the doctored ball. "If you swung your arm, it came out. I dropped it twice just picking it up. When you start to run with it, that water starts sloshing around in there, and every time you cut, the water sloshes. So it really simulates somebody tugging on the ball all the time."

Gray embraced it literally and figuratively. "If we forgot to bring the basket out with the water balls in it, Johnathan would run get 'em and bring 'em out," Buchanan said. "All the other kids are saying, 'Johnathan, why'd you do that?' But Johnathan knew it was going to make him better. And I'm not talking about just when he was a freshman. When he was a senior, 'Hey, Coach, where's the water balls?'"

The dividends showed up quickly. Aledo began the 2009 season with a 20–16 victory over Stephenville, the first of two times, according to Buchanan, that the Bearcats defeated the Yellow Jackets in that campaign, when Stephenville had the better team. But Aledo didn't escape the regular season unblemished. Weatherford handed the Bearcats a 28–27 loss in mid-September, which served as the jumping-off point for Aledo's twenty-nine-game winning streak.

Gray rushed for 2,813 yards and fifty touchdowns as a sophomore. And he served as a decoy on the pivotal play of the season. Trailing Stephenville in overtime after the Yellow Jackets kicked a field goal on their overtime-opening possession, the Bearcats lined up at the Stephenville thirteen. Johnathan's mother, Tonya Gray, identified the Stephenville playoff game from Johnathan's sophomore year as her all-time favorite. She gave me one of the best, most succinct descriptions of a play I've heard. "That was probably the best moment," Tonya Gray said. "That whole team went for Johnathan, and Matthew Bishop ran in."

Aledo won the 4A state championship in 2009 with thirty underclassmen, including thirteen sophomores, on the roster. It was clearly a prelude to an unbelievable 2010. Gray enjoyed the first of his two 3,000-yard seasons, gaining 3,221 yards and scoring fifty-nine touchdowns. But the Bearcats were versatile too. Bishop passed for more than 2,700 yards as a junior and connected with junior wide receiver Michael Mann more than fifty times for more than 1,000 yards.

Aledo definitely saved the best for the finale in 2010. Gray scored his seventh touchdown of the 4A state final early in the fourth quarter versus La Marque at AT&T Stadium in Arlington. The Bearcats led 62–34 late in the contest when Gray sneaked back onto the field for one final carry. "We had taken Johnathan out of the game," said Buchanan, whose Central Texas twang revealed that he's still a little mystified by the moment. "There was a turnover [on downs], and the backup running back was supposed to go in the game. He had an equipment problem, and Johnathan runs in the game. It just so happens we had already called the play. We didn't know we were going to score on it, and of course, Johnathan takes it to the house."

On the sideline, as the Bearcat defense was about to stop La Marque on a fourth-down play near the fifty, the Bearcat offensive linemen opened Gray's eyes to what was still on the table, even as Aledo led 62–34. The massive scoreboard at AT&T Stadium revealed that Gray had tied the state record for most touchdowns scored in a state-title game. That adds to the evidence that the players conspired to ensure that the backup running back had "an equipment issue," allowing Gray at least one more carry. "I was like, 'Great win. We need to finish this out,'" Gray recalled. "They were like, 'Do you know how many touchdowns you got? You got seven touchdowns, and we're getting ready to go back out there. Let's get you in the end zone again.' I was like, 'Let's do it.'"

Gray looked in the eyes of his teammates, including linemen Michael Wilson, Latham Johnson, Kevin Frantz, Hayden Lambert, Garrett Young, and tight end Justin Breshears, who were in on the final run, and knew he needed to go get one more for them. "The O-linemen were telling me that, so I was like, 'These guys want it, so let me get my butt in the end zone,'" Gray said.

The call Buchanan and the Bearcats' coaching staff sent in from the sideline, thinking they were calling a play for the backup, was a zone-blocked run to the right from the right hash mark. Given the crowded side of the field, it took just one key block—Breshears taking out the left defensive end—to spring Gray. Young put a block on the defensive tackle, and Johnson sealed off the outside linebacker and safety, allowing Gray to fly through a crease. "I was like, 'Wow!' I really couldn't see what was happening up front," Gray said. "I just knew there was a hole. You go back and watch film, and you're like, 'That one block made this whole run happen.' It made something special, like eight touchdowns in the state game. You go back to those people and you thank them and you praise them, because without that you have nothing."

Gray finished his high school career with 205 touchdowns. After identifying the national record for touchdowns in a career while sitting at the dinner table when he was in middle school, Gray broke it by one score. The championship game against La Marque, when Gray rushed for 325 yards to go with his eight scores, was the peak and epitome of his high school career.

But there was plenty left in the tank for the Aledo legacy. Although the Bearcats didn't make it through the 2011 season unscathed—they lost to Stephenville and Lake Travis early in the year—they hit their stride well before the postseason. Nobody came within three touchdowns of defeating Aledo in the playoffs in 2011. Gray rushed for 3,888 yards as a senior and completed his high school career with 10,889 yards. He was 343 yards shy of Kenneth Hall's astronomical career record.

Those 343 yards seem pretty irrelevant. It's clear from speaking with Buchanan and James Gray that Johnathan could've easily set a new mark. But it wouldn't increase his or the Bearcats' legacy by much.

Aledo added another state championship in 2013, the school's fifth title and its fourth in 4A. In that time, the Bearcats went from playing in a typical small-town stadium with mismatched bleachers to one of the high school football palaces that now dot the Texas landscape. What's more, the name "Aledo" rings out well beyond this state's borders. Buchanan recalled one of those serendipitous moments while on vacation with his family for his daughter's senior trip. "I was in Cozumel the summer of 2012 after winning three state championships, and there was a guy from New York City there, recognized my cap, and started talking to me about Aledo football and Johnathan Gray," Buchanan said. "Had no idea I was the coach. We stayed at the same place for a week. About the third day, one of the kids walked by and called me 'Coach.' The guy goes, 'Heck, you're a coach there?' I said, 'I'm actually the head football coach there.' And he goes, 'Man, I didn't know I was with greatness. I didn't know I was with a celebrity.' And I said, 'No you're not. All I did is stood on the sideline and talked to officials.'"

It only seems as if it was that easy.

# 40

# FORT WORTH

## 1983–1984

### *Trimble Tech's Glory Days*

As football fans, we mark time by the players who played for our teams. Through my high school (Waco Midway), college (Texas Tech), and NFL team (the Dallas Cowboys), I can recount the years in football like rings on a tree. I can tell you that Ben Hicks played quarterback for Midway while I was working on this project. Graham Harrell and Michael Crabtree carried the Red Raiders to their best season in my lifetime during the year I bought my first house. Emmitt Smith, Troy Aikman, and Michael Irvin spearheaded the great Cowboy teams that I use to define my high school years.

I trace my consciousness of the world around me by how far back I can remember watching players play for my teams. I was in early elementary school when Tony Dorsett and Danny White were the Cowboys' stars. I was nine when I reached the conclusion that Steve Pelluer was never going to be the guy to lead Dallas to a Super Bowl. Around the same time, the Red Raiders formed their death grip on my college football allegiance. I had a poster on my wall of the Red Raiders' Mighty Mites—Tyrone Thurman, Wayne Walker, and Eddie Anderson. Billy Joe Tolliver threw the ball to those guys, and he could absolutely light up a stat sheet.

But it was running back James Gray that enabled the Red Raiders to convert all that offensive firepower into wins. Gray ignited Texas Tech's offense in 1989, rushing for 1,509 yards and leading the Red Raiders to a 9–3 record, their best mark in fifteen years, and their first bowl win since the 1973 season. I was in the sixth grade, and as I changed classes between Mrs. Morris's English class and

Mrs. Klatt's Greek mythology class, I contemplated how far the Red Raiders had come since their dog days of the early 1980s.

On December 28, 1989, Gray finished his Texas Tech career by rushing for 280 yards as the twenty-fourth-ranked Red Raiders demolished the twentieth-ranked Duke Blue Devils 49–21 in the All-American Bowl at Legion Field in Birmingham. The game is stamped in my memory as one of my favorite football games of all time, and that goes a long way toward explaining why Gray was my first favorite running back.

It also explains what a thrill it was for me to meet with James and Tonya Gray at their home in Aledo to talk about their son Johnathan. From the beginning, I knew that the story of the Aledo teams, led by Matthew Bishop and Johnathan Gray, had to be told. I also knew Johnathan Gray could never surpass his father as my favorite running back. After all, Emmitt Smith hadn't. But I didn't plan on writing about James Gray. It wasn't until I interviewed Aledo coach Tim Buchanan and realized how big a role Johnathan's family life played in his success that I knew I wanted to write about the father's career. "James is a very unique daddy—fierce competitor, hates to lose," Buchanan said. "Johnathan has a mother with a drive and a father with a drive to excel and to work hard. Watching his mom and dad work and doing what was best for him, it instilled a heck of a work ethic in that kid."

It had been twenty-five years since Gray led the Red Raiders, and his accomplishments had been buried under an avalanche of Mike Leach–era gaudy passing stats. So to reminisce about James Gray the running back and to watch Johnathan run—a spitting image of his father, especially with a football tucked under his arm—brought a legend back from obscurity.

As I sat in Buchanan's office, I became convinced of the need to write about James Gray's Fort Worth Trimble Tech teams. Though Gray's college career has been overshadowed by the Air Raid attacks at Texas Tech, his high school career and the Trimble Tech teams he played for feel as though they came from an era that never really happened. But more than a decade before Aledo became a powerhouse of the Fort Worth area, Gray helped the Trimble Tech Bulldogs as they briefly ascended to relevance in the rough-and-tumble Dallas–Fort Worth Class 5A scene.

By the time I was covering Fort Worth schools in the early 2000s, Trimble Tech was still fielding a football team, but its games never amounted to anything of consequence. The Bulldogs were an afterthought, mere fodder for the more successful Dunbar, Wyatt, Arlington Heights, Eastern Hills, and Western Hills teams. It was difficult to imagine Trimble Tech producing a 5A team that had competed for a district championship and plowed ahead into the playoffs.

But that happened under head coach Quintin Robinson in 1983 and 1984—that's who the Bulldogs were. Gray and fellow junior running back Ervin Farris, who went with Gray to Texas Tech, played supporting roles on a senior-laden 1983 Trimble Tech team. The Bulldogs were led by quarterback Bobby McCoy and playmaking flanker Kevin Hobson. As a junior, Farris earned a reputation as an Earl Campbell–esque power back who was happier running through defenders than around them. Meanwhile, there was very little mention of Gray in the *Star-Telegram*'s archives. Gray ran for a six-yard touchdown in the Bulldogs regular-season finale, and it was the first time his name appeared in the game stories I scoured.

McCoy and Hobson made most of the plays that grabbed newspaper print as they led Trimble Tech to the playoffs for the first time in the school's forty-six-year history. But the Bulldogs weren't satisfied with that accomplishment. In the first round, Trimble Tech pulled off an upset of 5-5A champion Denton 24–14. The bi-district victory set up Trimble Tech versus longtime DFW powerhouse Euless Trinity. The Bulldogs kept up their momentum with a 33–29 victory over the Trojans, leading to a showdown with another rising program—the Midland Lee Rebels.

Tyrone Thurman signed with Texas Tech in the same recruiting class as Gray and Farris. Thurman was a junior tailback for the 1983 Lee Rebels, which reached the state finals before falling to Converse Judson. When I interviewed Thurman for the Midland Lee story, he said the most brutal game his team ever played in high school was the battle with Trimble Tech at TCU's Amon G. Carter Stadium. The Rebels prevailed on that Friday night 23–6, but the Bulldogs clearly made an impression. Lee coach Spike Dykes, who would soon join the Texas Tech staff, took over as the head coach in plenty of time to deploy Gray as the Red Raiders' star running back.

Trimble Tech graduated twenty-four seniors off the 1983 team, but Robinson and the Bulldogs had enough impact players coming back to build on the school's first playoff berth. Gray rushed for sixty-five yards and three touchdowns as Tech opened the 1984 season by tying Dallas Pinkston. It marked Gray's emergence as a go-to offensive weapon during his senior season.

On October 25, 1984, Gray broke through by tearing through the Western Hills defense. He ran for touchdowns of six, three, thirty-four, and eighty-five yards, finishing with 204 rushing yards on just nine carries. Although he was becoming a star, he stuck to the humble path, deflecting credit to teammates. "Anybody can do it when they get the blocking," Gray told *Star-Telegram* correspondent Christopher Fox. "I followed Ervin Farris mostly. He's a good blocker."

Farris gained 134 yards and scored a pair of touchdowns as the duo led Trimble Tech to a 47–9 win. That victory established the Bulldogs as a contender for the 6-5A title. The next week, Gray ran for 191 yards and Farris added 143 to propel Trimble Tech past Dunbar 46–14 and into the driver's seat for the school's first-ever district championship. In the regular-season finale, Gray rushed for 107 yards to help the Bulldogs defeat Eastern Hills and wrap up the coveted city crown. *Star-Telegram* reporter Jimmy Burch depicted Trimble Tech's victory celebration as one that reached the fervor of state-title glory. "I really can't explain the way I feel right now," Gray told Burch. "When the game ended, I wanted to cry, but I couldn't. I can't believe it. We've been waiting for this for four years and our fans have been waiting for 50 [actually, 47]. It feels great."

Trimble Tech's season ended in bi-district play as Denton exacted revenge for the 1984 playoffs by ousting the Bulldogs 50–26. Although I interviewed Gray thirty years after the fact, I could see the loss to Denton still stung.

In light of Johnathan Gray's enormous high school success at Aledo, the elder Gray was reluctant to boast about his high school career. His fondest memories were of traveling with teammates and enjoying postgame dinners of chicken-fried steak when they won on the road. Trimble Tech drew good home crowds in those days, and there was a sense of community within the school district. "Back then, it was more family," Gray said. "More support, more excitement."

Of course, the thousand or so fans that attended Trimble Tech games paled in comparison with the masses in the stands for Aledo's games, particularly when the Bearcats played another powerhouse. On the surface, Johnathan Gray's high school football experience overwhelms his father's teams' modest feats.

But looking at it from another angle, it seems the Grays might be closer in accomplishment than it initially appears. James Gray and his Trimble Tech teammates built a legacy, even if only a brief one, from scratch. Nothing told the Bulldogs that they were lined up for glory. Johnathan Gray, on the other hand, went into a high school program that had already won big. The Bearcats had consistently won their district and traveled deep into the playoffs for more than a decade before Gray arrived. The separating factor, ultimately, was that the Bearcats finished the job by winning three straight state titles.

James and Tonya, who met when they were at Trimble Tech, settled back in Fort Worth after college and Gray's pro career. When Johnathan was finishing middle school, they made a careful decision to move out of the Crowley school district to one that would demand more from Johnathan academically.

They moved to Aledo after researching the school and surveying parents and coaches. No doubt, James and Tonya's experiences gave them the lucidity to know what to want for Johnathan.

James Gray laughs about his football relationship with his son. From an early age, Johnathan has had a burning desire to top his father's accomplishments, so it's amusing that the son looks so much like his dad. Johnathan and James mirror each other in their ability to keep their upper body charging upfield while their legs dart here and there to avoid diving tacklers. Both possess the vision to see holes open and the body control to slip through unscathed. "It's kind of scary to actually watch," James Gray said. "You never can say we were similar, because that would devastate him. But it's so funny how you can see the way I ran, and then you could take a video and almost put us side by side. You couldn't tell except for he wears 32 and I wear a 31."

Perhaps the only person who senses a difference is Tonya Gray, though she feels it in her gut more than seeing it through her eyes. "I didn't worry about James," Tonya said. "He was my boyfriend, and I just cheered him when he played. Johnathan, on the other hand, I'm the worried mother. They're bigger, they seem faster, they seem stronger. Injuries—with James, I didn't even think about injuries. With [Johnathan], I think about every hit and every play."

Tonya, who was a year behind Gray at Trimble Tech, followed him to Texas Tech. Coming out of high school, Gray had offers from the Red Raiders and the University of Texas at Arlington, which would shut down its football program following the 1985 season.

Johnathan Gray chose Texas over his father's alma mater and other offers from as close as TCU and as far away as Auburn. As Gray's college career develops, the son still has a long way to go to surpass the father, in spite of his high school accomplishments. As I write this, Johnathan Gray just finished the 2014 campaign with 637 rushing yards and seven touchdowns. By comparison, James rushed for 938 as a junior at Texas Tech. By that time, he had led the Red Raiders in rushing for three straight seasons, including a 1,006-yard campaign as a sophomore. James Gray finished his Texas Tech career with 4,066 rushing yards. Going into the 2015 season, he was still second in school history and still the school's scoring king, with fifty-two touchdowns.

But it's sometimes hazy who is chasing whom. The Grays' man cave in their Aledo home is adorned with photos and memorabilia from Aledo, Trimble Tech, Texas, and Texas Tech, along with all-star and youth-league jerseys. As both an ex-player and a proud papa, James is content to let Johnathan's gear take over the lion's share of wall space in the man cave.

Their stories will always be intertwined, though, and at least one play from the highlight reel includes both father and son. When the 2009 Bearcats played in the 4A Division II state championship game against Brenham, James Gray found himself caught up in the hype of his son's first title-game appearance.

James was visiting with Dykes on the sideline as Aledo had the ball at its own nine-yard line. The two spectators were a little bit behind the offense, near the end zone on the Bearcats' sideline. "I got down on one knee," Gray said. "I was thinking I'm still out of bounds. When Johnathan got the ball and made a cut and then he got on that second level [into the secondary], we all took a step. When I took a step, now I'm on the field."

About the time the son crossed midfield, the father was nearing the players' box, where the Bearcats' coaches and players were also following the play, though most of them only with their eyes. "I'm running down the hash marks," James said. "I'm on the field, and I run past the official, and he just watches me go past, and he was getting ready to throw his flag. [Coach Buchanan] saw that, and when Coach Buck saw me, he came out and he pushed me. When he pushed me, he pushed me back into about four or five of the players, and I think I twisted my ankle, and I think Coach Buck kind of twisted his knee. I didn't realize where I was. Once one of the kids helped me up, he said, 'Did you realize you were running on the field?' I just kind of creeped back, limped back behind the stands. I said, 'Did he score?' And he was like, 'Did you hear the crowd?' I hurried up and exited stage left."

James and Tonya laughed as James diagrammed the play in their living room. While Tonya doesn't seem old enough to be the mom of a college football player, James definitely fits the appearance of a football dad.

As he said, he exited stage left, away from the football spotlight. But make no mistake, the old Tech running back still stays in mental shape for every down of the football season. "I don't do well during football season," Gray said. "I don't get very much sleep, and it's just because of nerves."

Like that senior running back who wanted to cry but couldn't, James Gray is still looking for the words. "That ride was something you can't explain," he said. And it's difficult to tell whether he's describing his own playing days or vicariously living through Johnathan as the son continues to chase the father.

41

———

# DENTON

## 2002

*Ryan Raiders Swipe Semifinal Victory from Ennis*

———

Denton Ryan coach Joey Florence took off his headset and sort of figured Gordon Wood was right again. Florence's 2002 Raiders were facing the Ennis Lions in a Class 4A state semifinal at Texas Stadium. Both programs had claimed state titles the previous season, Ryan winning 4A Division I and Ennis prevailing in Division II, so the lead-up to this clash was spectacular. Through forty-four minutes, it hadn't really lived up to the hype, however, at least for the Raiders, who trailed 14–3.

It had all started a week earlier, when the smoke cleared and it became apparent that Denton Ryan and Ennis would meet for the second time that season. Along with all the newspaper and TV-sports-show hoopla that built up the game, the opinions thrown around included an awkward exchange in the Texas Stadium press box a week before the contest. Ennis head coach Sam Harrell had played for Wood, the most exalted patriarch in the Texas coaching ranks, at Brownwood. Wood always backed his boys, so in an informal gathering of coaches in the Texas Stadium press box as Ennis's quarterfinal was wrapping up, the Brownwood legend let it be known he stood firmly in Ennis's corner.

"We were waiting on Ennis to finish their game, and I went upstairs to the press box," Florence remembered. "There's probably twenty-five old athletic directors, and they're all sitting around this big table. I go to get a drink out of the fountain, and I hear them talking about, 'Well, next week at one o'clock, Denton Ryan and Ennis are going to play.' And they'd already started bantering who's going to win, and I hear this voice. It's Gordon Wood. He said, 'Well, I've seen 'em both, and Ennis is going to beat Denton Ryan by two touchdowns.' I just went, 'Oh, my God.' About that time, Neil Wilson, who was the old athletic director at Lewisville, he said, 'Well, there's the head coach of Denton Ryan right there.' He said, 'Joey, come here. I want to introduce you to Gordon Wood.' Everybody was laughing, and Coach Wood was so gracious. He said, 'Don't take it personal. Sam Harrell is one of mine. Gotta root for him.' Neil Wilson wasn't going to let him off the hook. He said, 'I'll bet you a dollar that Denton Ryan wins.' Gordon Wood—he was so competitive if you knew him—he said, 'I'll bet you two dollars that Ennis wins.'"

A week later, Ennis had all but dismantled the Raiders. The Lions had a two-score lead when they punted and pinned Ryan at its own ten with less than five minutes remaining in the fourth quarter. Ryan's last-chance possession went nowhere fast. The Raiders narrowly gained a first down, but penalties turned a seven-play series into a net three-yard loss.

Florence listened to the play call on fourth-and-twenty-four from the seven, then the coach took off his headset and waited for what seemed certain to be a depressing finish. Upstairs in the coaches' box, offensive coordinator Dave Henigan at least had a reason to hope. "We had talked about it earlier in the game when we ran a similar play, that the fade had come open," Henigan said. "We didn't have an opportunity to get it to [wide receiver William Dowdy]. There's no good call at that point, so we felt like—I don't know that this was conscious, but that's a six-four receiver. Throw it up."

With the season hanging in the balance, Ryan quarterback James Battle scrambled to his left from the goal line to the two. From just outside the left hash mark, he heaved a pass deep down the left side, hitting Dowdy in stride. When Dowdy was dragged down from behind, the pass play had moved the Raiders from their own seven to the Ennis thirty-six.

New life. "You could feel the spirits and the energy and the excitement kind of rise on the sideline," said defensive lineman Derek Lokey, who went on to play at Texas and for the Kansas City Chiefs. "The anxiety went down. It was almost a feeling of kind of catching your breath and thinking, 'Okay, we got this. We're back in it.'"

The Raiders were accustomed to turning things around on a dime. Florence took over as Ryan's head coach before the 2000 season after the Raiders' 1–9 season in 1999. Every player in the program, not just the varsity, was struggling at the end of the last millennium.

Philip Jones, a senior wide receiver in 2002, remembered a strange dichotomy of growing up and playing football in Denton. As kids, he and his classmates believed they were the best anywhere, but then when their high school careers started, they received a much different message. "Our freshman year, we were horrible," Jones said. "I think the varsity team was, like, 1–9, the JV team was, like, 1–9, all four teams put together we were like 4 and 30-something. We were horrible. But then the new staff came in with a new defensive scheme and a new offensive scheme. I feel like those coaches took it to a whole 'nother level."

Indeed, the new coaching staff made a swift and dramatic change in the Raiders' fate. Florence led Ryan to a 12–3 record and the 4A Division I state title game in his first season as the Raiders' coach. Then Ryan finished the job by going 15–0 and winning the state championship in 2001.

So for a senior class that had gone 1–9 as freshmen and then 40–4 for the rest of their careers, a 14–3 deficit with less than four minutes left didn't seem like too high a hurdle, especially since they had the ball at the Ennis thirty-six.

Ryan needed eight plays to score from there. It had to convert a fourth-and-two from the thirteen, but Battle ran for an eight-yard gain to the Ennis five and on the next play hit Jones on a fade pass for Ryan's first touchdown of the contest, with a little more than a minute left. Battle connected with John Brice for the two-point conversion, and the Raiders trailed by only three.

They just needed to recover an onside kick when the opposition knew it was coming, perhaps the most difficult play in football. With the degree of difficulty and the stakes as high as they could go, Florence went straight to Jones. "He's the end man on the line," Florence recalled. "I said, 'Whatever you do now, if it goes out of bounds, the game's over.' I'll never forget, he said, 'Coach, I'm not going to let that ball go out of bounds.' He said, 'You get it to me, Coach, I'll get it.'"

Ryan kicker Connor Walling put toe to ball on the onside kick, and it definitely didn't take one of those crazy high bounces that improve the chances of recovering such a kick. "I don't think I could have kicked that any uglier, but it got there," Walling told Chuck Cox of the *Denton Record-Chronicle*. Walling kicked the ball to his right, a line-drive grounder headed for the sideline. The play is well preserved on the Raiders' season highlight film. An Ennis good-hands team member flashed past the ball but didn't grab it. "Every time I see it, I always say, 'If that was me, I would have took it the other way,'" Jones said. "It was like he jumped in front of it, but it was like he thought he was close to out of bounds and if he didn't touch, it would just go out of bounds. I don't know what he was thinking, but definitely I would have took it the other way."

In the instant between the Ennis player flashing in front of him and the ball flying through untouched, Jones made a reaction that saved the Raiders' season. "I just reached back for it, because I was falling to the ground," Jones said. "I just kind of reached back for it and grabbed it and fell on top of it. I just remember everybody coming up and grabbing me."

Jones's second game-changing play gave Ryan the ball at the Ennis forty-nine with sixty-eight seconds left. He was hot, and the Ryan coaches recognized it. On the second play of the ensuing drive, they shifted Jones from wide receiver to the left slot and sent him up the seam. Battle lofted a pass deep down the middle, toward a pack of three Ennis defenders and Jones. But Jones, who jumped the highest, came down with the reception at the Lions' four-yard line.

Lokey finished his career with a pair of state titles and a national championship ring from Texas's Rose Bowl victory over USC in 2006. He compared Jones's trilogy of plays in the Ennis state semifinal with another spectacular performance he witnessed firsthand. "Not a whole lot of times when I've seen anybody compile three phenomenal plays like that," Lokey said. "As far as three vital plays for one guy to kind of take control of the game, I haven't seen anything like that at any level, I don't think, other than playing with Vince Young and what he did in a couple of Rose Bowls."

Jones's forty-three-yard leaping catch put Ryan on the doorstep, and the Raiders finished their phenomenal comeback with a go-ahead touchdown. Brice scored on a four-yard run. "When we scored the touchdown to go ahead, we had to call a timeout because there was so much pandemonium," Florence said. "Kids were throwing helmets, kids were rolling. Coaches were hugging each other. I looked up and I said, 'There's still thirty seconds to go. It's 17–14. This is a very important extra point.' I thought, 'Man, it wouldn't take them long to get in field goal range.'" Walling nailed the extra point, extending the Raiders' lead to four points.

With only thirty seconds remaining to move the length of the field, Ennis quarterback Graham Harrell connected on a couple of passes to set up a Hail Mary attempt. But the Raiders picked off Harrell's desperation throw and won 18–14.

The Ryan sideline went berserk. "It was pandemonium after that game," Florence said. "It was insane. It was an unbelievable sequence of events."

Earlier that season in nondistrict play, Ennis had defeated Ryan at Denton's Fouts Field. The Raiders exacted the sweetest kind of revenge by winning when a berth in the state championship game was at stake.

While the Raiders players writhed with excitement and the thrill of victory, the opposite sideline stood in stunned disbelief. Graham Harrell had led his team to a pair of come-from-behind victories over Highland Park and

Southlake Carroll during the previous season on the way to the state championship. That was little consolation as the Lions' season ended on the Texas Stadium turf, but given a decade or so to reflect on it, Harrell had some appreciation for the way Ryan pulled off the win. "They made a lot of good plays, you've got to admit that," Harrell said. "When you're on the side where you lost, you see all the things that went bad, all the plays that y'all didn't make. When you're on the other side of it, when you're on the winning side, you see all the plays that you did make."

Ryan charged into the state championship game in the Alamodome, where the Raiders faced Brenham, coached by another Wood disciple, Glen West. Ryan prevailed, claiming its second straight state title with a 38–8 victory over the Cubs.

As mentioned, Lokey went on to add a college football national championship ring to his collection as a member of the 2005–2006 Longhorns. The multiple factors that went into acquiring such a unique jewelry collection aren't lost on Lokey. "There's a level of skill, and there's a level of timing, and there's a level of luck, and there's a level of being in the right place at the right time," Lokey said. "It's also an extreme honor and a blessing to be able to have done that. It's a small fraternity, but I feel blessed to have been in the situation to have an impact on both teams. It's very special to sit back and look at the artifacts and the relics and the rings. I look forward to talking to my sons about it. I've got three small sons. I look forward to reliving those memories with them."

Florence, who had stepped away from the sideline to become Denton ISD's athletic director by the time I spoke with him in the spring of 2015, displays the souvenirs from the 2002 championship run prominently on his office wall. Among them are a pair of framed two-dollar bills he received from Coach Wood. Although Wood didn't technically make his bet on the Ryan-Ennis game with Florence, the Brownwood legend went to significant lengths to commend Florence on the comeback victory. The two-dollar bills were for Florence and his father, Mickey Florence, whom Wood had known from the Texas coaching fraternity. Wood didn't know that Mickey Florence died in December 2001, so Florence kept both of the rare bills to commemorate the incredible victory and to pay homage to his father. Along with the token cash, Wood sent a letter congratulating Florence and likening the Raiders' victory to other great comebacks.

I got the feeling that if Florence's office caught on fire and he had to choose to save one over the other, he would leave the 2002 gold state championship ball and take Wood's two-dollar bills. "It's just one of my most prized possessions because he's by far the greatest to ever coach," Florence said. "There's always a connection with high school football, and that's part of its lore. That's why it's cool."

Wood's letter makes reference to Florence's success in 2002 against former Brownwood players. "If you quit playing my Ex-Players it will be easy to pull for you in your play-off games," Wood wrote.

# *Further Reading*

Telling high school football stories and writing about Texas high school football has captured the imagination of many authors, who have written from a variety of angles.

In the early 1990s, H. G. Bissinger's *Friday Night Lights* (New York: Harper Perennial, 1991) elevated to a new level the football legends of Odessa Permian, Texas high school football in general, and the idea that a sports book could have such an extensive audience. The film and television series that followed increased that audience while straying away from Bissinger's original slice of Americana. Bissinger's book described the role Permian football played in an oil-boom, oil-bust town in West Texas.

Jim Dent's catalogue of in-depth sports journalism includes two books, *Twelve Mighty Orphans* (New York: St. Martin's, 2007) and *The Kids Got It Right* (New York: St. Martin's, 2013), that unpack extraordinary moments in the history of Texas high school football, one that is unfathomable in its improbability and one that shaped the game moving forward. In an even more intimate look at small-town high school football, Carlton Stowers's *Where Dreams Die Hard* (Cambridge, Mass.: Da Capo, 2005) chronicles the resurrection of the six-man football program in tiny Penelope, Texas.

Others have taken a wide-angle approach, like that of *King Football: Greatest Moments in Texas High School Football History* (Birmingham, Ala.: Epic Sports Classics, 2003), in which editor Mike Bynum creates a collage of game stories that reach into many corners of the sport in the Lone Star State. Jeff Wilson's

*Home Field* (Austin: University of Texas Press, 2010) offers a subtler approach, with photographs taken from midfield of dozens of the state's unique stadiums.

In researching *The Republic of Football: Legends of the Texas High School Game*, I was pointed in the direction of many books about the sport. Three that I found especially helpful in telling some of the stories in these pages were John Carver's biography of Gordon Wood, *Coach of the Century* (Plano: Hard Times Cattle Company, 2001), *Dat: Tackling Life and the NFL* (College Station: Texas A&M University Press, 2005), and *Art Briles: Looking Up: My Journey from Tragedy to Triumph* (Chicago: Triumph, 2013).

# Acknowledgments

I would like to thank my mom and dad, Shana and John Conine, for being everything parents are supposed to be, and so much more. My dad played every sport with me from the moment I could walk, and it's the reason sports are a huge part of my life. Thank you to my sisters, Chaney Cockrell and Calley Durant, along with their families, for their enthusiasm for the journey of writing this book. Thanks to my brothers Jeremy, Tim, and Cory and the whole Webb herd (and in particular to Danny, for giving me the idea for the San Antonio game; and to Jeremy, for continually recommending that I talk to Bill Lane). Thanks to Shawn Skeen and his family for knowing where I was going with this and setting the bar high for me.

Thanks to Jacob Kyle Robinson, my first-read guy and the person who kept my head straight and directed consistency into this project. Thanks to Becky Murphy Simpson for making me want to keep fishing. Thanks to my high school journalism teacher, Kathi Couch, for teaching me, among other things, that cliches are the bane of a sportswriter's existence. Thanks to Zach McFarlen and his family for creative support and a place to stay in Indianapolis. Thanks to Brice Cherry, John Werner, and Jason Orts at the *Waco Tribune-Herald* for being great buddies in the business and letting me cover high school football every Friday night in the fall. Thanks to Jerry Hill and Kim Gorum for bringing me back to Waco. Thanks to Joben David, who asked the right question to help get this project started.

Thanks to Heath Nielsen at Baylor and Blayne Beal from Texas Tech, who helped me get the interviews that got the ball rolling. Thanks to all the subsequent media relations people who were willing to give time to a non-beat writer.

Thanks to the Texas Sports Hall of Fame and to *Waco Tribune-Herald* photo editor Rod Aydelotte for lending me photos.

Thanks to all the libraries and librarians across the state who helped me find the newspaper articles that played such an essential role.

Thanks to Robert Devens and the University of Texas Press, which provided the backing and momentum to take this project from an idea and four sample chapters to a forty-one-chapter book.

And finally, thank you to everyone I interviewed during this entire project. Very early on in the process, I realized that the fun of this book came from getting to have conversation after conversation with people who love high school football in Texas and love to tell stories about it. It didn't matter whether it was a Hall of Famer or a player who never played beyond the final game of his senior year, you were all fantastic. That's the heart of this book.

# Index

The letters *PS* indicate that an individual, team, or place is pictured
in the unnumbered photo section or is mentioned in one
of the accompanying captions.